Wittgenstein Archived

Gerhard Gelbmann

Wittgenstein Archived

Bergenser Essays

PETER LANG

Frankfurt am Main · Berlin · Bern · Bruxelles · New York · Oxford · Wien

Bibliographic Information published by Die Deutsche Bibliothek
Die Deutsche Bibliothek lists this publication in the Deutsche
Nationalbibliografie; detailed bibliographic data is available in
the internet at <http://dnb.ddb.de>.

Gedruckt mit Förderung des Bundesministeriums für
Bildung, Wissenschaft und Kultur in Wien.

ISBN 3-631-51286-4
US-ISBN 0-8204-6467-8

© Peter Lang GmbH
Europäischer Verlag der Wissenschaften
Frankfurt am Main 2004
All rights reserved.

Contents

Preface

This book is a collection of four essays I mainly wrote during my several stays at the Wittgenstein Archives at the University of Bergen in Norway between autumn 1997 and spring 2003, with valuable resources for research tools, foremost the Bergen Electronic Edition of Wittgenstein's Nachlass, at my disposal.[i] Their various themes all centre around Ludwig Wittgenstein's philosophy, which still enjoys a widespread reading and leads to animated discussions.

Yet my writings do not focus exclusively on what one might call 'Wittgensteinian philosophy'. There is not *one* thread running through the book; there are, rather, several intertwining trains of thought forming a network within which I move. Though I might appear like a fisherman wrestling with his own net, one should not forget that much of what fishermen do with their nets looks like as if it were in vain, while in fact they lay out the net to prepare it for further use.

The facets of Wittgenstein I have become acquainted with in the last years do not exhaust his writings. In fact they resemble a sea full of treasures that can apparently not be raised completely, however tightly knit our conceptual nets might be. As with every profound thinker, the attempts undertaken to understand him are in themselves rewarding, whatever their outcome.

Each of these essays has in some way already been exposed to criticism; they are the outcome of several stages of drafting, revising, rewriting. The result is *not* indented to be some semi-textual sort of "fragment". Besides, these essays of mine slightly overlap; the reader should not be surprised at encountering a passage again, quoted in some other section of the book. I did not attempt to get rid of this seeming redundancy, since it reveals on which texts and themes my thoughts focus and find centres of gravitation.-

This preface does not serve the purpose of clarifying what this book is about and why it was written (if this can ever be clarified by somebody with the warranted authority of being the author). I shall also expound my personal and philosophical standpoint: I am *not* an exclusive Wittgenstein scholar, I never wanted to be one. In addition, I am not solely devoted to the study of the literature by him or on him; in this sense I am not a Wittgensteinian[ii] at all, and I do not want to be considered as one. This does *not* mean that I have not read him, just as

---

[i] Oxford and New York: Oxford University press, 1998 ff.

[ii] In the sense of "belonging to a school or club or community".

it does not mean that I do not hold his thinking in high esteem. I respect this thinker, as I respect previous and contemporary Wittgensteinians, among whom I find promising and recognized scholars. I do *not*, however, worship Wittgenstein, I do *not* regard him as the wise, ultimate thinker, as sacrosanct, as one who gives definite answers to questions about life or just to philosophical disputes.

I find inspiration for tackling philosophical problems in Wittgensteinian thinking, in Wittgenstein's sayings and sources. But just as he does not belong to any current or former mainstream of academic philosophy, I am not a representative of any school. I am far more a drop of water swallowed by a stream, running into another current until finally reaching some lake of oblivion. I am certainly influenced by what is dubbed "Philosophy of Language", by analytic thinking, by the development of modern logic since Gottlob Frege and Bertrand Russell, by constructivism, by interdisciplinary thinkers like Gregory Bateson, by Charles S. Peirce and other semioticians (I cannot list all those thinkers I am indebted to). *I am a child of my time*, as happy as it is, as looming and dark as it can be, as shallow as it often appears and more often turns out to be.

Yet *I claim some autonomy*, especially with these essays on which I worked in a Northern country, that for a while was hospitable to me. I want to be taken seriously, not because of my particular biographical circumstances but because of what I ultimately tried to achieve. If I seem to be parroting Wittgenstein,[iii] the reader should kindly bear in mind that I do not always make my irony explicit, which is possibly the most European trait of my character.[iv]

These essays want to reveal the *complicated relationship between my reading of Wittgenstein and my writing* (it is somewhere between these two points that my philosophising is located). They are attempts at 'digesting' this philosopher as well as other, more recent influences on my thinking. With my doctoral dissertation I already embarked on a philosophical trip into new regions that had so far been ignored by philosophers. I had and have ideas about similar journeys in the future, some of which are connected to the name of Herbert Stachowiak, of which some traces can also be found in this book.-

---

[iii]   As Rush Rhees, Elizabeth Anscombe, or sometimes Norman Malcolm were.

[iv]   That Watzlawick 1983 is largely misunderstood or underestimated, is due to its ironic approach throughout. It has been said that Watzlawick was not successful with this book in America, in contrast to it being a bestseller in many European countries. So the implicitness of irony probably belongs to European culture and European contexts. What is the point of irony if it explicitly has to be declared as such?

My ways of referring to Wittgenstein must be explained. Bibliographic references will be rendered in the known Harvard-system. Passages left out of quotations will always be marked by three dots in brackets, as will my interferences into quotations.[v] Other comments to quotations will be attached to the source citations. From Wittgenstein's works I tend to quote the whole title in the language of the edition, and when referring to the Nachlass of Wittgenstein I abbreviate manuscripts with "*MS*", typescripts as "*TS*", and dictates as "*D*", followed by the item-number, according to the system of citation described by Georg Henrik von Wright.[vi] Yet for various reasons I will not always give a dating of these original source citations: the dating might be doubtful or superfluous. Where I find that the dating as rendered in the Bergen Electronic Edition is not reliable, yet important, I try to add other sources and conjectures.

Other remarks on my usage of typographical signs are necessary: I shall use abbreviations of Latin expressions for pointing at textual evidence: so "op. cit." means "the work quoted"; "loc. cit." denotes an already given citation or "locus"; "cf. inf." refers to what is going to follow; "cf. sup." indicates that something has been said above; "*nota*" is a note or footnote (in plural "*notae*"); "i.a." stands for "and others"; "ad" means "at"; "ad exemplum" hints at a specific case, the plural is "ad exempla"; "sec.", i.e. the Latin "secundum", is to be translated as "according to"; "et" as "and"; the known "e.g." as "exempli gratia", meaning "for the sake of an/the example" or just "for example"; whereas "cf.", "i.e.", "etc.", and "via" are still widely known Latin expressions and should need no explanation.

The reader should not be frightened by my use of other Latin phrases. Some of them sound a bit technical, but are still often applied. For instance, in modal logic a phrase qualified as "necessitas de re" refers to a necessary entity, whereas "necessitas de dicto" maintains the necessity of stating that something is the case. A "terminus ad quem" is a notion towards which some theoretical undertaking heads, a "terminus a quo" a concept from which such an enterprise sets off. Phrases like "argumentum ad hominem" and other Latin expressions are in all probability known among academics or are made clear implicitly within their context. The term 'unio mystica' means "mystical union", and talking of

---

[v] If I add footnotes in brackets in a quotation and mark it with "G.G.", then it is my footnote and not the rendering of a footnote by the author.

[vi] Cf. Wright 1982: 35-62. I shall introduce the terms 'item' or 'skript' as the over-all-concept, signifying manuscript, typescripts, and dictates. Cf. also *Essay II*.

'reification' or 'to reify' comes from the Latin word "res", meaning thing, cause, matter, or theme, thus the neologism 'reification' or 'to reify' expresses that something is turned into an object or regarded as a thing.

When I introduce formulae or new abbreviations for labelling statements or focussing on a notation, etc., it will always be at least implicitly explained, in more complicated cases there will be an explicit definition. But on the whole I try to keep technicalities at a low level.-

Sometimes I use dashes at the end of a sentence or paragraph (like this: "-", as after the last full-stop), hereby indicating the end of a thought. This should be distinguished from paraphrases – appositive phrases or whole periods built into a sentence – and intentional breaches marked by a long dash like: "–". They indicate a turn in my thinking – and should by no means confuse the reader, since I typographically indicate what is going on. If I sometimes use dashes within words like "re-organize" or "aspect-change", I either want to stress that they are "verba composita", or to emphasize a special accent attached to their meaning.

I do not intentionally try to avoid scholarly terminology, as I presuppose some degree of concentration and erudition on the part of the reader. It is, however, not my aim to make understanding more difficult than necessary. Yet I cannot yield to the fashion of simplification, lowering the standard of expression and style, and thus simplifying beyond acceptability – however elitist this attitude may appear.- Even though I have chosen to write in a foreign language, I hope to have managed to articulate myself fairly clearly, also with the help of a number of people and their corrections, who shall be acknowledged elsewhere.

I wrote this book for the so-called "sake of science". While I was working on it, I was often confronted with all kinds of problems and financial insecurity, with little or no prospects for the future. Remaining true to philosophy, being faithful and authentic to my chosen form of existence means hard work, and proceeding with my various writings is often a hardship not everybody would like to endure. It chiefly meant working through a lot of nights beside concentrating on various other tasks, and it was not done to earn me any merits. I would not refuse money, if my writings ever earned me some, and fame can hardly be refused, whether it be deserved or not. But I beg my readers to consider that certain philosophers write because it is their way of being and because philosophy requires this form of expression. I deeply respect the standards of scientific work; I try to adhere to them, and have sacrificed possible advancement and success for the sake of science. There are no additional or even hidden motives for my work.

Some of my fellow human beings have confronted me with baffled questions as to why in the world I spend my time on such 'stuff'. My answer, to them and others, is: *I do not have to justify my existence.* I claim this freedom, and, furthermore I claim that it is the duty of society and my fellow human beings to grant me this freedom, even if there is nothing they gain from my existence or the existence of philosophers as such,[vii] among whom I am just a dwarf.

I maintain that there is a certain originality in what I present here, not only in my approach to Wittgenstein, but also in showing how Wittgenstein was regarded as being 'available' by certain other thinkers, among them myself, who derived their philosophy from their preoccupation with Wittgenstein, and who read Wittgenstein on the background of their thinking. Even though this book is not written in the spirit of hermeneutics, every letter and space in it gives testimony to my hermeneutical commitment.

The reader is invited to elaborate on an understanding of Wittgenstein's writings along the lines of my writings, and I humbly ask my reader also to do me the honour of attempting to read and understand my writings.

Gerhard Gelbmann, October 2003 in Bergen, Norway

[vii]   I strongly doubt that there is nothing humanity can gain from the existence of philosophers. Many of the modern institutions of the Western World have their origin in philosophy, and nobody knows what fruits the philosophies of our days will bear for the benefit of all human beings. In this sense even some of the crippled apple trees I try to plant might bear fruit some day.

Essay I. Wittgenstein and Watzlawick.
Aspects of Selective Reading[viii]

I.I. Introduction

This essay will be devoted to the investigation of the influence of Ludwig Wittgenstein on the founders of the so-called Pragmatic Theory of Communication (hence abbreviated as *"PTC"*). This theory was formulated at the end of the sixties and the beginning of the seventies of the 20th century by a team around Don D. Jackson and Paul Watzlawick at the Mental Research Institute (*MRI*) in Palo Alto, Calif., who largely built on Gregory Bateson's groundwork.[ix]

An expert might assume that the *PTC*'s starting point immediately connects with Wittgenstein's ideas through the mediation of Maurice O'Connor Drury, the Irish friend of Wittgenstein,[x] who in his studies turned from Philosophy to Human Medicine and then to Psychiatry.

This assumption is, indeed, supported by Drury's career in academia: He was interested in semiotic matters,[xi] stressed the importance of empirical and mutually supportive data,[xii] spoke up for painstaking conceptual work,[xiii] was influenced by Gestalt-Theory,[xiv] took a stance against psychological behaviourism[xv] and was

---

[viii]   This essay has a background in Gelbmann 2001b, which I revised and translated myself from German into English. Some parts underwent fundamental improvements and alterations, though seldom on a large scale. It was written at the Wittgenstein Archives at the University of Bergen in its German version in 1998 and in the present version in 2003. Both times I made use of the valuable Bergen Electronic Edition.

    I often had to keep quotations of references to the sources available to me, which involves that I sometimes quote German translations of works that were originally written in some other language (cf. the bibliography). From Wittgenstein's works I either quote from known English editions, or I give my own translation, which I always mark.

[ix]   I shall refer to this group of people as "Watzlawick et al.".

[x]   Cf. Monk 1990: 264.

[xi]   Cf. Drury 1996: 2 ff.

[xii]   Cf. Drury 1996: 6 ff.

[xiii]   Cf. Drury 1996: 29 ff.

[xiv]   Cf. Drury 1996: 45 ff.

[xv]   Cf. Drury 1996: 49 ff.

open to the relativity of the concepts 'normal' and 'pathological'.[xvi] All these traits move Drury close to the psychological constructivism developed and advocated by Bateson, Watzlawick et al.-

Apparently, however, there are not any references by Bateson, Watzlawick et al. to Drury. Drury does not seem to have been in touch with the British psychologists Ronald David Laing and Gregory Bateson, both very important sources for Watzlawick et al. With Laing and Bateson Drury shared some central thoughts that can also be found in Wittgenstein's writings, but from Wittgenstein's point of view they depict only arbitrary parallels to their work.- How Wittgenstein would have faced his own influence, is quite a different matter: probably disapprovingly.-[xvii]

The following investigations are chiefly devoted to the question, *as to how the authors (and forerunners) of the PTC made use of what we today call their sources*. Research on such forms of reference in the face of the complexity of the source materials is only partially possible. The mass of what was implicitly turned into a basis or whose source verification is unclear yet nevertheless had an effect on what is being investigated here, are often not easy to survey. In addition, the authors of the *PTC* do not always make research easier, since, not coming from a distinctive philosophical tradition themselves, they do not attach importance to explicit citations to an extent one wishes to encounter when fulfilling one's reconstructive task.[xviii]

From the point of view of the task we have set ourselves, it is doubtlessly of the greatest importance to investigate what the authors in question thought and to whom they referred. Bateson, Watzlawick et al. do *not* emulate or even copy Wittgenstein's procedure; they bring quotations, but they do not quote everything, and not all of it is accurate.

When inquiring into the relationship between Wittgenstein's Philosophy of Language and the *PTC*, one is confronted with the problem that to my knowledge nobody has as yet found any contact between Wittgenstein and Watzlawick et al. Moreover, Watzlawick, in spite of being well-read, was not acquainted with

---

[xvi]   Cf. Drury 1996: 112 ff.

[xvii]   Cf. Wright 1986: 207.

[xviii]   Cf. here Wittgenstein's attitude as expressed in the Preface to his "Tractatus Logico-Philosophicus", cf. Wittgenstein 1992a: 3. The anticipation of his thoughts is a matter of indifference to him.

Wittgenstein's Nachlass more than to the extent of what was published at the time. Still, Watzlawick can doubtlessly be said to have been influenced by Wittgenstein.

We have to elucidate what *forms of quoting* can be found in the writings of Watzlawick et al., who use a variety of differently relevant authors in the presentation of their own tenets. In their reference to Wittgenstein, direct or indirect citations outweigh those that do not interpret Wittgenstein by way of comment. Most of the citations are limited in origin to a few locations in the many-facetted *opus* of Wittgenstein. To my mind it must be ascribed to Watzlawick to have brought this knowledge about Wittgenstein to bear, as he alone of the authors concerned can boast an academic study of Philosophy in Venice, Italy.-

We shall hence prefer a contextual, at times multistage form of quoting, trying to demonstrate by inserted and marked comments where else in the writings of Watzlawick et al. the very same citations from Wittgenstein's writings are entered. Citations from Wittgenstein's published works in their most important variants are always compared with the Bergen Electronic Edition of Wittgenstein's Nachlass, which I had at my disposal at the Wittgenstein Archives at the University of Bergen in Norway in spring and summer 1998 and again in winter and spring 2002/2003. In doing so, I kept to the catalogue of Georg Henrik von Wright, described in Wright 1982.-

I.II. Aspects of Reconstruction

We shall take a close look at the relationship of Watzlawick (et al.) to Wittgenstein according to three points of view, denoted by Greek letters:

(α) according to a *heuristic aspect*, by which the *question about the genesis of ideas* is to be understood, in so far as it definitely applies to Wittgenstein, whereas it otherwise applies to any taking over of leitmotifs in Wittgenstein for the process of Theory-construction in (Bateson) Watzlawick et al.

In *(β)*, the *utilitarian aspect of instrumentalization* has to be outlined, with strategic references to passages in the text that according to an explicit or safely inferable opinion offer either the backing of acknowledged authorities or a formulation suitable for the current purpose.

Finally we have to ask for *(γ)*, the *aspect of parallel evolution(s)*, which is the most speculative aspect, especially considering the incompletely elaborated genesis of Wittgenstein's texts. It has to be added that this aspect *(γ)* on the one hand leads to the unfolding of an aspect *(δ)*, i.e. the aspect of *convergence of lines of thoughts*, yet on the other hand it reveals odd *coincidences* between otherwise disconnected factors of epistemology and cognitive psychology.-

I.III. From the Anthropologic to the Systemic Perspective

When confronting phenomena that at first sight seem to be incomprehensible, Wittgenstein has occasionally been ascribed a method comparable to anthropology (or ethnologoy).[xix] This so-called 'ethnological perspective' often assumes the form of *an activity in imagination*, which is not without a comical component (and amused Wittgenstein himself[xx] when using it in lectures). It shows that *under different circumstances the "normal" or "given" loses the apparent character of being a matter of course* in order to reveal characteristics inherent to it.[xxi]

[xix] Cf. Bartley 1974: 103 *et* 126, Glock 2000: 21, besides Monk 1990: 261, who dates Piero Sraffa's known influence on Wittgenstein's around 1932 (cf. *MS 117*: 114 from June 27th 1938 and the "Vorwort" zu "Philosophische Untersuchungen", Wittgenstein 1984, Band 1: 232).

Examples of Wittgenstein's anthropological or ethnological method can be encountered in "Vermischte Bemerkungen", Wittgenstein 1984, Band 8: 502 (*MS 162b*: 67v from July 2nd 1940), "Philosophische Untersuchungen" I § 206 ff., Wittgenstein 1984, Band 1: 346 (*TS 241*: 3 § 11 from Jan. 1944, *MS 129*: 30, *TS 227*: 147 § 206, etc.), in "Bemerkungen über Frazers *Golden Bough*", Wittgenstein 1967a (*MS 110 et TS 211*), further in "Eine Philosophische Betrachtung (Das Braune Buch)" ad exempla 51 ff., Wittgenstein 1984, Band 5: 147 ff. (i.a. *MS 115*: 153 ad exemplum 43 *et* op. cit.: 160 ad exempl. 52 from Aug. 1936) or in "Letzte Schriften über die Philosophie der Psychologie" I § 203, Wittgenstein 1990b: 29 (*MS 137*: 98 from Nov. 17th 1948).

Cf. also Rudich & Strassen 1971, and K. T. Fann 1969: 48 ff., a source I owe to Alois Pichler from the Wittgenstein Archives at the University of Bergen, who together with the guest researcher Andrzej Orzechowski had worked on the "anthropological approach", yet so far unfortunately without publishing any documentation of their results.

In his doctoral dissertation, Pichler 2001a: 220 f. distinguishes between "anthropological perspective" and "ethnological perspective", the first being explained as a context-oriented principle rooting human thought and conduct into a practice, in contrast to Frazer's universalism and rationalism. The latter, ethnological approach is then a specification of the anthropological method, which consists in assuming counterfactuals, giving fictive examples, presenting thought-experiments, and which in the narrower sense pertains to the habits, rituals, demeanour, cultural peculiarities of a foreign, imagined tribe.

[xx] Malcolm 1966a: 29.

[xxi] Doubt and criticism of 'normality' are inherent in the advancing constructivist paradigm in psychotherapy, cf. e.g. Jackson 1967.

No direct adoption of this Wittgensteinian anthropological perspective by Bateson, Watzlawick et al. can be located. Yet it wins a methodically decisive role in Wittgenstein's later philosophy – which was obviously not known to them. It was certainly not reading Wittgenstein that induced them in their therapeutic and conceptual activity to take a view which, in the confrontation with observing incomprehensible and deviant behaviour, lets them regard this as the form of conduct of an alien culture, thus suddenly gaining from their systemic organization a rich potential for explanation as well as intervention. But under the title "systemic" or "transactional analysis" respectively, a large number of factors in the *PTC* are only intelligible from this approach, namely to regard observed systems as micro-cultures in their own right.

Perceived thus, we have come across a parallel in the sense of *(γ)*, but at the same time this is blended with *heuristic* constituents resulting from this perspective, which does not however allow reading them according to *(α)*, since *no direct heritage* of Wittgensteinian ideas can be proved.

We shall, firstly, come to a story Bateson tells,[xxii] pointing out how he came to learn to form his *contextual understanding of psychopathology* by being exposed to the immediate milieu and living conditions of one of his patients. Besides Milton H. Erickson, it was Bateson who introduced the systemic approach into the psychotherapeutic practice.[xxiii] At once and in their entirety, the form of life and the language-games belonging to it on the part of the patient become the *meaningful context* that has to be identified in order to let a disturbance or so-called 'disease' appear in a different light, under which it becomes explainable as being placed into a certain context. The deviant conduct of the individual and indicated 'patient' gains in lucidity in regard to the situations and constellations in which it occurs, *not so much as a feature of a single person, but as a feature of the internal organization of this observed person's social system.* Concomitantly, it loses the veneer of going too far and leaving the ordinary framing, because it is embedded in exactly the frame in which it actually takes place.

This allows gathering a *formation of hypotheses* from a perspective focussed on *the sequences of behaviour in the micro-social system*, thus not trying to

---

[xxii] This is a nosology, which as a personal report has to be qualified as purely qualitative, based on personal experience, like many of their kind that are often to be met in psychiatry (V. E. Frankl 1973 is a good example of the importance of such nosological presentations in the writings of new movements within medical sciences).

[xxiii] Cf. Nardone & Watzlawick 1994: 47 f.

explain the pathology of the so-called index-patient as stemming from a traumatic experience in the child's aetiology, but *to look for characteristic patterns of the sequences of such noticeable or even unusual demeanour.*[xxiv] Here it is worth mentioning that Bateson himself has a background in cultural anthropology.[xxv]

This case-study is directed against the tendencies of psychoanalysis to tie down observable deviances to qualities of the analysed individual, thus perceiving patients in isolation and as mere products of their personal biography.- In the following Bateson is visiting the client's family with his patient:

"The house looks like what is called a »model« home – a house which has been furnished by the real estate people in order to sell other houses to the public. Not a house furnished to live in, but rather furnished to look like a furnished house.

I discussed his mother with him one day, and suggested that perhaps she was a rather frightened person. He said, »Yes«. I said, »What is she frightened of?« He said, »The appeariential securities«. [...]

After his mother arrived, I felt a little uncomfortable, intruding in this house. He had not visited there for about five years, but things seemed to be going all right, so I decided to leave him there and to come back when it was time to go back to the hospital. That gave me an hour in the streets with absolutely nothing to do, and I began to think what I would like to do to this setup. What and how could I communicate? I decided that I would like to put into it something that was both beautiful and untidy. In trying to implement that decision, I decided that flowers were the answer, so I bought some gladioluses. I took the gladioluses, and, when I went to get him [Bateson's patient, G.G.], I presented them to the mother with a speech that I wanted her to have in her house that was »both beautiful and untidy«. »Oh!« she said, »Those are not untidy flowers. As each one withers, you can snip it off.«

Now, as I see it, what is interesting is not so much the castrative statement in that speech, but the putting me in the position of having apologized when in fact I had not. That is, she took my message and reclassified it. She changed the label which indicated what sort of a message it was, and that is, I believe, what she does all the time. An endless taking of the other person's message and replying to it as if it were either a statement of weakness on the part of the speaker or an attack on her which should be turned into a weakness on the part of the speaker; and so on.

[xxiv]   Cf. the fundamental study Bateson & Jackson & Haley & Weakland 1956 and see Laing 1969: 91-119.

[xxv]   Cf. e.g. Bateson 1934, Bateson 1936, etc.

What the patient is up against today – and was up against in childhood – is the false interpretation of his messages. If he says, »The cat is on the table«, [[xxvi]; G.G.] she replies with some reply which makes out that his message is not the sort of message that he thought it was when he gave it. His own message identifier is obscured or distorted by her when the message comes back. And her own message identifier she continually contradicts. She laughs when she is saying that which is least funny to her, and so on.
Now there is a regular maternal dominance picture in this family, but I am not concerned at the moment to say that this is the necessary form of the trauma. I am only concerned with the purely formal aspects of this traumatic constellation; and I presume the constellation could be made up with father taking certain parts in it, mother taking certain other parts in it, and so forth.
I am trying to make only one point: that there is here a probability of trauma which will contain certain formal characteristics. It will propagate a specific syndrome in the patient because the trauma itself has impact upon a certain element in the communicational process. That which is attacked is the use of what I have called the »message-identifying signals« – those signals without which the »ego« dare not discriminate fact from fantasy or the literal form from the metaphoric." (Bateson 1972f: 198 f.;[xxvii] punctuation slightly improved)

Not only did the peculiar conduct of this woman provide Bateson with a clue as to the latent situation of conflict his patient had to comply with, but such experiences also invoked his sensitive search for features of a form of suffering that is marked as 'schizophrenia' in psychopathology. I personally think that Bateson did not only have such experiences from his time as a therapist to lead him to his revolutionary understanding of schizophrenia and to his 'double-bind'-theory. (Incidentally, this understanding was not only formulated by him, Jay Haley, to name only one, deserves to be mentioned in this connection.)

There is also another source Bateson certainly had: a patient's personal historical or even biographical account of his own schizophrenia. There we find a similar insight into the strange role metaphors play in the modes of communication one finds with "lunatics", especially the point that metaphors and similar non-literal ways of expression are taken too literally (as is also the case

---

[xxvi] In Gelbmann 2002b, I discussed the famous example of the statement "The cat is on the mat", yet without quoting this passage from Bateson 1972f, which strikingly makes the same transactional point as I tried to reveal by looking into the possible contexts for such a 'pure' locution about a certain state of affairs.

[xxvii] German in Bateson 1994f: 266 ff.

with religious fanatics or fundamentalists). First let me briefly describe the account in question:

This classic report is from John Thomas Perceval, the son of Spencer Perceval, a former Prime Minister of Great Britain, who was assassinated in May 1812. The report was (re-)edited by Gregory Bateson in 1961, and in his introduction he explains the circumstances of how John Perceval came to write his book. The British Parliament passed a law which left the family and the widow of the murdered man a generous sum of money, which was used for John Perceval's confinement to a lunatics' asylum when he, years later, began to show deranged behaviour in public and signs of mental illness, probably immediately caused or rather triggered off by a religious experience and his involvement in praying-circles after he had spent part of his youth in the British Army.

Bateson's edition abbreviates Perceval's moving narrative about his schizophrenic phase, which lasted from about 1830 until early 1834. Perceval's story came out in 1838 (first volume) and 1840 (second volume) and is probably the *first published self-account of a schizophrenic experience*. The thrust of the book deals with the intolerable and "ungentlemanly" treatment he had to suffer in asylums − parts of what he and we today would call torture. Other parts consist of descriptions of his treatment as a will-less and immature person, which probably contributed to the development of his disease, a treatment that might have been similar in young John Thomas' own family. In addition, he makes observations on the reasons for his mental problems with an astonishing degree of (recollected) self-awareness one does not readily tend to ascribe to these deplorable people.

In his introduction,[xxviii] Bateson comments on Perceval's report from the point of view of his understanding of schizophrenia, which is preliminary to *PTC* and understands schizophrenia *not so much as an illness but as a deep experience of undergoing a change of personality*, brought about in Perceval's case by a double-bind situation in his family and triggered off by the contact with fanatic Protestant circles with a strong tendency to uncritical, literal reading of the Bible and queer forms of public confession. This induced Perceval to see his suffering as *something intended by himself*, a sort of punishment, fitting into the sinister frame

---

[xxviii]   Cf. Perceval 1961: v-xxii, itself an interestingly early document about Bateson's development, only a few years after the famous double-bind-hypothesis was approached in Bateson 1955a, Bateson 1955b, Bateson & Jackson & Haley & Weakland 1956, Bateson 1959.

of such confessions. Bateson loc. cit. furthermore most interestingly states that at Perceval's time the so-called "treatment" of lunatics was *not so very different from today*. It consisted of a sort of punishment and imprisonment, which was at that time pretty brutal, whereas doctors in 1961 (or today) have more refined ways of medication at their disposal. Yet *in both cases*, at the time of Perceval's case in the 19th century or more than hundred years later, *the response the patient needs*, viz. *the understanding of the world he lives in, is rarely given*. Some of Perceval's letters from the time of his insanity, edited in his writings, and his comments show that he was aware of this lack as a cause which furthered his illness.

I see Bateson's grand editorial work in immediate connection with the account of double-bind and the Theory of Schizophrenia which he, together with J. Haley and others, developed and published in 1956. It is one of the reasons why I talk about *PTC* and forerunning undertakings as "rehumanization".[xxix] There are numerous passages one could quote showing the striking insights the 'patient' Perceval gains during his sufferings. I shall quote only a passage which is connected to the situation described above, namely to *the problem of metaphors and the disguised mixing up of metaphors with literal ways of talk* in the immediate milieu and also in the thoughts of the patient:

> "I suspect that many of the delusions which I laboured under, and which other insane persons labour under, consist in their mistaking a figurative or a poetic form of speech for a literal one; and this observation may be of importance to those who attend to their cure." (J. Th. Perceval 1961: 270)

Yet in what sort of reality does a person live who mixes up metaphors with words meant literally? What might be the adapted way of living in a circle of fanatic Bible-readers, is certainly not the sane and safe way in other circumstances. It was Bateson et al. who not only searched for common characteristic features in the behaviour of schizophrenics (or persons so called), but who also *gave up framing the concept of such characteristics individually by attaching them to the patient's personality*. In an often quoted passage this becomes a sort of key issue in the methodology of what later on was to be called 'systemic perspective':[xxx]

[xxix]   E.g. in Gelbmann 2000b.

[xxx]   Cf. Watzlawick & Beavin & Jackson 1967: 119 ff., Watzlawick 1988a, Nardone & Watzlawick 1994: 52 ff. or Marc & Picard 1991: 27 ff.

"The specificity for which we search is to be at an abstract or formal level. The sequences [of observed behaviour; G.G.] must have this characteristic: that from them the patient will acquire the mental habits which are exemplified in schizophrenic communication. That is to say, *he must live in a universe where the sequences of events are such that his unconventional communicational habits will be in some sense appropriate.* The hypothesis which we offer is that sequences of this kind in the external experience of the patient are responsible for the inner conflicts of Logical Typing. For such unresolvable sequences of experiences, we use the term »double bind«." (Bateson & Jackson & Haley & Weakland 1972: 206;[xxxi] italics original)

There is no evidence for Bateson here referring to Wittgenstein, although Bateson himself once interprets the term 'transaction' with "»language game« in Wittgenstein's sense".[xxxii] Correspondingly, the view of a parallel development sec. *(γ)* is not entirely free from an aspect of the genesis of ideas according to *(α)*, which on Bateson's part is made use of in a way of what I might call "instrumentalizing form of quoting" according to aspect *(β)*. So far the genesis of hypotheses is indeed something Wittgenstein in an epistemological remark called *a system of mutually supportive consequences and premises.*[xxxiii]

This gives rise to the conjecture that *Bateson's idea of the transactional view* (or systemic perspective, respectively) *is tightly knitted to the Wittgensteinian conception of 'language-game' and 'form of life'*, and probably influenced him just as strongly as his own experiences with patients and Perceval's narrative did. Wittgenstein's "Tractatus logico-philosohicus"[xxxiv] is consulted as an *epistemological basis for psychiatric theorizing*[xxxv] and for Bateson's model of a *hierarchy of types of the levels of communication* (which, of course, originates with Bertrand Russell).

Yet these are what I shall call *'references ex post'*, applied and made useful when looking back from an already gained standpoint. Therefore they do not match condition *(α)*, since they are instrumentalized in so far as they serve to

---

[xxxi] German in Bateson 1981: 275 f.

[xxxii] Cf. Bateson 1990: 131.

[xxxiii] Cf. "Über Gewißheit" § 142, Wittgenstein 1984, Band 8: 149 (*MS 174*: 30v f. from April 24th 1950).

[xxxiv] Besides works by Bertrand Russell and Alfred North Whitehead, R. Carnap, B. L. Whorf and others.

[xxxv] Sec. Bateson 1981: 241.

equip oneself with the authority of background-knowledge, without this fulfilling the purely utilitarian prerequisite *(β)*. Even though a historical independence of the theory-formation in question can be assumed, an astounding similarity can easily be detected that reaches beyond the aspect of a parallel development sec. *(γ)*.-

There is a biographical detail from Wittgenstein's advanced years, remarkable as a fascinating parallel to the enfolding of the systemic perspective, which holds according to aspect *(γ)* as well as *(γα)*; the latter insofar as, independent from each other, *the same heuristic process of forming methods* seems to have been at work in these two cases, in both *prompted by the realization of a lack of conceptual clarity with practical consequences.* Although about an incident not directly linked to the school of Palo Alto and the circle around Gregory Bateson, it elucidates the problem of a concept of a certain *diagnosed* illness:

It was David L. Rosenhan who stated that the diagnosis 'schizophrenia' is not only too readily applied, but obviously used *without clear criteria* and hence misused in the hospitalisation of *alleged* patients. This, in turn, has had an impact on the constructivist approach to the research on schizophrenia in regard to the criticism of the hitherto applied methods in conceptualisation and diagnostics.-[xxxvi]

On the other hand Wittgenstein's youngest biographer, Ray Monk, talks about Wittgenstein being confronted during his wartime-service at Guy's Hospital with a conceptually unclear application of the diagnosis "shock" as applied to soldiers and victims experiencing shelling in the war.[xxxvii] Wittgenstein's criticism, sharp, sustained, and to the point as usual, had a strong influence on the responsible doctors, Basil Reeves and Dr. Grant:[xxxviii]

> "In fact we found that the diagnosis of shock seemed to depend on the personal views of the individual [...] rather than on generally accepted criteria. [...] We were led, therefore, to discard the word »shock« in its varying definitions." (sec. Monk 1990: 452)

It was Wittgenstein's criticism that led to a revision of this concept for clinical work, it revealed what Watzlawick et al. would have called a "reification". The symptoms accounted for with the pseudo-term "shock", which – to express it in familiar Wittgensteinian terms – maximally shared family-resemblance, had *by*

[xxxvi]   Cf. Rosenhan 1973, Watzlawick 1988a: 88 *et* 104, Kreuzer 1982: 65 f.

[xxxvii]   Cf. Monk 1990: 451 ff.

[xxxviii]   Cf. Reeves' "Observations on the General Effects of Injury in Man", January 1941 (sec. Monk 1990).

the act of problematic diagnosis created a reality that immediately affected not only the current state of medical art, but even more so the treatment of the patients concerned, which could hardly be called adequate.

Strikingly similar is Rosenhan's report from about forty years later, which I mentioned earlier.[xxxix] Retold by Watzlawick, it is about an American research project

> "[...] in the course of which eight of his collaborators voluntarily requested admission into mental hospitals, claiming that they heard voices [[xl]; G.G.] and needed psychiatric care. Immediately after their admission they declared that the voices had stopped and from that moment behaved in a way which outside of a psychiatric clinic would have been considered perfectly normal. The length of their »therapy« varied [...] and all of them were discharged with the diagnosis »schizophrenia in remission«. Not one of them was unmasked as a pseudo-patient; on the contrary, every aspect of their behavior was judged to be further proof of the accuracy of the diagnosis. Instead of being based on observable facts, the diagnosis *created* a »reality« sui generis, which in turn necessitated and justified special clinical procedures. The crowning irony was that the only people who did not participate in this reality construction were several »real« patients. »You are not crazy – you must be a journalist or a professor.« This and similar remarks were made repeatedly and sometimes vehemently." (Watzlawick 1990c: 132 f.;[xli] italics original)

In both cases *the mere diagnosis constituted a clinical reality*, sufficient for severe intrusions into the lives of the people concerned; here, thorough conceptual work has inveighed against and remedied things that were wrong.[xlii] From this it cannot be concluded that Wittgenstein was a constructivist, nevertheless there are amazing parallel modes of inference sec. *(γ)*, which dispelled with objectifications or reifications. In other words, *fatal inferences were drawn from the existence of a linguistic expression to the existence of what was thereby signified.* The point is that Wittgenstein's opinion on theoribilization does not differ from that represented by Watzlawick et al. and Rosenhan in practice.-

---

[xxxix] Cf. Rosenhan 1973, Watzlawick edited Rosenhan's article in English and in German.

[xl] This hearing of voices, by which 'lunatics' are "desired" to do certain things, is typical of a schizophrenic psychosis, as already mentioned by John Perceval 1838-1840.

[xli] German in Watzlawick 1988c: 104. Cf. David L. Rosenhan 1973.

[xlii] In the case of Perceval, op. cit., one might ask whether his abominable treatment did not partly contribute to turning him into the lunatic as which he was regarded.

Above, the central term 'double-bind' was introduced, whose function and genesis within the *PTC* has been retraced in other writings.[xliii] The question as to how far a 'pragmatic paradox' can be noticed in the circumstances described, takes one to a different level of referring to Wittgenstein's philosophy, viz. *to questioning the pragmatic role of a contradiction in a system*, i.e. its effect on those exposed to it. Thereto Watzlawick at al. contribute with a citation (loc. cit. inf.) that makes us aware that the utilitarian outlook *(β)* in *usefully illustrating a rhetorical dimension of intertextuality depicts a value*, that consists not so much in the humble reconstruction of original thoughts and in philologically faithful unlocking the door to grasping what Wittgenstein might have thought originally, but which applies a constructive moment straight to the lecture and presentation of modes of reading, which allow taking a different view of the quoted author. Without this form of reference, this parallel to Wittgenstein sec. *(β)* would not be visible at all.

In other words, *parallels are produced*, they *are not just simply there*. In this case at least the authors themselves push the aspect of parallel evolution to the fore, without thereby claiming to have substantially profited in their own achievement from preparatory work. Yet in hinting to such a parallel development more plausibility is gained for one's own thoughts, thus firmly fixing one's own edifice of ideas to a background in sociology and history of science. This is a widely distributed procedure which, indeed, has a rhetorical component. It should be distinguished from the common and practical illustration of one's thoughts with the aid of a quotation taken from another author.-

---

[xliii]   Cf. Gelbmann 2000b: 411–422.

I.IV. The Functionality of Error

That rhetorical, hence pragmatic components play a decisive role in paradoxes occurring in communication, is, according to Watzlawick et al., not new to Wittgenstein, who, interestingly enough, comes to talk about this in his philosophy of mathematics:

"To the best of our knowledge, it was Wittgenstein who first speculated on the practical, behavioral implications of paradox: »The various half-joking guises of logical paradox are only of interest in so far as they remind anyone of the fact that a serious form of the paradox is indispensable if we are to understand its function properly. The question arises: what part can such a logical mistake play in a language game?« [xliv; G.G.] Wittgenstein then makes reference to the paradox of the king (who had promulgated a law according to which every arriving foreigner had to state the true reason for his entry into the kingdom; those who did not tell the truth were to be hanged, which prompted a sophist to state that his reason for coming was to get hanged on the strength of this law) and asks the crucial question: »What kind of rules must the king give to escape

---

[xliv] Cf. "Bemerkungen über die Grundlagen der Mathematik" VII § 29, Wittgenstein 1984, Band 6: 397 (*MS 124*: 110 f. from March 9th 1944). Also brought in Watzlawick 1988a: 23 und Watzlawick 1975: 118 f. Watzlawick et al. quote loc. cit. from the English translation by G. E. M. Anscombe, i.e. Wittgenstein 1956: 179 (the only deviation I traced in Wittgenstein 1994b: 397 is that they render "question is" as "question arises").

It is worth commenting that in the German version, Watzlawick & Weakland & Fisch 1974a: 84 f. quote Wittgenstein loc. cit. as "Es fragt sich: welche Rolle kann ein solcher logischer Irrtum in einem Sprachspiel spielen?", whereas the Bergen Electronic Edition in *MS 124*: 110 f. has "Es fragt sich: Welche Rolle kann ein solcher 'logischer Irrtum' in einem Sprachspiel spielen?", with inverted commas added and a big capital letter after the colon, as required in German grammar, whereas the Suhrkamp edition has the same as *MS 124* loc. cit., yet without inverted commas for "logischer Irrtum".

The original handwriting of *MS 124* loc. cit. is, with regard to the text string in inverted commas, hardly readable, since it is scribbled into the lower right corner in the margin of the page, yet I agree with the reading of the transcriber(s) in the Bergen Electronic Edition (cf. Cornell copy Vol. 26 loc. cit., the source for the transcription of *MS 124*). The English edition of loc. cit., Wittgenstein 1994b: 397, has no inverted commas either, so the book editions of this passage are bad and do not render the fact that Wittgenstein might have meant this "logical mistake" a bit ironically.

To my mind he did mean it ironically, because a real logical mistake, what I called an 'illogicity' – in German "Illogizität" in Gelbmann 2000b – *could not occur in a language-game*, it would be impossible. Yet the occurrence of *pragmatic paradoxes* as such "logical mistakes" would not be impossible, they can be (pragmatic) components of a language-game.

henceforth from the awkward position which his prisoner has put him in?–
What sort of a problem is this?« [...] [[xlv]; G.G.]" (Watzlawick & Weakland &
Fisch 1974b: 63[xlvi])

A pragmatic paradox produces a situation of insecurity; the person exposed to
it finds her/himself in the absurd situation that *every* form of behaviour (even
every attempt to avoid behaviour at all) becomes (absolutely) impossible (for a
human being).[xlvii] Here we obviously have to distinguish 'possibility in the sense
of modal logic'[xlviii] or 'possible in principle' from 'possible for a human being'.
According to G. H. von Wright,[xlix] what is 'possible for a *human being*' or,
shorter, 'the humanly possible', is defined as what human beings can accomplish
by action, what "can be done", as he puts it. For our purposes I would even like to
see this rendered as 'that which can be accomplished by human *behaviour*'.[l]
Correspondingly we get *an alternative to the first axiom of PTC*, whose several
versions run as

[xlv]   Cf. "Bemerkungen über die Grundlagen der Mathematik" VII § 34, Wittgenstein 1984,
        Band 6: 400 (*MS 124*: 118 from March 10th 1944). Watzlawick et al. quote loc. cit. from
        the English translation by G. E. M. Anscombe, i.e. Wittgenstein 1956: 181.

[xlvi]   German in Watzlawick & Weakland & Fisch 1974a: 84 f.

[xlvii]   Cf. Watzlawick 1976a: 30, Watzlawick 1988a: 28.

[xlviii] I am talking here about what Oskar Becker 1930 calls 'alethic modal logic' (in German:
        "alethische Modallogik").

[xlix]   Cf. Wright 1986: 189-205 (re-translation and italics mine); the original edition of Wright
        1982: 183-200 has:
        "From among everything logically possible one can single out the *physically* possible, and
        from this again the *humanly* possible (that which can be achieved through action) [...] the
        fact that something is achieved in action proves that this is humanly possible (can be done).
        Since that which is physically or humanly possible is *also* logically possible, a plausible
        view concerning the relation between existence and truth on the one hand and physical and
        human possibility on the other hand, may induce us to take an incorrect view of the relation
        between factual truth and logical possibility." (Wright 1982: 191).

[l]   It is not clear whether Wright would exclude from his definition of 'human possibility' (viz.
        "that which can be achieved by action") the case of something that can be achieved by any
        behaviour, with or without intention. In my opinion the realm of 'the humanly possible'
        includes everything that can be achieved or "done" by human beings, by intentional action
        or any behaviour.
        Even if I disagree with Wright and endorse a different concept of 'human possibility', this
        does not really concern us here.

"one cannot not communicate" or "one cannot not behave", or that "all behaviour is communication" (Watzlawick & Beavin & Jackson 1967: 48 ff. and Beavin & Watzlawick 1966/1967),

by formulating

> "It is absolutely impossible for human beings to avoid behaviour, since every form of behaviour produces communication; entire abstinence from behaviour is no behaviour that is humanly possible, and neither is any complete avoidance of communication."

With this reformulation it lies near at hand to read Watzlawick et al. in such a way as to purport that *it is inherent to the concept of 'person' that the attempt to achieve the humanly impossible by action leads to inconsistencies*, whereas the behavioural achievement of the logically impossible is per definition humanly impossible. This holds because *what is humanly possible is a sub-class of what is logically possible*, whereas what is humanly impossible could belong to the class of the logically possible as well as to the class of the logical impossible, since *not all that is rationally conceivable can be achieved by human beings.-*[li]

Bateson formulated it a methodical principle to regard the index patient's "crazy" behaviour as *adequate to a double-bind-like situation*. Cannot one then make out an effect of rehumanization[lii] in both approaches – Bateson, Watzlawick et al. on the one side, Wittgenstein on the other –, by substituting the dogmatic ban on any contradiction by inquiring into the behavioural effects within

---

[li] This is an interesting *conceptual intertwining of modal logic with pragmatics of human behaviour*. Conceiving logical possibilities (possible worlds or possible constellations of states of affairs) does not entail that human beings can bring about (all of) these fancies. The limitation to what human beings can bring about is empirical, practical, as well as conceptual, but to draw the line between the first, the second, and the third sense is a difficult matter. I admit that I doubt whether this line is fixed and not itself dependent on the dynamics of (micro-)cultural development.

It is conceivable and hence logically possible to talk about possible worlds, yet I am quite certain that not only particular fellow human beings are restricted in their imagination in this respect, but that *the human mind as such has certain restrictions*, due to, firstly, its own finiteness, beyond which we rationally cannot conceive anything (a Kantian notion, by the way), secondly, due to the ways it can express itself by means of the language and representations available at its time.

This has to be distinguished from *the impossibility in principle to achieve certain forms of behaviour or imagination at all*, about which we have no notion, although we know of certain examples (taken mainly from mathematics, e.g. contradictions).

[lii] Cf. inf. *nota xl.*

the language-game or the interactive system itself?- Putting the argument the other way round:

The person diagnosed as 'schizophrenic' has to be regarded as somebody who finds himself in a situation that continuously undermines any confidence in the meaningfulness of his own behaviour and who tries the humanly impossible – at the cost of ultimate failure, because *one just cannot succeed* in this attempt. This incapability to succeed in attempts to do something impossible holds in principle; so the 'schizophrenic' commits a logical-pragmatic mistake. (One feels a touch of tragedy here, doesn't one?)

There is, indeed, a remark by Wittgenstein, from the "Big Typescript" of 1933 (i.e. *TS 213*) which was quite certainly not known to Bateson, Watzlawick et al., stating that

> "[h]uman beings are deeply mined in philosophical, i.e. grammatical confusions. And, to free them from these, would *presuppose* that they became disentangled from the enormously multitudinous network which holds them captive. One would, so to speak, have to rearrange their entire language." (translation by Georg Henrik von Wright from *TS 213*: 423, sec. Wright 1982: 209;[liii] italics taken from original)

Just as an aside and for our evaluation of the parallel we recognize: those entrusted with administering the heritage of Wittgenstein's Nachlass, the so-called "trustees", did not permit any publication of *TS 213* together with the edition of the collected works. Yet the unpublished skripts were not accessible to Bateson, Watzlawick et al. either.

So even though Wright 1982: 209 quotes and translates this passage (*TS 213*: 423) quoted above, we cannot conclude that Bateson, Watzlawick et al. took their ideas directly from Wittgenstein, since the authors mainly dealt with here did not know Wright's book, at least this essay's author could not find any traces or hints in this direction. Hence, this parallel most likely is *a mere coincidence*, nothing more. But the fact that one and the same insight is accessible from different angles makes it even more plausible.-

The schizophrenic's behavioural confusion can be seen as *the confusion of the grammar of the internal relations manifest in the pragmatics of the interactive system concerned*. The effort of pulling him/her out of this entanglement or of

---

[liii]   Cf. *TS 211*: 570 *et MS 113*: 23v.

changing this bewitched situation, respectively becomes a task for therapy (including a criticism of the language applied), and that for Wittgenstein is the method of philosophy.[liv]

Even if Wittgenstein might have some reservations about this interpretation, it cannot be denied that there was an influence of a certain reading of Wittgenstein's early, tractarian thinking on the conception of the *PTC*, even though this interpretation is certainly considered wrong by specialists in the philosophy of Wittgenstein.

We know, for instance, of Wittgenstein's dislike for set-theory,[lv] which is an important prerequisite for the Theory of Types, and although he did not like the latter either, it certainly plays a fundamental role in *PTC*, which would be *inconceivable without a theory of the hierarchy of levels of language*. Bateson's introduction of Bertrand Russell's concept of a Theory of Types into the behavioural sciences[lvi] might have prepared what can be called a fruitful case of taking over the (positivistic) misinterpretation of "Tractatus" in Russell's preface from 1922 to the English edition[lvii] by Watzlawick et al.[lviii]

I am well aware that Russell's preface, firstly, was seriously attacked and refused by Wittgenstein,[lix] secondly, that it misreads "Tractatus". Moreover, I know that Watzlawick et al. lack scientific seriousness when checking the reliability of Russell's reading, on which they base their utilization of it. One cannot deny, however, that the acceptance of this misreading had fruitful or at

---

[liv]   In this respect I see "Tractatus Logico-Philosophicus" § 4.0031, Wittgenstein 1984, Band 1: 26 in kinship to "Philosophische Untersuchungen" I § 109, op. cit. 298 f. (cf. *MS 142*: 102 § 110 from Nov. 1936, *TS 220*: 76 f. § 96 from Jan. 1937, *TS 239*: 76 f. § 114 from Jan. 1942, and *TS 227*: 84 § 109 from Jan. 1945; this famous § 109 is also discussed in my essay on J. Hintikka, cf. inf. *section IV.IX.*), and of course to the last paragraph of "Philosophische Untersuchungen" I § 133, op. cit. 305 f. (cf. *MS 116*: 186 from Sept. 1937, *MS 120*: 85r from Feb. 23rd 1938, *TS 227*: 91 *et TS 228*: 38 from Jan. 1945, *TS 230*: 135 from Aug. 1945).

[lv]   Cf. Wright 1986: 210, Bartley 1974: 49, Fann 1969: 25 ff. or Monk 1990: 62 ff. See also Wittgenstein's letter to Bertrand Russell from Jan. 1913, furthermore "Notes Dictated to G. E. Moore in Norway", Wittgenstein 1979b: 109 (i.e. *D 301*: 4 from April 1914), and "Philosophische Bemerkungen" XV § 174, Wittgenstein 1984, Band 2: 211 (i.e. *MS 106*: 155 from Feb. 2nd 1929, *TS 209*: 91 from Jan. 1930, *TS 208*: 40 March 1930).

[lvi]   Cf. Watzlawick & Weakland & Fisch 1974a: 47.

[lvii]   Cf. Fann 1969: 9.

[lviii]   Cf. Watzlawick & Beavin & Jackson 1967: 193.

[lix]   Cf. his letter to Russell from May 6th 1920, partly printed in Wright 1986: 100.

least supportive consequences for the constellation paradigmatically forming the *PTC*. With hindsight to a genesis of ideas, this has to be assessed as permissible, yet we cannot talk of a parallel development according to *(γ)*.[lx]

This even holds good when, firstly, the uncritical usage of Russell's interpretation cannot be seen under aspect *(α)* as being justifiably rooted in Wittgenstein himself, and when, secondly, a utilitarian reading sec. *(β)* of Wittgenstein by Russell in his known "Introduction" was adroitly instrumentalized by Watzlawick et al. for their own work, who most likely did not know about Wittgenstein's reaction towards Russell. Thus we here have an instrumentalized utilization of an already utilized reading sec. *(ββ)*. At the same time it can be assumed that for Watzlawick et al. there are *no doubts* about the correctness of Russell's reading of Wittgenstein, hence from their point of view the situation could be symbolized with *(βα)*.

This *stratification of aspects*, as I would like to term it, shows that Russell's reading of "Tractatus" revealed to him those structures in thinking that matched Russell's own course of thinking at the time.[lxi] If one regards the widest possible understanding of 'reading' as a form of mediated communication, we here encounter the *phenomenon of pragmatic punctuation*, with which the *PTC*'s third axiom deals.[lxii] Russell invests Wittgenstein's thoughts with a pattern that lets them appear as relevant to him. This interpretation, regardless of whether it is 'true' or not, turns out to be effective for Russell's understanding of Wittgenstein's thinking. We should not be too amazed if I now draw a conclusion by detecting a close connection between the known theme of 'seeing as' in Wittgenstein and the phenomenon of 'reading as'.

I moreover link both of them conceptually to the pragmatic concept of punctuation by Bateson, Watzlawick et al. Wittgenstein himself enfolded his considerations on aspect-change in his critical analysis of Wolfgang Köhler's

---

[lx]   It is worth mentioning that with Spencer-Brown 1969 we are presented with a proto-logical calculus that does not only depict a formal development of a constructivist epistemology besides distancing type-theoretical methods, but also has some parallels to "Tractatus": cf. Varga von Kibéd & Matzka 1993.

[lxi]   However, he could not cope with the mystical parts of "Tractatus", as Russell admits to Ottoline Morrell in his letter from Dec. 20th 1919, cf. Monk 1990: 182 f.

[lxii]   Cf. Bateson 1981: 387 ff.; Watzlawick & Beavin & Jackson 1967: 54 ff.; Gelbmann 2000b: 489 ff.

'Gestaltpsychologie'.[lxiii] In daily communication there is no safeguard procedure against a confusion of language levels, which was successfully given in the syntactical theory of artificial languages by Russell's Theory of Types.[lxiv] It appears as a basic heuristic idea to use the *confusion of language levels as a model of the explanation of communicative disturbances*, to which the mentioned pragmatic paradoxes have to be counted.

Yet if (some) problems in communication and forms of disturbed behaviour can be explained as violations against the rules of the grammar of pragmatics, then the next step is to look at systemic communication per se as a pragmatically implemented calculus – which, indeed, is the novel idea of the *PTC*.[lxv] This represents a parallel sec. *(γ)* to a station in Wittgenstein's philosophy, where he marks language as a calculus characterized by linguistic activities.-[lxvi] This, again, raises the question as to the role of this analogy to the foundational theories in logic and mathematics in *PTC*.

Here we encounter methodological considerations on the parts of Watzlawick et al., who in principle always ground their meta-theoretical awareness with regard to their own undertaking in the exemplariness of the structural methods of the Formal Sciences. This paradigm could be seen under the parallel aspect *(γ)* in the sense of re-encountering a line of thought from one area of research in another, to which it is transferred as a blending of *(βγ)* and *(αγ)*. Historically, this becomes obvious with the stimulating effect of cybernetics. This awareness of *a shift of*

[lxiii]   For this there is ample evidence, firstly among commentators: cf. Monk 1990: 489 ff. *et* 544; ter Hark 1990: 160-190, secondly in his own works:

Cf. "Tractatus Logico-Philosophicus" § 5.5423, Wittgenstein 1984, Band 1: 64 f.; "Eine Philosophische Betrachtung (Das Braune Buch)" II ad exempla 16 *et* 19, Wittgenstein 1984, Band 5: 252 ff. *et* 260 ff.; "Philosophische Untersuchungen" II xi, Wittgenstein 1984, Band 1: 518-577 (i.e. *MS 144*: 38-106 from Jan. 1949); very often in what was edited as "Bemerkungen über die Philosophie der Psychologie" I *et* II, Wittgenstein 1998a *et* Wittgenstein 1998b, last but not least in "Letzte Schriften über die Philosophie der Psychologie" I *et* II, Wittgenstein 1990b *et* Wittgenstein 1992b, etc., issues he focussed on in the forties.

[lxiv]   Cf. Gelbmann 2000b: 428-439.

[lxv]   Cf. Watzlawick & Beavin & Jackson 1967: 13 ff.

[lxvi]   Cf. "Philosophische Grammatik" I, X § 140, Wittgenstein 1984, Band 4: 193 (*MS 114*: 172 f. from June 5th 1932).

Yet *this* parallel aspect *(γ)* is none to which references can be found that could be symbolized with *(αγ)* or *(βγ)*.

paradigms,[lxvii] which was performed by transgressing to the systemic perspective and discovering the autonomy of transactional communication,[lxviii] deeply affects the conceptual foundation, at the same time finding its justification in a utilitarian appeal to Wittgenstein sec. *(β)*, that cannot be authorized and is cut out of its context, as the following citation shows:

> "The question *why?* has always played a central, virtually dogmatic role in the history of science. After all, science is supposed to be concerned with explanation. Now, consider the sentence: »We are not competent to explain *why* scientific thinking conceives of explanation as the precondition for change, but there can be little doubt *that* this is the case.« This statement is both about the principle under examination and at the same time an example of it. [[lxix]; G.G.] The awareness of the *fact* that the question *why?* is being asked and that it determines scientific procedures and their results is not predicated on a valid explanation of *why* it is being asked. That is, we can take the situation as it exists here and now, without ever understanding why it got to be that way, and in spite of our ignorance of its origin and evolution we can do something with (or about) it. In doing this we are asking *what?*, i.e., what is the situation, what is going on here and now. [...] [[lxx]; G.G.] However, the myth that in order to solve a problem one first has to understand its *why* is so deeply embedded in scientific thinking that any attempt to deal with the problem only in terms of its present structure and consequences is considered the height of superficiality. Yet in asserting this principle within our theory of change we find ourselves in good company. It is certainly not our discovery; all we can claim is that we stumbled over it in the course of our work. Only gradually did we realize that it had been enunciated before, albeit in different contexts.
>
> One source is Wittgenstein, whose work we have already mentioned. In his *Philosophical Investigations* he takes a very strong stand against explanations and their limits. »Explanations come to an end somewhere. But what is the meaning of the word 'five'? Meaning does not enter here at all, only how the word 'five' is used.« [...] [[lxxi]; G.G.], he states initially, and later in the same

---

[lxvii]   Cf. Th. S. Kuhn 1962, a book, which Watzlawick et al. certainly read (as shown in Gelbmann 2000b).

[lxviii]   Cf. Watzlawick & Weakland 1980: 12 ff.

[lxix]   Cf. to the theme of self-reference also Watzlawick 1990d.

[lxx]   Here comes a footnote 3: "It is amazing how rarely the question *what?* is seriously asked. Instead, either the nature of the situation is taken to be quite evident, or it is described and explained mainly in terms of *why?* by reference to origins, reasons, motives, etc., rather than to events observable here and now." (Watzlawick & Weakland & Fisch 1974b: 84).

[lxxi]   Cf. "Philosophische Untersuchungen" I § 1, Wittgenstein 1984, Band 1: 238 (*MS 142*: 1 f.

work he returns to this theme in a formulation which goes far beyond the abstractions of the philosophy of language into territory that appears very familiar: »It often happens that we only become aware of the important *facts*, if we suppress the question 'why?'; and then in the course of our investigations these facts lead us to an answer.« [...] [[lxxii]; G.G.] For the later Wittgenstein, what becomes questionable is the question itself; this is an idea that has great affinity with our investigations into change, and one that he had touched upon in his most important early work, the *Tractatus Logico Philosophicus*: »We feel that even if *all possible* scientific questions be answered, the problems of life have still not been touched at all. Of course, there is then no question left, and just this is the answer. The solution of the problem of life is seen in the vanishing of this problem« [[lxxiii]; G.G.]

We need mention mathematics only very briefly. It, too, does not ask *why?* and yet is the royal road to penetrating analyses and imaginative solutions. Mathematical statements are best understood as interrelated elements within a system. An understanding of their origin or causes is not required to grasp their significance and may even be misleading.

Another area in which causal explanations or questions of meaning play a very supordinate role is cybernetics. [...]" (Watzlawick & Weakland & Fisch 1974b: 83 ff;[lxxiv] italics original, punctuation slightly changed)

We need not expound how far cybernetics and mathematics were preliminary for *PTC*,[lxxv] apart from stating that with Gregory Bateson a personal connection to the circle of early cyberneticians around Norbert Wiener was given – a circle to which Heinz von Foerster, a friend of Paul Watzlawick and a nephew of the Wittgensteins, also belonged. He is another source[lxxvi] for constructivism in re-

---

from Nov. 1936, *TS 220*: ii § 2 from Jan. 1937, *TS 239*: 2 § 2 from Jan. 1942, *TS 227*: 6 § 1 from Jan. 1945). The quotation follows the English edition, cf. Wittgenstein 1991: 3.

[lxxii] Cf. "Philosophische Untersuchungen" I § 471, Wittgenstein 1984, Band 1: 426 (*MS 129*: 199 from Aug. 17th 1944, *TS 227*: 252 § 471 from Jan. 1945, *TS 228*: 103 § 365 from Jan. 1945, *TS 230*: 146 § 524 from Aug. 1945, *TS 235*: 8 § 139 from Jan. 1951). The quotation follows the English edition, cf. Wittgenstein 1991: 134.

[lxxiii] Cf. "Tractatus Logico-Philosophicus" § 6.52, Wittgenstein 1992a: 73. Although, Watzlawick et al. use a non-standard edition of "Tractatus" (cf. inf. *nota cxxviii*), this difference is irrelevant here.

[lxxiv] German in Watzlawick & Weakland & Fisch 1974a: 105 ff.

[lxxv] Cf. Gelbmann 2000b: 152–359.

[lxxvi] Cf. i.a. Foerster 1973, Foerster 1979, Foerster 1981, Foerster 1991, Foerster 1993a, Foerster 1999a, Foerster & Glasersfeld 1999.
I have entered into these more historical connections and the establishment of a disciplinary matrix (in terms of Th. S. Kuhn) in the first chapter of my doctoral

applying the Theory of Types in his famous concept of 'second-order cybernetics' to a socio-epistemic field, by conceiving of the inter-action of social subjects in terms of cybernetics.-

From Wittgenstein's limiting infinite questioning by his conception of language-games, Watzlawick et al. derive their justification for envisioning the traditional model of explanation[lxxvii] with scepticism, hence their approach in this respect is a mixture of the aspects *(α)* and *(β)*.[lxxviii] The discovery of the aforementioned shift was *not* brought about by a systemic reading of Wittgenstein. It rather stems from clinical experience and practice; hence it is a parallel sec. *(γ)*, and in reflection on its own course is projected on Wittgenstein's philosophy. So from this point of view it can be symbolized as *(βγ)*.

The procedure is similar when, in explaining a certain therapeutic technique conceived under a type-theoretical view-point, reference to Wittgenstein is evoked by the *need for illustrating* one's estimation as to which methods should be either construed or applied. Here we have a double aspect in the way that *one tends to see one's own insights as discoveries* according to *(αγ)*, in order *to make use of certain handy formulations for one's explicative comments*, sec *(β)*. A good case-study of this kind of utilising heuristic reference is the technique of re-interpretation[lxxix] or reframing. This technique is applied in the communication between therapist and patient(s), which on both sides has to be understood as *a rhetoriccal experience*. The technique of reframing orients itself to the mathe-

---

dissertation, i.e. Gelbmann 2000b.

[lxxvii] This is the covering law model according to Hempel, cf. Hempel 1965 or Braithwaite 1968, to which Bateson 1967 already advanced the cybernetic alternative. The criticism of Hempel's covering law model of explanation in Hintikka & Halonen 1995 neglects Bateson 1967.

[lxxviii] If this is supposed to be some kind of progress, at least detectable in the spirit of Baeteson's writings, we should keep in mind that Wittgenstein did not have much sympathy for the modern belief in progress, the bond between industry and science, as witnessed by Wright 1986: 213 and traceable in Wittgenstein's critical attitude towards (our) modern civilization in his writings.

Cf. the Preface to "Philosophische Bemerkungen", Wittgenstein 1984, Band 2: 7 (*MS 109*: 205 ff. from Nov. 1930), re-edited in "Vermischte Bemerkungen", Wittgenstein 1984, Band 8: 459, but see also op. cit. 529 (*MS 133*: 46r from Jan. 7th 1947) and op. cit. 538 f. (*MS 135*: 13 f. from July 14th 1947).

[lxxix] The term 're-interpretation' is my tentative translation of the German "Umdeutung", which originally seems to have its source in the English "reframing".

matical Theory of Sets in a type-theoretical form, just along the lines of Bateson's notion of 'deutero-learning'[lxxx] and the concept of layers or levels of 'solution'.[lxxxi]

Here the reader has to be told in advance that in the case of system-therapy there might be a definite index-patient to which a manifestation of symptoms can be attributed, yet the object of therapy and what is to be altered towards a less (psycho)pathogen organization is *the entire system itself*. When talking about marking the modes and metaphors of communication, including the framing of the situation of therapy, Bateson et al. now speak in terms of (their understanding of) Russell's Theory of Types, but also relate to B. L. Whorf and L. Wittgenstein.[lxxxii]

> "The reader who has had the patience to follow us through these rather tedious considerations will by now see their relevance to reframing as a technique for achieving second-order change: In its most abstract terms, reframing means changing the emphasis from one class membership of an object [[lxxxiii]; G.G.] to another, equally valid class membership, or, especially, introducing such a new class membership into the conceptualization of all concerned. If, again, we resist the traditional temptation of asking *why* this should be so, we can then see *what* is involved in reframing:
> 1. Our experience of the world is based on the categorization of the objects of our perception into classes. These classes are mental constructs and therefore of a totally different order of reality than the objects themselves. Classes are formed not only on the basis of the physical properties of objects, but especially on the strength of their meaning and value for us.
> 2. Once an object is conceptualized as the member of a given class, it is extremely difficult to see it as also belonging to another class. This class membership of an object is called its »reality«; thus anybody who sees it as the

---

[lxxx]   Cf. Bateson 1942, Bateson 1972d, Bateson 1982: 148 ff., etc.

[lxxxi]   Cf. Watzlawick & Weakland & Fisch 1974a.

[lxxxii]   Cf. i.a. Bateson & Jackson & Haley & Weakland 1956 *et* Bateson 1959. Bateson 1972d even goes beyond Russell in considering the possibility of a ramified Theory of Types, which in the area of philosophical logic was approached e.g. by Tichý 1988 in his account of Gottlob Frege.

[lxxxiii]   Here comes a footnote 8: "*Object* should be taken in its most abstract connotation, as including events, situations, relationships between people and between people and objects, patterns of behaviour, etc." (Watzlawick & Weakland & Fisch 1974b: 98; italics original).
In terms of Herbert Stachowiak's 'General Model Theory' (in short: *GMT*) one could talk about this term 'object' as about "everything that is modellable" or as "everything that can be modelled", taken from the domain of what occurs in communication or of what communication consists. (Some thoughts about 'modellability' – *via GMT* – can be found in Gelbmann 2002d.)

member of another class must be mad or bad. Moreover, from this simplistic assumption there follows another, equally simplistic one, namely that to stick to this view of reality is not only sane, but also »honest«, »authentic«, and what not. »I cannot play games« is the usual retort of people who are playing the game of not playing a game, when confronted with the possibility of seeing an alternative class membership.

3. What makes reframing such an effective tool of change is that once we do perceive the alternative class membership(s) we cannot so easily go back to the trap and the anguish of a former view of »reality«. [...]

It seems that the first to draw attention to this – albeit in the context of games and the awareness of rules – was again Wittgenstein. In his *Remarks on the Foundations of Mathematics* [[lxxxiv]; G.G.] he writes:

»Let us suppose, ... [[lxxxv]; G.G.] that the game is such that whoever begins can always win by a particular simple trick. But this has not been realized;– so it is a game. Now someone draws our attention to it;– and it stops being a game.

What turn can I give this, to make it clear to myself?– For I want to say: 'and it stops being a game'– not: 'and we now see that it wasn't a game.'

That means, ... the other man did not *draw our attention* to anything; he taught us a different game in place of our own.– But how can the new game have made the old one obsolete?– We now see something different, and can no longer naïvely go on playing.

On the one hand the game consisted in our actions (our play) on the board; and these actions I could perform as well now as before. But on the other hand it was essential to the game that I blindly tried to win; and now I can no longer do that.« [[lxxxvi]; G.G.]" (Watzlawick & Weakland & Fisch 1974b: 98 ff.;[lxxxvii] italics original, punctuation corrected)

'Re-interpretation' or 'reframing' provide insights into what shall be called the customariness and ordinariness that so far ruled the game and forms of behaviour in this system – provided that it is comprehended in its efficacy *within the*

[lxxxiv] In German the title is misquoted, it should be "Bemerkungen über die Grundlagen der Mathematik", yet Watzlawick & Weakland & Fisch 1974a: 123 wrongly quote it as "Grundlagen der Mathematik".

[lxxxv] Watzlawick et al. indicate loc. cit. with three dots that they left out a part of the text.

[lxxxvi] Cf. "Bemerkungen über die Grundlagen der Mathematik" III § 77, Wittgenstein 1984, Band 6: 203 f., (*MS 117*: 205 f. from March 1940). Watzlawick et al. loc. cit. followed Anscombe's translation, to be found in Wittgenstein 1994b: 203 f.

[lxxxvii] German in Watzlawick & Weakland & Fisch 1974a: 122 ff., cf. also Watzlawick 1975: 125; Watzlawick 1977: 95; Watzlawick 1981a: 108; Watzlawick 1988a: 28 ff.; Watzlawick 1993: 124.

interactive system and not merely taken in isolation as a change undergone by an individual person. The notion that with exactly the same system-elements under the same presuppositions a different game, different forms of behaviour shaping the interactive system, become possible – a re-organization which minimizes suffering and helps to get rid of behavioural disturbances – bears strking similarity to a line of thought found in Wittgenstein.

The sujet of aspect-change depicts a parallel sec. *(γ)*, reminding us of the famous rabbit-duck-double-picture.[lxxxviii] At once we recognize the connection with the therapeutically motivated modification of (pragmatic) punctuation, as envisaged in the third axiom of *PTC*.[lxxxix] The rules implemented into a social system and the (mental) models of reality that select a certain succession of events from the variety of what is realizable as so-called second-order realities,[xc] are then – due to reframing – suddenly seen as something optional that can be substituted by other, more viable alternatives. Accordingly, the exclusiveness of one aspect of experiences is relativized in its monolithic incontrovertibility.

So *reframing as a second-order solution*[xci] rests on the possibility of actualizing and accepting a change of aspects in such a way that the current situation (as a reality of first order) allows for both (and perhaps further) interpretations (as realities of second order). These only become incompatible with each other if their mutual exclusiveness and the uniqueness of the corresponding reality-construct is defended at all costs (in an unresolvable conflict). Hence the constructive solution

---

[lxxxviii] Cf. "Philosophische Untersuchungen" II xi, Wittgenstein 1984, Band 1: 520 or "Bemerkungen über die Philosophie der Psychologie" I, § 70, Wittgenstein 1998a: 16 (cf. *MS 130*: 133 May 26th 1946, *MS 134*: 58 from March 21st 1947, or *MS 144*: 39 from Jan. 1949).

Wittgenstein took it from Joseph Jastrow 1900.- Incidentally, Jastrow was a student of Ch. S. Peirce, cf. Jastrow 1916. Cf. for this picture also Aldrich 1958: 73, Gombrich 1960: 5 and Savigny 1993: 268.

[lxxxix] Cf. Watzlawick & Beavin & Jackson 1967: 54 ff.

[xc] Cf. Watzlawick 1993: 42 ff. Second-order-realities are the ways of experiencing and living that are not reducible to a purely physical or biological level, but are autonomous products of social interaction between personal subjects. They are *results of communication* (Watzlawick 1990c: 138).

The term 'first-order-reality' corresponds to a physically describable, materially organized constitution of 'world'. In communication, communicators might agree on a view of first-order-reality, but by communicating they construe a second-order-reality influencing the way they perceive their socialising and interaction. Implemented in social systems, the same first-order-reality might lead to different or even conflicting second-order-realities.

[xci] Cf. Watzlawick & Weakland & Fisch 1974a: 99 ff.

consists in abandoning the claim that this or that is the only correct or possible point of view.- With Wittgenstein, yet not with Watzlawick et al., the following can be said under aspect *(γ)*:

> "We see, not change of aspects, but change of interpretation." ("Zettel" § 216, Wittgenstein 1990c: 38[xcii])

Systemic-pragmatically speaking, this change of interpretation becomes apparent in the disappearance of the disturbing sequences in the succession of inter-action and hence of the communicational disturbances that produced or badly influenced disturbed behaviour. One actually perceives the effects of a change of inter-pretation invoked by becoming aware of a change of aspects, and these results become visible in concrete interpersonal interaction. Here the solution of a problem can be realized in its vanishing.[xciii]

This reframing has an injunctive, even commanding form and takes one aspect as absolute. It consists in prescriptions of conduct, and even in giving orders as to how to behave or act.[xciv] The problem was *not* that *the* reality was not realized, cognated, but that only *one* possibility of construing a realization of reality was construed and that this was considered *the only one*. The problem is not a wrong aspect of a cause, but the wrong interpretation, i.e. that there is only one aspect under which a case can be seen. Watzlawick's *credo* has to be read in this constructivist understanding, contained in one of Wittgenstein's often quoted metaphors. We shall bring it as a quotation in a quotation, by introducing explanations Watzlawick gives:

> "»What is your aim in philosophy?– To show the fly the way out of the fly-bottle.« [...] [[xcv]; G.G.]

[xcii] Cf. the German original in "Zettel" § 216, Wittgenstein 1984, Band 8: 319 (i.e. *TS 233a*: 45 § 520 from Jan. 1946, *TS 232*: 733 § 520 from Jan. 1948, *MS 137*: 32 from Aug. 3rd 1946). It was also edited in "Remarks on the Philosophy of Psychology" II § 521, Wittgenstein 1998b: 93e.

[xciii] Cf. "Tractatus Logico-Philosophicus" § 6.521, Wittgenstein 1992a: 73.

[xciv] Cf. e.g. Watzlawick 1988d.

[xcv] Cf. "Philosophische Untersuchungen" I § 309, Wittgenstein 1984, Band 1: 378 (*MS 118*: 71r from Sept. 8th 1937, *MS 117*: 92 from Sept. 11th 1937, *TS 227*: 190 § 309 from Jan. 1945, *TS 228*: 105 § 368 from Jun. 1945, *TS 230*: 48 § 179 from Aug. 1945). The quotation follows the English edition, cf. Wittgenstein 1991: 103, except that Anscombe has "shew" instead of "show". This quotation is also used in e.g. Watzlawick & Weakland & Fisch 1974a: 99 *et* 114.

Old fashioned fly-bottles had a funnel-like opening whose large outer mouth made it appear safe for the fly to venture into the excitingly smelly (but gradually narrowing) interior. Once inside the inner chamber, the only way back out was through the same narrow inner opening of the funnel through which the fly had entered. But seen from the inside, this hole now appeared even more confining and dangerous than the chamber in which it found itself caught. Following Wittgenstein's metaphor, it would now be necessary to convince the fly that the only solution to its dilemma was the seemingly least likely and most threatening one.
How do we find the way out of the fly-bottle of an ill-fitting reality construction? And is there any hope of freeing ourselves if all conceivable solutions only lead to »more of the same« and enantiodromatic fatality seems to ordain that they only make worse what they are meant to improve?" (Watzlawick 1984a: 249[xcvi])

This 'more of the same', with its *sudden change to the opposite of what was intended* – the so-called 'enantiodromy'[xcvii] – is a first-order-solution, repeatedly attempted by those concerned in order to solve their problems, without realizing that they hereby aggravate the problematic situation. *Second-order-solutions then consist of abandoning first-order-solutions* and of trying some alternative so far overlooked. This often succeeds after the circular structure of the communication constituting the situation has been disrupted – e.g. by a therapeutic intervention, applying simple instructions instead of a long-winded and paralysing analysis.[xcviii]

It is evident that here a striking metaphor of Wittgenstein has been adopted, recycled and aptly used for one's own purposes. *This is the only reference to Wittgenstein that clearly sets the two aspects (α) and (β) on a par.* So the conjecture is not improbable that we can locate an aspect *(δ)*, going beyond what we signified with *(γ)*, since here a convergence of the train of thoughts of Watzlawick et al. with Wittgenstein's becomes apparent.-

---

[xcvi]   German in Watzlawick 1981a: 229.

[xcvii]   The German term is 'Enantiodromie'. This term has a Greek origin, and despite its artificial construction I think it is a useful expression.
One should not forget that Watzlawick received the classic Austrian education from a "Gymnasium" with a humanist background, studied linguistics in Venice, was or still is able to do therapy in at least five languages and spoke or even still speaks at least seven languages fluently; so I credit him with enough linguistic knowledge to invent such terms.
The reader also finds this term in Watzlawick 1981c, which is translated into English as Watzlawick 1984c and as Watzlawick 1990e.

[xcviii]   Cf. Watzlawick & Weakland & Fisch 1974a: 51 ff. *et* 99 ff.

The cited passage also fits the sub-theme, i.e. the question in how far it can be recognized at all whether failing with a first-order-solution has a functionality for a construction of what is to be taken as real. In creating and prolonging a crisis, this failing offers a chance, namely to facilitate discarding those assumptions that produced and stabilized the problem but were not recognized or accepted in this function. Hence this failing, *if once realized*, becomes the first step towards a fundamental improvement of a self-perpetuating situation.-

This takes us to the next point in our investigation of Watzlawick et al.'s relation to Wittgenstein.-

I.V. World, Subject, Object

Watzlawick expresses his view on the essence of human relationships in a very characteristic way:

"In contrast to objects, however, human relationships are not phenomena which exist objectively, in their own right, as it were, nor is it possible to have a consensus about their properties. Above all, if there are differences of opinion about the characteristics of a human relationship, it cannot be proved that one of the partners is right and the other wrong, or, to anticipate one of our main topics, that one partner is »normal« and the other »crazy«. Relationships, the contents of our *interpersonal*, pragmatic reality, are not real in the same sense as objects are; they have their »reality« only in the perception of the partners, and even this reality is shared only partially by the partners. When A defines his relationship with B by the statement: »I know that you don't like me«, and B answers with his definition of their relationship by saying: »You always think the worst of me«, then, in the nature of human communication, there is no possibility of solving this controversy by objective proof. Pragmatic events cannot be determined monadically. [xcix; G.G.] If this is attempted anyway and if relationship phenomena are either ignored altogether or seen as epiphenomena, the monad will inevitably acquire hypothetical properties, which either do not exist at all or cannot be proved. It is especially significant that this problem runs like a red thread through the conceptions of man and his behavior, no matter how incompatible these views might be in every other

---

[xcix] This view on interpersonal relationships and especially on the so-called 'transactions' (performed in the communicants' mutual reference to their relationship) is the main theme of Gelbmann 2002b.

respect." (Watzlawick 1990b: 15 f.;[c] italics original, tiny mistakes in punctuation corrected)

This quotation is the proper, concisely formulated foundation of the often discussed, often misunderstood, often criticized so-called 'constructivism' of Watzlawick et al. It concerns the perception of relationships in contrast to the perception of objects.[ci]

Without making demands on Wittgenstein in favour of constructivism as it can be encountered in Watzlawick et al., Glasersfeld, or Foerster – although some of the entries collected in "On Certainty" could be interpreted in this direction[cii] –, we have to state that on one point fundamental to the constructivist approach, Wittgenstein's ideas were obviously an important source for Watzlawick et al.: I mean the interdependent relation between the (mental) constructions of the concepts 'world', 'object', and 'subject'. This stems from a not totally interest-free interpretation sec. *(β)*, yet at the same time its promoting effect on the constitution of theorizing according to *(α)* should not be overlooked.

The objectivistic distinction between 'subject' and 'object' cannot be maintained for a constructivist epistemology if the perception of relationships besides the perception of objects becomes constitutive for the reality-construing function of communication, and if at the same time that which is the epitome of the existence as 'world' itself cannot be grasped by knowledge or even experience. The recourse to Wittgenstein's "Tractatus" supports the thoughts of Watzlawick et al. by conceptualising the delimitation of the knowable as non-objectifiable and

---

[c]   German in Watzlawick 1975: 106 f.

[ci]   Another source for this constructivism has its background in formal sciences (yet not an explicitly intuitionist background): it is the well-known relativation of the *tertium non datur* (the Latin expression for the principle of excluding the third, viz. a third truth-value). Wittgenstein flirted with this weakening of a basic semantic principle, which is worth mentioning sec. *(γ)*. In this he was influenced by Luitzen Egbertus Jan Brouwer, who gave a lecture at the University of Vienna in March 1928, cf. Monk 1990: 249, Malcolm 1986: 41 ff, or Hintikka 1996d: 81 ff.
This to be reflected in "Philosophische Untersuchungen" I § 352, Wittgenstein 1984, Band 1: 391 f. (*MS 116*: 149 ff. from Sept. 1937 which refers to Hermann Weyl, yet not so in *TS 227*: 208 f. § 352 from Jan. 1945, but again in *TS 228*: 32 f. § 121 from June 1945 and in *TS 230*: 97 f. § 360 from Aug. 1945). But allusions to Brouwer's name in Wittgenstein's skripts can be found even earlier, cf. e.g. *MS 106*: 245 from Feb. 1929, *MS 113*: 99v f. from May 9th 1932, etc. (this has been edited in "Philosophische Bemerkungen").

[cii]   Cf. Wright 1986: 170 ff.

accompanying the relativizing qualification of the subjective with the relativizing qualification of the objective. This leads them to a discussion of what could be called *the problem of intelligibility and effability*, i.e. the problem where to draw a limit around what can be said or thought in meaningful terms and where it becomes necessary to understand what is inexpressible. Look at the following quotation:

"Man is ultimately subject and object of his quest. While the question whether his mind can be considered to be anything like a formalized system [...] is probably unanswerable, his quest for an understanding of the meaning of his existence *is an attempt at formalization*. In this and only in this sense we feel that certain results of proof theory (especially in the areas of self-reflexiveness and undecidability) are pertinent. This is by no means our discovery; in fact, ten years before Gödel presented his brilliant theorem [*ciii*; G.G.], another great mind of our century had already formulated this paradox in philosophical terms, namely Ludwig Wittgenstein in his *Tractatus Logico-Philosophicus*. [*civ*; G.G.] [...] Probably nowhere has this existential paradox been defined more lucidly nor has the *mystical* been accorded a more dignified position as the ultimate step transcending this paradox.
Wittgenstein shows that we could only know something about the world in its totality if we could step outside it; but if this were possible, this world would no longer be the *whole* world. However, our logic knows of nothing outside it:
»Logic fills the world: the limits of the world are also its limits.
We cannot therefore say in logic: This and this there is in the world, that there is not.
For that would apparently presuppose that we exclude certain possibilities, and this cannot be the case since otherwise logic must get outside the limits of the world: that is, if it could consider these limits from the other side also.
What we cannot think, we cannot think: we cannot therefore say what we cannot think.« [...] [*cv*; G.G.]
The world, then, is finite and at the same time limitless, limitless precisely because there is nothing outside that together with the inside could form a

---

ciii   Cf. K. Gödel 1931.

civ   Cf. inf. *nota cxxviii*.

cv   I put this second-order-quotation into the corresponding quotation marks, Watzlawick et al. loc. cit. render it in print with indented margins. I kept their paragraphing.
       The reference is "Tractatus Logico-Philosophicus" § 5.61. The translation and also punctuation used by Watzlawick et al. loc. cit. insignificantly differs from D. F. Pears and B. F. McGuinness given in Wittgenstein 1992a: 56 f.- This passages is also cited in Watzlawick 1976a: 74 f.

boundary. But if this is so, then it follows that »The world and life are one. I am my world« [...] [*cvi*; G.G.] Subject and world are thus no longer entities whose relational function is in some way governed by the auxiliary verb *to have* (that one *has* the other, contains or belongs to it), but by the existential *to be*: »The subject does not *belong* to the world, but it *is* a limit of the world« [...] [*cvii*; G.G.]." (Watzlawick & Beavin & Jackson 1967: 270 f.;*cviii* italics original)

What conclusions in favour of constructivism are to be drawn from Gödel's discovery in the field of mathematical logic? When understood as meaning that the 'paradox of human existence' consists in inevitably occurring, undecidable situations, this is a rather uncontroversial exploitation of Gödel's proof for *PTC*. Gödel's article from 1931 showed in a sufficiently rich calculus encoding arithmetic, firstly, that the consistency of this logical system cannot be proved with the means this system itself provides, therefore such a system is *incomplete,*[cix] and secondly, that there are formulae derivable from the system's axioms whose truth-value can in principle not be determined, hence the talk of *undecidability.*[cx]

What Watzlawick et al. now come to claim is that by looking at social systems of communicants and their interactions as logical or even symbolic systems that encode the structure of a logical system – whose richness is of such a degree that it depicts a logical situation analogous to the logical situation one is confronted with when formulating a calculus for fundamental branches of mathematics – one realizes the undecidability and incompleteness inherent to human communication and the 'paradox of human existence'.[cxi] (There is no doubt

---

[cvi]   "Tractatus Logico-Philosophicus" § 5.621 *et* § 5.63, cf. Wittgenstein 1992a: 57.

[cvii]   "Tractatus Logico-Philosophicus" § 5.632, cf. Wittgenstein 1992a: 57 (again, loc. cit. differs in the translation used by Watzlawick et al. from the one I use, but the difference is not important).

[cviii]   German in Watzlawick & Beavin & Jackson 1969: 252 f.

[cix]   So David Hilbert's dream of absolute consistency was refuted.

[cx]   This put an end to the logicists' strife to find the ultimate logical axioms for arithmetic (here the names of Gottlob Frege and Bertrand Russell are the most prominent representatives).

[cxi]   What about a game-theoretical description of communication-situations, applied by Watzlawick himself, e.g. in Watzlawick 1976b? Are they also incomplete and undecidable in principle?
The possibility of such descriptions already presupposes the reduction of the communication situatation to be described to a rational decision procedure. But it is exactly the point of *PTC* that not only rational decisions account for the "moves" in the great game

that Watzlawick et al. had at least more than a philosophical layman's acquaintance with Gödel's results.) In comparing *PTC* with a logical calculus of a complex sort they are provided with the means of expression to *characterize by analogy* the complexity of human systems of communication and interaction; so in a certain sense the authors of *PTC* use Gödel's proof as *measure*.

William W. Bartley mentions[cxii] that through Gödel's famous work it became clear to Alonzo Church and Stephen Kleene[cxiii] that the assertion "riddles exist" holds *in principle*, in contrast to what Wittgenstein maintained in "Tractatus" § 6.5.[cxiv] The far reaching implications of the logical discovery of undecidability and incompleteness had not been foreseen by Wittgenstein.[cxv] This sets certain limits to optimism about knowability that are firmer and less metaphysical as Immanuel Kant tried to draw with his *Critique of Pure Reason*.[cxvi]

What we have just quoted from Watzlawick et al. is meant to show that, within the frame of subjectivity, subjectivity itself cannot meaningfully be conceived of. *Here the limit of effability becomes apparent*, and with it the realization of the limitations of any effabilization of the premises for the construction of second-order-realities (which are themselves third-order-premises),[cxvii] i.e. *it becomes impossible to make them expressible*. The complexity of second-order-realities, which are *social products of the communication embodied in interactive systems*, is to a certain degree analogous to the one given in undecidable arithmetic calculi.[cxviii] To have to accept the situation of

---

of human communication. That is why the game-theoretical approach by Hintikka & Sandu 1997, despite its marvellous insights into a formal characterization of language-games, does not provide us with any means to understand *communication* in the sense of *PTC*.

[cxii] Cf. Bartley 1974: 50 ff.

[cxiii] Cf. Church 1936 and Kleene 1943.

[cxiv] Cf. Wittgenstein 1984, Band 1: 84.

[cxv] But that the post-tractarian Wittgenstein had some knowledge of these proofs and pondered on their effect on his philosophy of mathematics, that he even commented them, is shown in e.g. Charles Sayward 2001.

[cxvi] Cf. Kant 1781.

[cxvii] These third-order-premises are premises for second-order-realities and hence a highly abstract matter, ruling the ways and forms of how the social world is organized in second-order-realities. A therapy, in the psychological as well as philosophical sense, then has to alter, apprehend, and align the third-order-premises that are detectable and conjectured in the social system taken under consideration.

[cxviii] I.e. propositional calculi of first order or a reduction of set-theoretical mathematics to the axiomatization attempted by David Hilbert, Guiseppe Peano, or Bertrand Russell and Alfred North Whitehead. These axiomatizations are, in contrast to Hilbert's original claim,

undecidability in principle in the face of the "paradox of human existence" is a situation where 'the mystical' is transcended in so far as the materialization of third-order-premises evades any predictability. *We cannot catch up with the creativity of the constructive.*

Permit me speculating: In anology to Gödel's proof we might find ourselves in the (epistemological) situation that at any point of time in communication a second-order-reality is constructible that is not completely explainable in terms of third-order-premises or derivable from any postulated knowledge of third-order-premises. *We can construe more in communication than we can know about communication in a certain situation.* It is exactly at this point that the therapeutic approach of Watzlawick et al. starts off, implementing a series of elaborated methods of intervention, whose purpose is not the attainment of a pre-conceived aim or prescribed premises of second or third order, but only to *make those premises leading to a pathogenic situation alterable.*

This does not only shed light on what Friedrich Kainz[cxix] called "seduction by language" – easy to detect by an inclination to say "one has subjectivity" or "one has world" –, it also demonstrates that the relation between subjectivity and the world, between the abstract essence of 'the subject as such' and the abstract essence of 'being in the world as such', is a relation of mutual constitution and mutual limitation. (I am not trying to hint at Martin Heidegger, he was definitely no source for Watzlawick et al., in contrast to Jean-Paul Sartre.)

Thus an interpretation can easily gain ground that lies in the interest of constructivism sec. *(β)* which, with the concept of the limitation of the subject, understands the existence of subjectivity as a viabilization of its mundanity, within which those objectifications of reality (of whatever order) take place that account for self-reference and reflectivity in constituting subjectivity. The subject can understand itself because it is only by being in the world that it construes those ideas that make the reflective and self-referential constitution of its autonomy possible. *The objectified 'world as such' is a construction necessary for the subject which brought this idea about, in order to enable it to constitute itself as the*

---

    not able to prove their own consistency. Cf. Nagel & Newman 1958, a work quoted by Watzlawick et al. themselves.

[cxix]   Cf. Kainz 1972. With "seduction by language" or "linguistic seduction" I translate Kainz' German term "Sprachverführung".

autonomous centre of its own world.[cxx] The frame within which one can speak of 'subject' and 'world' is seen as reframed.

That this framing cannot be transcended *puts an end to modelling further meta-levels*, since these arc always relative to a framing. So to talk about a framing can only produce a further framing, but then there would be no talk about the framing of the framing. It is exactly because the concept of the limitation of the 'subject and world' frames the relation these two notions have to each other, within which they can be labelled and marked off, and moreover because *this frame coincides with the entirety of what can be said* in a tractarian manner of speaking, that there cannot be any further intelligibilization by widening the region or horizon of what is effable. That which is effable, belongs to the framing of world and subject within the language construed and available. In this sense, 'subjectivity' and 'world' are interdependent with the intelligibility of that which can be said. *We cannot get rid of the language-games of 'subject' and 'world', although we know that we construe the social reality in which they are applied.-*

This interactional perspective was already introduced at the *MRI* in Palo Alto, initiated by Bateson as one of its most creative precursors.[cxxi] It is *one* view on investigating psychic and communicative phenomena. New possibilities of theorizing about human behaviour as constituted by communication arise by trying to explain behaviour not purely intrinsically from the individualized position of the subject and its intra-psychic dynamics, but from communication itself, and hence from a particular situation of interacting people. Now it becomes clear what it is that takes one beyond the so far perceived section of reality.

The result is that in many ways the semantisation of the conceptual apparatus is re-organized, yet concomitantly it becomes expressible or effable, whereas it hitherto could not even be indicated as non-existent, to say nothing about it being describable.- Hence one could *not* inquire at which degree of abstraction within the hierarchy of types one had arrived at a level which superseded the hierarchy of types itself. For the *PTC* there appears a boundary to theoribilization, since what, in terms of Kant, constitutes the subject as a 'Ding an sich' (a 'thing for itself'),

---

[cxx]   Cf. Hejl 1985.

[cxxi]   Yet this was not its only result. The unfolding of system theory had various origins, whose background for theorizing on communication is enlightened by Ruesch & Bateson 1951, Bertalanffy 1968, Bateson et al. 1969, Watzlawick & Weakland 1980, Marc & Picard 1984.

respectively the world per se, does not only remain ineffable, but even beyond being intelligibilizable.

The metaphysical notions 'existence', 'world', 'reality' reveal themselves as unavoidable constructions or temptations to take them as such.[cxxii] Regardless of the indication of a person as "patient" on whom the properties of a social system are projected, *the subjectivation of the interpersonal sphere of pragmatics presents itself as an alienation* that inevitably ascribes to the monade 'patient' hypothetical qualities and properties, which genuinely emerge from the whole system itself and *manifest themselves only symptomatically where they can be observed in an objectifiable way.*[cxxiii] What is revealed here is what used to be regarded as "metaphysical" by negative delineation.

Watzlawick et al. quote "Tractatus" § 6.4312 (about the riddle of current and eternal life) *et* § 6.5-7 (about the fact that there are only answerable questions, the unsayable, the famous ladder-metaphor, cf. inf., and the final metaphysical taciturnity)[cxxiv] in referring to the frame that allows for asking and answering meaningful questions that arise within it.[cxxv] Subjectivity as such cannot remain the *terminus ad quem* for *PTC* (yet the question whether it was a *terminus a quo* is to remain open). A strong motivation for this form of constructivism sec. aspect *(α)* might lie in reading "Tractatus" in a similar way. Watzlawick et al. are aware thereof, when, alluding to experiences that lead to the loss of a habitual and customary view of the world – think of *unio mystica* or having been near to death – they write:

[cxxii] I do not use the term 'metaphysical' in the sense of G. Baker 2002, who to my understanding apprehends it along the lines of traditional philosophy as accounting for necessary and impossible attributes. (He might be right however in reading Wittgenstein's usage of the term 'everyday use' as 'non-metaphysical use', where 'metaphysical' is understood in the traditional sense by Wittgenstein).

 In contrast to Baker, I apply the term 'metaphysical' as qualifying a word-use which is *not testable*, refers to very general, yet unclear notions via their reification, furthermore transgress the Kantian boundary of reason, and in this case seem to be unavoidable (probably more in the meaning of 'humanly necessary' than of 'necessary de re').

[cxxiii] Cf. Watzlawick 1975: 107.

[cxxiv] Cf. Wittgenstein 1984, Band 1: 84 f.

[cxxv] Cf. Watzlawick & Beavin & Jackson 1967: 270 f., Watzlawick & Weakland & Fisch 1974a: 77 *et* 105 ff., Watzlawick 1976a: 237, Watzlawick 1981a: 219, Watzlawick 1988a: 154 f., etc.

"But all [...] anthological references [...] [[cxxvi]; G.G.] all these [...] vague and subjective descriptions, sound [...] »mystical« in the bad sense of the word, and yet their mystical character cannot be altogether denied if by this term we mean those brief moments during which, inexplicably, subject and object merge into what may be called their primordial unity. The problem is their description. The so-called mystics either fall silent – as Wittgenstein recommends – or they are forced to use the language of the great symbols governing their era: religion, mythology, philosophy, and the like. [...] In the incomparable simplicity of his style, Lao-Tsu [[cxxvii]; G.G.] expressed this paradox in the first chapter of the *Tao Te Ching*: »The Tao that can be expressed is not the real Tao; the name that can be named is not the real name.« Whoever is capable of writing a sentence like this [...] knows that all attribution of sense and significance creates a particular reality. But to arrive at this knowledge he had to catch himself [...] in the very act of constructing that reality; [...] he had to discover [...] how he remained unaware of this act of creation, how he then experienced that world »out there« as being independent of himself, and how, finally, he constructed – self-reflexively – himself in relation to the »suchness« of this supposedly objective world. The inevitability of this quest makes its senselessness meaningful. The wrong track must be taken in order to reveal itself as wrong. Wittgenstein must have had this in mind when he wrote the following:

»My propositions are elucidatory in this way: he who understands me finally recognizes them as senseless, when he has climbed out through them, on them, over them. (He must so to speak throw away the ladder, after he has climbed up on it.)« [...] [[cxxviii]; G.G.]

[cxxvi] Watzlawick loc. cit. has brought several literary examples in this epilogue to Watzlawick 1984a by quoting i.a. F. M. Dostojevski, H. Hesse, Robert Musil, and Ludwig Wittgenstein. This line reads as a self-comment on the lines of my essay here.

[cxxvii] In German this name is transcribed from Chinese as "Laotse", and the title of his book in German as "*Tao Te King*", where "Tao" is translated with the German "Sinn" (which in English would be "meaning" or "sense").

[cxxviii] Watzlawick loc. cit. quotes from an edition not available to me: Wittgenstein, Ludwig (1951): *Tractatus Logico-Philosophicus*. New York: Humanities Press. Obviously this is some non-standard translation, a bi-lingual edition English-German, since Watzlawick several times quotes it in his German writings as "Ludwig Wittgenstein, *Logisch-philosophische Abhandlungen*, Humanities Press, New York 1951, zweisprachige Ausgabe", which is a strange title, because Wittgenstein's original heading has a singular, not a plural: "Logisch-philosophische Abhandlung".
The cited passage is "Tractatus Logico-Philosophicus" § 6.54, and the translation by D. F. Pears and B. F. McGuinness in Wittgenstein 1992a: 74 does *not* essentially deviate from the quotation rendered. Loc. cit. is also quoted in e.g. Watzlawick 1988a: 154.

We now see that the question, that this epilogue attempts to answer (»What reality is construed by constructivism itself?« [[cxxix]; G.G.]) is a fundamentally wrong question. But we also see that this mistake had to be committed in order to reveal itself as a mistake. Constructivism does not create or explain any reality »out there«; it shows that there is no inside and no outside, no objective world facing the subjective, rather, it shows that the subject-object split, that source of myriads of »realities«, does not exist, that the apparent separation of the world into pairs of opposites is constructed by the subject, and that paradox opens the way into *autonomy*." (Watzlawick 1984a: 329 f.;[cxxx] italics original, slight errors in orthography and punctuation corrected)

At a meta-theoretical level one can see therein *a further function of failing*, since in the necessity of being committed the error *shows* that those presuppositions from which one started to realize what went wrong can themselves be shaken and belong just to one of many possible views of the world, which is inevitably taken as real as long as one stays and dwells within the system of the according world-view.[cxxxi]

Even if this is a realization to which one could have come without constructivism, it shows the enactment of constructivist considerations. *Constructivism distinguishes itself from other philosophies by providing insights into the fact that questioning its concept and content presupposes exactly those differentiations that according to its doctrine cannot be indicated as 'real' or 'true'.* Herewith the 'heaven of objectivity' has not been achieved − to stay within the drastic picture drawn by Wittgenstein − if one pushes away the ladder for one's ascent, since there is no such reified 'objectivity'. Correspondingly, we face a

---

[cxxix] This is a key-question for any philosophical approach towards this form of contructivism and towards an interpretation of *PTC*. This is not the place to deal with it, but I have done so in the core of Gelbmann 2000b.

Summarizing, I would today simplify my statements just for the current purpose in such a way as to state that there are objectively, i.e. intersubjectively binding rules for construing (higher order) realities in interpersonal communication − principles which govern our communicating and of which we are not completely aware, just as we do not have to be aware of the Laws of Gravitation in order to be able to walk. I call these Principles of Pragmatic Communication "Pragmalogies", to give the English version of a term I coined in German. I also mentioned this in e.g. Gelbmann 2001a, and on occasions of public talks, lectures, and in private conversations (not least with my Bergenser friends and colleagues).

[cxxx] German in Watzlawick 1981a: 313 f.

[cxxxi] Cf. "Über Gewißheit" §§ 95-99, Wittgenstein 1984, Band 8: 139 f. (*MS 174*: 21v ff. from April 24th 1950) and Wright 1986: 183.

confusion of logical levels – that could – in those forms of criticism of Wittgenstein's metaphor that see in this picture of the ladder an *actual* impossibility, since nobody can climb up a ladder while throwing it away without falling.[cxxxii]

This picture has not been invented to support a common-sense comprehension of how ladders work and are to be used, but in order to function as a *metaphor* for revealing that the whole process of thinking in "Tractatus" leads to the insight that it *had to* start from certain conditions and premises in order to be able to, eventually, give them up. As Watzlawick 1984a: 330 says: " The wrong track must be taken in order to reveal itself as wrong."

In my opinion, this principal insight applies to the reading of "Tractatus" as well – a performative reading, as I feel tempted to call it. *To have recognized the statements of "Tractatus" as lines that, if they are true, should not ever have been permitted to be written, exactly presupposes the process underlying their creation.-*[cxxxiii] Wittgenstein himself adds to the aforementioned quotation:

> "He must transcend these propositions, and then he will see the world aright."
> ("Tractatus Logico-Philosophicus" § 6.54, Wittgenstein 1992a: 74)

The overcoming or surmounting of these statements (to improve the translation offered by D. Pears and B. F. McGuinness) is quite informative if one forgets about the "positivistic misunderstanding"[cxxxiv] that there was a paradox. The puzzling situation was pedagogically necessary and led to an important insight due to a self-reference which would have asserted nothing if there had not been a riddle or puzzle from which it arose.- Watzlawick himself dealt with self-reference. He writes:

> "[...] So we see in more than one respect that we draw close to Wittgenstein, who in the *Tractatus* [...] states, »It is quite impossible for a proposition to state that it itself is true.«[cxxxv; G.G.] The trouble is that this proposition is itself a proposition that says something about itself, just like the proposition I

[cxxxii]   Quite similar the metaphor of Münchhausen's pigtail, alluded to in e.g. Watzlawick 1988a.

[cxxxiii]   Cf. McGuinness 1988b: 463 ff.

[cxxxiv]   Cf. Kraft 1950: 25 f.

[cxxxv]   Cf. "Tractatus Logico-Philosophicus" § 4.442, Wittgenstein 1992a: 33.

have just stated. Level and metalevel, communication and metacommunication paradoxically intermingle, and one is forever reminded of the dog chasing its tail [...]" (Watzlawick 1990d: 193;[cxxxvi] italics original)

This (kind of) pragmatic paradox was originally grasped by means of the *double-bind-hypothesis* by Bateson et al. Bateson himself uses the metaphor of throwing away the ladder:

"The Buddhists claim that the self is a sort of fiction. If so, our task will be to identify the species of fiction. But for the moment, I shall accept the »self« as a heuristic concept, a ladder useful in climbing but perhaps to be thrown away or left behind at a later stage." (Bateson 1980: 145[cxxxvii])

It remains unclear whether Bateson is here alluding to Wittgenstein in order to give an illustration sec. *(β)* or whether he merely sec. *(γ)*, by a historical coincidence, uses the same metaphor.[cxxxviii] Yet what we just quoted from Bateson's writings is informative as to *how* an aspect *(α)* becomes viable: heuristics can carry with it a form of reference which is only used as long as it is fruitful for a certain train of thoughts or vein of reasoning. *Concepts used heuristically are not dogmatically immunized or invariably lexicalized*; the conventionalistic touch adhering to them is not kept alive at all costs.

Watzlawick et al. cannot be reproached for taking the positivistic attitude prevailing during the early reception of "Tractatus", which read it only as a source for inspiration[cxxxix] sec. *(β)*, although these first readers, who themselves did not know much about the rest of Wittgenstein's works and what his Nachlass revealed about his transitional phase in the thirties, were probably subjectively convinced they were on the right track.[cxl] Watzlawick et al. at least know how to make use of converging lines of thinking, as becomes obvious from the following:

"The reality of the second order, which determines our idea of the world, our thoughts, feelings, decisions, and actions, is the result of a specific order, which

---

[cxxxvi] German in Watzlawick 1988e: 145 f.

[cxxxvii] German in Bateson 1982: 168.

[cxxxviii] That Bateson was acquainted with the English translation by K. C. Ogden in 1922, is shown by a remark in Bateson 1972g: 177; he obviously used this translation.

[cxxxix] Cf. Wright 1986: 190.

[cxl] This kind of reading and interpretation of "Tractatus" can also be found in i.a. Karl. Raimund Popper 1934, Popper 1945a, Popper 1945b, und Popper 1979, despite Popper's criticism of (neo-)positivism and the "Wiener Kreis".

we impose on the kaleidoscopic, phantasmagorical multiplicity of the world, and which is therefore not the result of understanding the »real« world but which, in the strictest sense of the word, *constructs* a specific world. We are, however, not aware of this construction and assume naively that it exists independently of us. The way these realities emerge is of the highest interest to researchers as well as clinicians. Again, Piaget's pioneering work [...] [*cxli*; G.G.] comes to mind in this connection.

At approximately the same time as Piaget, Wittgenstein too was studying this subject. At the beginning of his work *On Certainty* [...] [*cxlii*; G.G.] we find the sentence: »From its seeming to me – or to everyone – to be so, it does not follow that it *is* so« [...]. [*cxliii*; G.G.] And further: »But I did not get my picture of the world by satisfying myself of its correctness; nor do I have it because I am satisfied of its correctness. No: it is the inherited background against which I distinguish between true and false« [...]. [*cxliv*; G.G.]

And finally even more explicitly:

»We do not learn the practice of making empirical judgements by learning rules: we are taught *judgements* and their connexion with other *judgements*. A *totality* of judgements is made plausible.

When we first begin to *believe* anything, what we believe is not a single proposition, it is a whole system of propositions. (Light dawns gradually over the whole.)

It is not single axioms that strike me as obvious, it is a system in which consequences and premises give one another *mutual* support.« [...] [*cxlv*; G.G.]

The study of these systems, in which postulates and conclusions reciprocally and recursively support and confirm each other, is one of the main concerns of communication research. Second-order realities can be considered the result of communication. No higher life form could survive if it had to comprehend the

---

cxli   Watzlawick loc. cit. quotes Piaget 1954.

cxlii   Watzlawick loc. cit. quotes the standard English edition, cf. Wittgenstein 1969b.

cxliii   Cf. "Über Gewißheit" § 2, Wittgenstein 1984, Band 8: 119 (*MS 172*: 1 from Jan. 1950; *MS 173*: 22r from March 30th 1950); in English edited in Wittgenstein 1969b: 2. The quotation given by Watzlawick loc. cit. differs from the German as well as the English edition in lacking italics for "seeming".

cxliv   Cf. "Über Gewißheit" § 94, Wittgenstein 1984, Band 8: 139 (*MS 174*: 21r f. from April 24th 1950); in English edited in Wittgenstein 1969b: 15.

cxlv   I put this second-order-quotation into the corresponding quotation marks, Watzlawick et al. loc. cit. render it in print with indented margins. I kept their paragraphing.
The reference is "Über Gewißheit" §§ 140-142, Wittgenstein 1984, Band 8: 149 (*MS 174*: 30v ff. from April 24th 1950); edited in English in Wittgenstein 1969b: 21. There are slight differences in spelling and in italicising.

world solely on its own. Lower forms of life seem to come with a genetic »set of instructions« and are wiped out mercilessly by death when their genetic program no longer fits. In human beings socialization has always taken precedence over predisposition. And socialization is based on communication, i.e. on instructions as to how to see the world.
All this is by no means relevant only to the reality of the second order. How would we fare if we had only our own immediate sense perceptions to rely upon, even on the level of the first-order reality? What certainty would I ever have that anything whose existence I have not verified myself does in fact exist?" (Watzlawick 1990c: 137 ff.;[cxlvi] italics original)

Again, by distinguishing between a reality of first order and a reality of second order, Watzlawick et al. apply what shall be called a type-hierarchical method of abstraction.[cxlvii] Yet aided by Wittgenstein's texts, these second-order-realities sec. *(β)* are regarded as a system of mutually supporting, interwoven assumptions – regardless of the first-order-reality being co-determined in a complex manner by the socio-cultural, biological, and psychological formation of perception.

Since what is prevalently regarded as 'real' emerges from *unquestioned assumptions about the perceived*, or *about the assumptions on the part of the respective 'other'*, and since at *the same time it becomes a constituent of a certain interpersonal relationship*, the presuppositions for the interpersonal events and for one's own realization of 'realities' by that very act are not something those involved can easily comprehend. This *hierarchy of assumptions (about assumptions [about assumptions {about assumptions …} …] of the respective other person) about the respective other person*, which mostly establishes itself tacitly among the people communicating in a continual relationship stretching over longer periods of time, can best be demonstrated with the example of an intercultural communication-situation. Even if the reader might feel bored, a

---

[cxlvi] German in Watzlawick 1985: 94 f.; see also Watzlawick 1988a: 107 f.- Hejl 1985 gives a good background reading about the construction of realities through the means and medium of socialising, or towards (as he calls it) *parallelization as collective selection of maladapted or not viably fitting realities.*

[cxlvii] This gradation or typisation is based on Bateson's concept of 'deutero-learning', cf. sup. *nota lxxx* and Ruesch & Bateson 1951: 214 ff., Bateson 1981: 229 ff. *et* 356 f.-) This method of constituting and changing so-called third-order-premisses was applied by Watzlawick et al. in their conceptualization of the construction of reality (or realities), cf. Watzlawick & Beavin & Jackson 1967: 260 ff.

longer citation shall be presented to show how Watzlawick et al. study a historical, even paradigmatic case:

"During the last years of World War II and the early postwar years, hundreds of thousands of U. S. soldiers were stationed in or passed through Great Britain, providing a unique opportunity to study the effects of a large-scale penetration of one culture by another. One interesting aspect was a comparison of courtship patterns. Both American soldiers and British girls accused one another of being sexually brash. Investigation of this curious double charge brought to light an interesting punctuation problem. In both cultures, courtship behavior from the first eye contact to the ultimate consummation went through approximately thirty steps, but the sequence of these steps was different. Kissing, for instance, comes relatively early in the North American pattern (occupying, let us say, step 5) and relatively late in the English pattern (at step 25, let us assume), where it is considered highly erotic behavior. So when the U. S. soldier somehow felt that the time was right for a harmless kiss, not only did the girl feel cheated out of twenty steps of what for her would have been proper behavior on his part, she also felt she had to make a quick decision: break off the relationship and run, or get ready for intercourse. If she chose the latter, the soldier was confronted with behavior that according to *his* cultural rules could only be called shameless at this early stage of the relationship.

If we were to commit the mistake of looking at the girl's behavior in isolation, without taking into account its interactional nature, we would have no difficulty making a psychiatric diagnosis: if she suddenly runs, she is behaving hysterically; if she offers herself sexually, she is a nymphomaniac. Here again we are faced with a conflict that [...] must not be reduced to the madness or badness of one partner, since it lies exclusively in the nature of their communication impasse. [...] It is in the nature of these disinformation problems that the partners cannot resolve them, for, as Wittgenstein once remarked, »What we cannot think, we cannot think; we cannot therefore say what we cannot think« [...] [[cxlviii]; G.G.]" (Watzlawick 1976b: 63 f.[cxlix])

[cxlviii] Cf. "Tractatus Logico-Philosophicus" § 5.61, which reads in Wittgenstein 1992a: 57 as "We cannot think what we cannot think; so what we cannot think we cannot *say* either", which is a rather simple translation of the original German text, edited e.g. in Wittgenstein 1984, Band 1: 67 (*TS 202*: 40 from Jan. 1918): "Was wir nicht denken können, das können wir nicht denken; wir können also auch nicht *sagen*, was wir nicht denken können". This German text is consistently brought in the German edition of Watzlawick 1976a: 75.
Although, Watzlawick et al. use another English translation of "Tractatus" (cf. inf. *nota cxxviii*), the difference is irrelevant here.

[cxlix] German in Watzlawick 1976a: 74 f.

Without taking into closer consideration that here we again meet the *refutation of isolating observables*, it is remarkable and evident that the formation of assumptions about "how to behave" or "the correct conduct", moulded by the cultural circumstances in which it takes place, contains potential for conflicts. This potential grows the less conscious the people involved are of their own assumptions, viz. assumptions about what the respective 'other' should do or think, based on some kind of imperturbable certainty about their own, mostly implicitly accepted premises from which their forming of assumptions usually commences. *Being entangled in such a situation can make it humanly impossible to give expression to what oneself regards as matter of fact and hence would never question, not even put into words by making one's basics explicit in order to give others a chance to understand one's principles and priorities.*

At the same time, the situation's *aporia* and lack of any exit-strategy leading out of ensuing conflicts consist in the human impossibility of claiming that one should avoid assuming anything. I even feel tempted to put it as follows: Making assumptions about people with whom we communicate and about their making assumptions about their fellows, among whom we find ourselves, is a sort of destiny. One might even take an existentialist attitude towards it. It belongs to the *conditio humana*, and is not a problem of theorizing but of the existential condition of being a human being, of being a person. *I think it is a very idealistic and unrealistic demand many thinkers tend or tended to make that one should not presume anything about one's fellows.*

Enlightenment and liberal philosophy are liable to criticize prejudices; they ask for meticulous argumentative reasoning for one's opinions, to which I whole-heartedly agree in all matters concerning scientific striving for knowledge. Yet the situation in communication involves several vague elements, and one enters it just as one enters a hermeneutical situation: with a certain horizon and from a certain standpoint. Recognizing that others experience these situations in the same manner entails having to accept that, despite their problematic corrigibility, prejudices and wrong assumptions are *practically necessary* and a component of our factuality.[cl]

In practical life one cannot always account for one's assumptions, one just starts from what one regards as matter of fact. It is neither by trying to prepare

---

[cl]   Cf. for the term 'factuality' the classic study of existentialism, i.e. J.-P. Sartre 1943.

oneself for a task of complete rationality by doubting everything in a Cartesian manner, nor by trying to sort out where one is prejudiced that one complies to rationalistic attitudes so inapplicable to practical matters. *We usually get rid of prejudices in confrontation with the opinions and attitudes of others*, i.e. *by communication*, which can even assume the form of conflicts. But in order to arrive at this *practical* outcome, which consists in learning about one-self and others, one has to enter and be in communication.

So if I decide to broaden my horizon by climbing a mountain, I will not get rid of any "horizon as such", although I will have to alter my standpoint, and my assumptions and attitudes in practical matters. If I read a text, I might start from a preconceived opinion, even misread and misinterpret it, *yet any understanding of the text I gain can later on be used as a standard for further attempts at understanding.* Texts, even if reencountered, do not usually change, they remain typographically, syntactically, probably even semantically what they are. They are very *practical invariants.*[cli]

But people and communication *do* change; so the hermeneutical situation just mentioned is even more complicated than in the classic case of texts and books, since *what enters one's horizon of understanding is itself a horizon of understanding, in which I am perceived as an intruder or perceiver.*[clii]

Let us take up the thread again: Where is the connection to Wittgenstein? Well, does it not resemble *the situation of the visual field being incapable of perceiving its own borders?-*[cliii] Watzlawick compares this with the pragmatic

---

[cli]   I belong to those people who can open a book at a marked page at which they stopped reading some time ago, go on reading, and are then surprised that the lines they have just re-read are still the same as those they read some time ago and whose meaning they now recall. Elsewhere I have written about recollection and memory from a Wittgensteinian point of view, cf. *sections III.I.* ff., here I just want to state that the attitude in reading is similar to the attitude in communication:

Why am I surprised that the text is the same?- This is because in communication the "text" is never the same, even if a situation or a constellation, a social system, might be the same as one already experienced. *The sameness of meaning does not depend on the stability of expression or one's understanding of the message, it rather depends on the way construing it and how it is constituted!*

[clii]   I have elsewhere dealt with the intertwining of observing observers. Cf. Gelbmann 2002b and Gelmann 2002e.

[cliii]   Cf. Wittgenstein's diary from Aug. 4th until Aug. 12th 1916 in "Tagebücher 1914 - 1916", Wittgenstein 1984, Band 1: 174 f. (*MS 103:* 40*r* f.) and "Tractatus Logico-Philosophicus" § 5.633 ff., Wittgenstein 1984, Band 1: 68.

situation of disinformation arising from the complex interaction of mutual assumptions. He describes this form of disinformation in the words of Ronald D. Laing's, another forerunner of psychological constructivism:

> "»If I don't know I know, I think I don't know«. [...] [[cliv]; G.G.]" (Watzlawick 1976b: 64[clv])

Laing's aphorism is of interest here insofar as it demonstrates *interlocking epistemic modalities in their pragmatic effect on communication,*[clvi] which (independently of the structure of the references of Watzlawick et al. to Wittgenstein) reveals a loose connection with later thoughts of Wittgenstein dealing with the theme 'certainty', which is *not a matter of logical analysis alone* but is *in need of a pragmatic analysis of the assumptions and attitudes of those people mutually involved in interaction.*

In other words, one's certainty of being properly informed about the ways and motives of and reasons for a certain form of behaviour in somebody else turns into its opposite as soon as one has grasped that it consisted merely in assumptions, even if they be plausible ones; vice versa, disinformation about certainty with regard to the behaviour of others brings about the assumption that one is in a situation of uncertainty and lack of proper knowledge, hence one feels insecure.

These refined (informational) semantic differences of epistemic modalities operating in multiple ways can lead to the most complicated pragmatic and psychological consequences.[clvii] Without comprehending one's own state of disinformation, an opinion prevails or is pushed through on the basis of mere conviction, whereas disinformation about one's certain knowledge brings with it an insecure appearance towards others. Accordingly, one's own behaviour will produce in one's interlocutors certain assumptions about one's state of knowledge,

---

[cliv]   Cf. Laing 1970: 55.

[clv]   The German edition in Watzlawick 1976a: 75 quotes "Laing definiert diese Form der Desinformation wie folgt: »Wenn ich nicht weiß, daß ich nicht weiß, glaube ich zu wissen. Wenn ich nicht weiß, daß ich weiß, glaube ich nicht zu wissen«." In the English edition, the first sentence is missing.

[clvi]   These epistemic modalities are in actual language verbalized in expressions of propositional attitudes like "You doubt that ...", "He knows that ...", "I believe that ..." and can be analysed as modal logic operators put in front of well-formed formulas, by themselves producing complete sentences. So the three dots, i.e. "...", in our examples stand for a whole proposition.

[clvii]   I do not talk about formal semantics or truth values (logical values) here.

on the basis of which they then behave and choose a reaction, in merely putative knowledge about one's state of information or disinformation.-

As a logical consequence, *all certain knowledge about the state of information of one's interloctur(s) can always be doubted*, even if one cannot doubt one's entire knowledge (due to a practical limit to scepticism). Equally, *every impression of uncertainty on the part of another person about oneself can be wrong*, although the degree of information might justify this impression. This is *not* unconditional relativism in regard to the state of (mutual) information in communication-situations, but relativism that might serve as a maxim for rationality in assessing behaviour.

It is of great importance to grasp that, simply due to its interlocked, epistemic-pragmatic structure, every communication-situation conceals a factor that makes the rules according to which this 'game' is played ineffable. But this, again and for itself, does *not* entail that the partners in this situation are forced to go on with their "game". On the contrary, a termination is thinkable, even possible at any time, although this option is not always practically realized. *The incapability of putting an end to such a game makes it a pathogenic case*, viz. a case with a ban of terminating the game built into the situation as part of the rules of the interaction in such a relationship.[clviii] In the case of the 'Game Without End' there is *mutual certainty that the game has to be continued*, against all conventions and knowledge of the usually applied behavioural répertoire for terminating contacts, finishing relationships, exiting from a situation.-[clix]

In my opinion, it is easy to perceive that Watzlawick et al. enlist the aid of Wittgensteinian reasoning – again according to *(β)* – in order to transport their theory. Yet it should not be overlooked that the development of ideas that can also be found in "Tractatus" was needed to form the convictions from which the perspective of constructivism that prompted the theorizing of Watzlawick et al. was constituted. The genesis of ideas cannot be assessed as being directly generated under Wittgenstein's influence sec. *(α)*, it appears in the guise of a parallel sec. *(γ)*. It cannot be supported exegetically or biographically, but has to be regarded as reconstructed, as if one does not have the utopian expectation that a

---

[clviii] This is the case of the so-called 'Game Without End', cf. i.a. Watzlawick & Beavin & Jackson 1967: 179 ff., 232 ff., 240 ff. *et* 269; Watzlawick & Weakland & Fisch 1974a: 41, 58 f., 77, 109, 157 ff. *et* 183; Watzlawick & Weakland 1980: 12 *et* 415; Watzlawick 1977: 96 *et* 114; Watzlawick 1981a: 140; Watzlawick 1988a: 26 ff., 55, 61, 128 *et* 138 ff., etc.

[clix] Cf. i.a. Watzlawick & Beavin & Jackson 1969: 74 ff.

PTC in the understanding of Watzlawick et al. *must* come from an exegetic and coherent interpretation of Wittgenstein's philosophy.

The self-reliant and original validity of the *PTC* has to be recognized even when one has arrived at the conclusion that one cannot conceive of fundamental pre-conditions for it without Wittgenstein's philosophy leading the way.-

I.VI. Premises in Relative Terms

Towards the end it appears to be appropriate to investigate some points which might make one prone to ascribe some constructivist traits to Wittgenstein's thinking, were it not anachronistic. That Wittgenstein probably felt attracted by some ideas of solipsism and at least felt invited to discuss it, is well-known.[clx] To say it in advance: subjective idealism or a form of solipsism is *not* the metaphysical position of (psychological) constructivism, it is not true that Watzlawick et al. maintain that "everything is just a construction", although they take a certain ontological stance. *Sound realism is not to be seen as being in ontological contrast to this kind of constructivism.*[clxi] Watzlawick et al. claim the objective validity of their theses in a realistic manner.-

In other places – as an instrumentalized parallel under double aspectivity *(βγ)* – we can associate (systemic) constructivism with Wittgenstein in so far as from an often quoted passage one can read the dubious nature of *what* a message is intended to purport. Here it is worth mentioning that, similar to Ludwig Wittgenstein, Charles W. Morris – in whose 1938 conception of semiotics *PTC* is rooted[clxii] – speaks up for an elimination of the term 'meaning'.[clxiii] At the time Morris was writing within the frame of Otto Neurath's project of a "unified science",[clxiv] only Wittgenstein's "Tractatus" could be quoted, as Morris duly does. Whether Wittgenstein ever read Morris, remains open, as so much of his reading

---

[clx]   Cf. "Tractatus Logico-Philosophicus" 5.6 ff., Wittgenstein 1984, Band 1: 67 ff., McGuinness 1988b: 476 ff., Bell 1992.

[clxi]   This is a basic point of my interpretation and reconstruction of *PTC* in Gelbmann 2000b.

[clxii]   Cf. Watzlawick & Beavin & Jackson 1967: 21.

[clxiii]   Cf. Morris 1938: 43 ff.

[clxiv]   Cf. Stadler 1997.

does.[clxv] But back to the quotation, taken from a much later time than "Tractatus" and probably the most constructivist citation ever to be found in Wittgenstein:[clxvi]

"[...] Suppose everyone had a box with something in it: we call it a »beetle«. No one can look into anyone else's box, and everyone says he knows what a beetle is only by looking at *his* beetle.- Here it would be quite possible for everyone to have something different in his box. One might even imagine such a thing constantly changing.- But suppose the word »beetle« had a use in these people's language?- If so it would not be used as the name of a thing. The thing in the box has no place in the language-game at all; not even as a *something*: for the box might even be empty.- No, one can »divide through« by the thing in the

---

[clxv] Yet isn't it, just as an aside, interesting that Morris 1975 quotes Watzlawick et al.?

[clxvi] Cf. *TS 241*: 17 § 61 from Jan. 1944, *TS 242*: 5 f. § 242 from Jan. 1944, *MS 124*: 256 f. from July 3rd 1944, *MS 129*: 59 f. from Aug. 17th 1944, *TS 227*: 184 f. § 293 from Jan. 1945 (all dates taken from the Bergen Electronic Edition).
It is interesting in this long row of source-citations that according to the Bergen Electronic Edition's dating, it is a *typescript* which brings the first occurrence of the bug-example, thus making it the oldest occurrence of the bug-example hitherto known to us (*TS 241*: 17 or *TS 242*: 5 f., both are of about the same age).
But did Wittgenstein invent this example when his texts were typed, possibly when dictating it? I am inclined to believe that *a manuscript-source got lost*. When discussing this problem with Alois Pichler at the Wittgenstein Archives at the University of Bergen in spring 2003, he drew my attention to his own publication, Pichler 1994: 134 and to M. Nedo 1993: 43 (quoted by Pichler loc. cit.); both say that *TS 241* was dictated after *TS 242*. Furthermore, also according to Wright 1986: 58, *TS 241* was not typed after 1945. Pichler 1994: 134 dates *TS 241* back to September 1944 and *TS 242* to January 1945 (nine and twelve months later than the dating found in the current Bergen Electronic Edition), which means that *TS 241* and *TS 242* would be *younger* than *MS 129*, which Pichler 1994: 134 dates as not after 1945 and Nedo 1993: 43 as between March and Sept. 1944.
It seems to be reasonable to assume that *MS 129* was the direct source of *TS 242*, which was then rewritten as *TS 242*, also in the light of the evidence from the skripts. So *the Bergen Electronic Edition's dating does not seem to be reliable*.
Yet if *MS 129* was a source for *TS 241*, it is strange that even then the first occurrence of the bug-example, according to the Bergen Electronic Edition in *MS 124*, is to be found in a fairly unchanged and clear-cut text, looking as if it had itself just been copied from some other source which must then have got lost (and here I again have to thank Pichler for agreeably pointing this out to me), or Wittgenstein really just wrote this part almost without any scribbling over, without much self-correcting, and without other usual signs of his re-writing. *I keep up my hypothesis that the original of the bug-example got lost*, or *MS 124*: 256 f. is the original occurrence (Pichler 1994: 1234 dates it at partly March and April 1944, partly July 1944). *MS 129*: 59 f. seems to me to be younger than *MS 124* loc. cit.; in the latter skript there are at least some improvements of the passage. Wittgenstein was obviously satisfied with his famous bug-example from the start.

box; it cancels out, whatever it is." ("Philosophical Investigations" I § 293, Wittgenstein 1991: 100)

This is the famous "bug"-paragraph, which is *not* referred to by Bateson, Watzlawick et al. That they could have cited it is, however, made manifest by an observation the young and anthropologically oriented Bateson once made, as his friend Watzlawick relates:

"Bateson (personal communication) reported that the inhabitants of a certain coastal region in New Guinea availed themselves of heavy millstone-shaped rocks for larger transactions (for daily cash they used seashells). One day one of these rocks, as payment for a major purchase, was transported from one village to the next across a broad estuary. The boat capsized in the surf and the rock disappeared into the deep water, never to be seen again. Since this event was common knowledge, the rock kept functioning as currency, even though it now existed, as it were, only in the heads of the people concerned." (Paul Watzlawick 1990b: 19[clxvii])

By convention of the legitimate usage of the means of payment "stone" the situation was dealt with as if the corresponding expression still had its old meaning (viz. reference to the transportable, available, demonstrable object "stone"), although the thing to which this meaning referred was no more available. Today we know bank deposits, bank accounts, foreign exchange, virtual money instead of coins, bank notes, valuta, to draw a comparison to the loss of any concrete reference while maintaining real meaning.

[clxvii]   German in Watzlawick 1975: 109 f. One could point out here that the rock did still exist, even though invisible in deep water.

Yet the existence of the rock is not the issue here but its function as a means of financial transaction. Due to a socially shared abstraction, the reality of this means of transaction was made independent from the object, i.e. from the stone itself; this very separation *in mente* is responsible for the subsistence of the means of currency or transaction called "stone". Thus the people in Bateson's account discovered *the possibility of de-reifying institutional devices for communication*. That such an abstraction can maintain its reality and serve as an institutional device for a social community, is an observation that amazed Bateson, Watzlawick, et al.

The semantic invariance on which this cultural progress depends is the meaning of transactional value, of currency, yet the reference of this meaning to a certain thing or object and its availability, its movability, need not be given. By practice and language one can refer to this meaning and its function without referring to any concrete or physical object entrusted with this function. Such a presupposed agreement is, indeed, a normal practice.

This shows that the language-game of 'using money', 'paying', and 'financial transfer' works, *independently* from whether the meaning that corresponds to the word applied, 'exists factually or objectively'. The institution, the convention has to prevail. Embedded in such a conventional practice, the reference of the expressions is unimportant for their meaning. *Playing a language-game means sharing a common practice,* viz. a *practice of how reality and that to which language refers have to be construed.* Conventions are just an outcome, an expression, a manifestation of this practice, an indication of its existence.

'Meaning as reference' just drops out of the framing of such a situation as irrelevant; *by postulating meaning as reference, the first step towards reification is already taken.* By introducing and inaugurating a language-game, 'meaning as reference' has to commit this 'intellectual crime', since the object "stone" is then used as *signifying a paradigm,* but not as the paradigm itself, since every primitive aboriginal just as a modern yuppie from Wall Street knows that money is not the same as stones and does not consist of stones. The first step can only be taken once (but neither Bateson, Watzlawick et al. nor Wittgenstein are interested in this first occasion).

The paradigm signified by the object is here clearly the paradigm of the first or original (financial) transaction, namely the quite *concrete and observable form of a reference to a certain form of relationship by exchanging goods against some abstract, but commonly accepted value* called 'money' and represented by the "stone".[clxviii] The (only, correct, true, authentic, legitimate, real) meaning of what is "communicated" annuls itself in so far as within the language-game and in a commensuralized application of some sign-usage the hypostasizing of the object referred to remains a matter or fact, implicit and invisible just as meaning itself, due to the parallelization of the construction of assumptions. These people did not pay with stones but with the meaning stones had in their world, just as we do not pay with paper or metal but with the meaning these devices have: i.e "money". So *meaning is the outcome of a common practice called "the parallelization of the construction of assumptions",* and *conventions are just the rules for this practice.*

When saying that this is "implicit", I mean that in everyday circumstances nobody asks what words like "bug" or "pain" mean.[clxix] So the aforementioned

---

[clxviii]   Cf. also Gelbmann 2002b.

[clxix]   Provided they know the language in which these words occur as *sememes.*

practice is just followed, unhesitantly and without further ado; what is construed can easily be objectified if constituted on the same basis of construing assumptions. This basis is exactly what is brought about by sharing a form of life and by taking part in language-games. Yet philosophy is *not* an everyday business, even thinking about the everyday use of language is not, and in this sense philosophy has no meaning, because it undercuts the matter-of-fact parallelization of construing assumptions just by attacking its assumptions.

With the above argument we obtain a possibility of interpreting the so-called private-language-argument[clxx] in the terminology of *PTC*, to which we have just alluded. It was Ivor Armstrong Richards and Charles Key Ogden[clxxi] who came up with the idea of such a "private language", probably not as the first, but as definite influences on Wittgenstein – besides Bertrand Russell[clxxii] – and they were particularly influential in their account of firstly, how a language is learned, and secondly, of the internality of sense-data. Both views were attacked by Wittgenstein.

A private language cannot exist, since the second-order-reality to which it pretentiously would have to refer is never private but is always rooted in the corresponding possibility of relationships to others. One can imagine that in a sort of speculative Robinsonade a language is applied and used by a single person alone, under the tragically lonesome circumstances of complete and prevailing social isolation – this would be an empirical contingency without any effect on the concept. (Daniel Defoe's famous novel certainly did not rouse Wittgenstein's resistance to the notion of a 'private language'.) Yet the scope for interpreting what is preferably objectified as 'the inner sphere' is *not* a private region which solipsistically provides exclusive access for the individual in question. On the contrary, it is *constituted as a second-order-reality through and by interpersonal communication.*[clxxiii] The individual acquires the concept of the inner sphere as an abstraction from communicative experiences, as communication is not derived from the inner or private expression of feelings and sense-data; *instead the*

[clxx]   Cf. "Philosophische Untersuchungen" I §§ 241 ff., Wittgenstein 1984, Band 1: 356 ff.; see i.a. Kripke 1982, ter Hark 1990: 25 ff. *et* 73 ff., Costa 2000, Garrett 2001, Savigny 2002, etc.

[clxxi]   Cf. Ogden & Richards 1923: 210 ff. (I am indebted to Alois Pichler for having drawn my attention to this forgotten book, either in autumn 1997 or spring 1998).

[clxxii]   Cf. M. ter Hark 1990 and ter Hark 1995a.

[clxxiii]   Cf. Wright 1986: 210 and Savigny 1991.

expression of feelings in behaviour is, as behaviour itself, genuinely communicative.

According to Georg Henrik von Wright or Eike von Savigny, the individual is embedded in a social reality, has a 'social soul'. It is an abstraction from the phenomenon as well as from one's experience to conceive of an isolated individual. From the point of view of *PTC*, each individual in his/her behaviour and with his/her habits is always to be conceived of as an element of at least one social system – usually of several interacting and overlapping systems.-

I.VII. A Final Observation on the Interpretative Potential

In the case of *PTC*, we are confronted with a new understanding of theorizing,[clxxiv] which is different from a classical empirical collection of data or from a descriptive classificatory approach and proceeds towards a relativizing the so far fundamental category of '*the* reality'. Theories cannot then be construed with the claim of giving the only true, objective form of a theory, clearly distinguished from all other options. This does *not*, however, mean that any claims on validity have been discarded, or that "anything goes".

The very limits of one's language – which according to a Wittgensteinian dictum[clxxv] often quoted by Watzlawick et al. *are* the limits of one's *world* – are now redrawn in a certain but not absolute sense, by making them somehow newly measurable *in conceptualising language as limiting itself in its operativity.-*

Having dealt with the direct references to Wittgenstein found in Watzlawick et al., it appears relevant to focus on the study of some indirect references and the ideas connected with them. The purpose is to try to bring the *PTC* even nearer to Wittgenstein's thinking and draw an analogy between the two, or at least to show how far this is feasible. Comprehending *communication as consisting of all behaviour observable within an interactive system* on the one hand, and

---

[clxxiv]   I am not thinking of Stachowiak's "General Model Theory" (*GMT*) here, from whose point of view *PTC* could be envisaged as within its explanatory scope. Cf. i.a. Herbert Stachowiak 1973.

[clxxv]   Cf. Wittgenstein's diary from May 23rd 1915 in "Tagebücher 1914 - 1916", Wittgenstein 1984, Band 1: 141 (*MS 102*: 101*r*); "Tractatus Logico-Philosophicus" § 5.6 ff., Wittgenstein 1984, Band 1: 67 f. (*MS 104*: 59 ff. from June 1915); "Philosophische Bemerkungen" XIII § 152, Wittgenstein 1984, Band 2: 178 (*MS 105*: 32 Feb. 1929).

conceptualising it with its verbal and non-verbal constituents as a *pragmatic calculus* on the other, are the two characteristic principles of *PTC*.

> "Now, if it is accepted that all behavior in an interactional situation [...] has message value, i.e., is communication, it follows that no matter how one may try, one cannot *not* communicate. Activity or inactivity, words or silence all have message value: they influence others and these others, in turn, cannot *not* respond to these communications and are thus themselves communicating. It should be clearly understood that the mere absence of talking or of taking notice of each other is no exception to what has just been asserted." (Watzlawick & Beavin & Jackson 1967: 48 f.; italics original)

With this we are not only presented with an anticipation of the first axiom but are concomitantly given *an implicit definition of what for such a systemic or transactional perspective appears to be an 'interactive situation' or an 'interactive system'*. We shall accept this to be the case if, and only if, *the behaviour of other system-elements in any case is perceived or observed by the system element under consideration, which in its own behaviour and conduct cannot be left uninfluenced by this perception or observation.*[clxxvi]

This means that (a.), there is *an internal relation between the observation of the behaviour of others and their "internal", mental states,* allowing for the inferences on the part of the observing system-element from a pragmatic and behavioural unit to a semantic dimension, and that (b.), *an internal relation specifying the interactive system under consideration is prevalent between the reception and registration of the behaviour of others and the reaction to it by one's own behaviour*. These internal relations are *not* mediated by a third, external, instance such as by a *meaning per se* or by 'the' reality as such.

From this one *cannot* draw behaviouristic conclusions. *PTC* is a behavioural, though not a behaviouristic theory, since the reaction of a system-element (i.e. a person in communication) to an observed behaviour attributed to another system-element is not determined by what was observed or by the counterpart's behaviour. In every reaction several forms of behaviour leading to the same aim, so-called equifinal forms of behaviour, are possible.[clxxvii] This is quite contrary to what

---

[clxxvi]   This sophisticated step of reconstructing *PTC*'s first axiom as a definition of the intra-theoretical term 'interactive system', originally was enacted in Gelbmann 2000b: 402-414.

[clxxvii]   The term 'equifinality' is taken from Bertalanffy 1968. Cf. Watzlawick & Beavin & Jackson 1967: 127.

behaviourism assumes, although the répertoire will often be limited by the co-construction of assumptions about the respective 'other'.

The terminology of *PTC* often leans closely towards the language formed by the Cybernetic Revolution, and by adopting the *metaphor* of 'black box',[clxxviii] the authors of *PTC* might have helped to interpret their texts as maintaining tendencies of behaviourism or even holding behaviouristic tenets. But there is no reason to accept such reproaches. In the face of the constructivist background of *PTC* such a reading is completely absurd. The construction of second-order-realities as a social and communicative undertaking and the conception of the social system in view of the first axiom of *PTC* provide enough reasons for *refuting* this allegation, namely that the individual as a system-element is only conceived of as a functional mechanism or even machine, about whose inner structure we need not know anything in order to regard its behaviour as a conditioned and calculable reaction.

How a system-element reacts and behaves within the complexity of an interactive system and what is communicated thereby, is to a large degree dependent on the conventional organisation of communication and the personal intelligence involved, not to mention the mental sphere providing the semantics for all devices and means, such as language and signs shared by the system-elements. The implementation of the two internal relations I talked about above is the best precaution against a behaviouristic account of communication. 'Internal relation' is here be understood in the way defined by Michel ter Hark:[clxxix]

> "(i) It is impossible that both relata do not have this relation to each other. (ii) The relation is not mediated by a third term. (iii) The internal relation exists in a practice, in a language." (ter Hark 1990: 47)

From the point of view of *PTC*, and of Watzlawick et al. respectively, the 'practice' or 'language' in ter Hark's third condition corresponds to communication itself, since the latter systemically shapes interpersonal relationships. The arising

---

[clxxviii] Cf. e.g. Watzlawick & Beavin & Jackson 1967: 43 f. or Watzlawick & Weakland & Fisch 1974b: 85.

[clxxix] Michel ter Hark refers to "Philosophische Untersuchungen" II xi, Wittgenstein 1984, Band 1: 518-577, and to "Philosophische Bemerkungen" III §§ 21 ff., Wittgenstein 1984, Band 2: 63 ff., and he criticizes not only Ogden and Richards for their behaviouristic tendencies, but also Bertrand Russell. Cf. also ter Hark 1995a. (The reader will kindly forgive me for omitting the original skript-citations, but ter Hark already worked this out long ago.)

question whether observable behaviour constitutes a system, has to be negated at first glance, yet one one could go deeper by stating that interpersonal behaviour per se includes its observability. *Internal syntactic-semantic or mental processes inevitably have to materialize into external, behavioural, and pragmatic manifestations* to make talking about behaviour as ascribable to a person possible.

In other words, in order not to fall into the trap of the behaviouristic physicalism of neo-positivism and Carnap's logical empirism,[clxxx] self-observation has to be regarded as observation. Behaviour either has to be observable for external people, i.e. people who do not take part in the communication-system under investigation, or can be externalised by means of self-observation by turning what was observed into inter-subjectively communicable behaviour which leads to a loss of immediacy. In this sense the term 'behaviour' is only meaningful if its grammar is systemic-transactional. *Behaviour can hence only be conceived of as being given for an observer*.

Correspondingly, Watzlawick et al. earlier expressed their first axiom by stating that *one cannot not behave*.[clxxxi] This is a strikingly fitting reformulation. Behaviour that is not systemic-pragmatically manifest and hence does not knit the so-called Inner to the Outer by an internalised relation would be "privately ostensive", as Wittgenstein calls it.[clxxxii] Behaviour of subjects, objectified by subjects observing it – by taking it as *manifestations of the subjectivity of other people* – has its own multiplicity only in the interpersonal sphere. The grammar of the word 'behaviour' would be violated, if behaviour merely took place in pure internality, without manifestation within the relatively external, performed by relatively external, objectifiable subjects.

If it is to be distinguishable from solipsistic or intra-psychic dynamics, the term 'behaviour' can only be applied in such a way as to signify something that is *not* of the nature of a private language. *Hence even sensations can be regarded as forms of behaviour.-*

The addition of the pragmatic-transactional dimension to the syntactic-semantic perspective allows, firstly, conceiving the manifestation of the internal relation between semantic-mental internal life and syntactic-pragmatic external

---

[clxxx]   Cf. the brilliant criticism in Kraft 1950: 149 ff.

[clxxxi]   Cf. Watzlawick & Weakland 1980: 97.

[clxxxii]   Cf. "Bemerkungen über die Philosophie der Psychologie" I § 200, Wittgenstein 1998a: 41 (*MS 130*: 265 from Aug. 4th 1946, *MS 131*: 222 from Sept. 9th 1946, *TS 245*: 171 *et* 210 from Jan. 1947; *TS 229*: 237 *et* 284 from Sept. 1947).

world in terms of observability, and, secondly, externalising it into the semantisations performed by other people, i.e. other intellective subjects. As an externalisation of my inner world my behavioural and observable output is, as my behaviour, the input for another subject perceiving me (or for my own, self-distancing subjectivity). Yet the way this subject interprets the manifestations of my expressions and utterances, how it sets it into a meaningful frame against the background of its reality-constructs – in a way manipulating it in its mental life – can neither be predicted by me nor can it be explained by the reacting outputs of this other subject whose behavioural reaction I perceive.

A private-linguistic misuse of the word 'behaviour' would be the result if semantisation on part of the subject took place in the way that everything perceived would only be solipsistically realized as a self-produced manifestation, hence as an internalisation of everything external, and that this would *not* be observable itself. *The ostensive character of interpersonal behaviour only makes sense if another subjectivity is always already presupposed*, which attributes subjectivity in a mutually comprehensible way to the subject in his behavioural appearance. Behaviour would not show anything about the internal life of a person if the internal relation between behaviour and internal life were externalised into a strangely encoded medium, which itself would be inaccessible and without visible manifestation. Behavioural display does not only presuppose the reality and effectiveness of what was shown, but the efficacy of showing it in an inter-subjective sphere. The consequence would be infinite regress, if we required the act of showing itself to be shown.-

In a transactional-pragmatic understanding of communication, we find internal relations between expectation and fulfilment,[clxxxiii] action and rule,[clxxxiv] execution and instruction,[clxxxv] expression and sensation, e.g. pain,[clxxxvi] and these internal relations are *manifest as structurands of interactive systems*. What

---

[clxxxiii] "Philosophische Grammatik" VII §§ 85 ff., Wittgenstein 1984, Band 4: 132 ff.; "Philosophische Untersuchungen" I §§ 444 f., Wittgenstein 1984, Band 1: 419 ff.

[clxxxiv] "Philosophische Untersuchungen" I §§ 201 ff., Wittgenstein 1984, Band 1: 345 ff.

[clxxxv] "Philosophische Untersuchungen" I §§ 431 ff., Wittgenstein 1984, Band 1: 415 ff.

[clxxxvi] "Philosophische Untersuchungen" I §§ 244, Wittgenstein 1984, Band 1: 357; "Bemerkungen über die Philosophie der Psychologie" I §§ 200 ff. *et* §§ 304 ff., Wittgenstein 1998a: 41 ff. *et* 61 ff.; "Bemerkungen über die Philosophie der Psychologie" II § 63, § 499, § 574, Wittgenstein 1998b: 12 ff. *et* 90 *et* 101; "Letzte Schriften über die Philosophie der Psychologie" I § 203 *et* § 549, Wittgenstein 1990b: 29 *et* 71.

becomes evident thereby as *pragmatic redundancy* in an interactive system – for example as repeated behaviour in rituals and in other regularities,[clxxxvii] endowing it with a typical pattern – will then be ascertainable by an external observer and hence be determinable as an *essential structure* of this system, according to the degree it gains by being characteristic of this system.

That internal relations can thus only persist in practice, implies that the internal relations between inner life and expressions of a subject demand an internal structure of the frame for the interactive system within which behaviour can work as communication: That, for instance, a facial expression is understood as delight and is correspondingly answered by a form of behaviour on the part of whoever perceives this expression – e.g. by ignorance, envy, astonishment, or happiness – shows that a common language of verbal as well as non-verbal interaction is available within the system for every system-element. At the same time this indicates that *the interactive system itself can be conceived of as constituted by internal relations between the system-elements* in a social practice.

Yet this is exactly in what the systemic-pragmatic (or: transactional) perspective of *PTC* consists, namely that under this perspective internal relations and interpersonal relationships can be regarded as the constituents of an interactive system. Externally they can only be observed in the *form of an organization of redundancies, from them they are abstracted as structures*. The structure of an interactive system is described in the language of the observer, which thus gains a *meta-linguistic character*. This shows the relative meta-linguistic function of observer-language.[clxxxviii] The moment the observer becomes part of the system by his/her behaviour becoming observable and her/him thus becoming an interactive system-element, s/he loses the exclusive status of the external or even objective observer, and by the observer entering the system as a new element, the system itself is altered.

This is the main reason why Watzlawick et al. developed methodical instruments in therapeutic practice to turn the role of the observer – often the so-called 'therapist' or the therapist's supervisor – into a function that is usable for therapeutic purposes and interventions, with the aim of disposing of certain pathogenic traits of the system by re-organizing it. Yet these lines are not to be

---

[clxxxvii]   Cf. Watzlawick & Beavin & Jackson 1967: 32 ff.
[clxxxviii]   Cf. Cherry 1965: 90 ff.

read as purporting that only an external observer can observe the system. *The double role of observer and observed can, indeed, be ascribed to every system-element.* The degree of consciousness of *being observing observer and observed observer in every interaction,* essentially determines the transactional process. Only external observers shielded from all system-elements so that they cannot be observed within the system, will be without a (transactional) influence on the system and the system's reality.-

The clarification of this deeper connection between conceptual preparations by Wittgenstein (chiefly in his later philosophy) on the one hand and the characteristics of *PTC* on the other, cannot be based on definite evidence or on interpreting the connection as parallel lines of thought reaching beyond mere heuristics, neither can it be dismissed as some dark intuition or as based on a psychology of research or some other empty formulation enlightening the epistemological situation. One rather finds support for the opinion – which achieves more than the reconstructive aspect *(γα)* – that there is a *meta-theoretical equifinality,* not of the form of demonstrable *convergence,* but of a development starting from different points and leading to approaches which present themselves as related or similar, even though not all details can be inferred from biographical or textual material.

With this careful statement, the vague phrase about certain discoveries in the history of ideas "lying in their times" loses its mystical force. *That Watzlawick et al. can discover and use Wittgenstein's works as an interpretative potential for their own work at all, obviously required some principal convergences that are not only comfortable for founding one's own line of argumentation on an authority, but which are mainly to be found in the matter itself.* In this view, the aspects of a genesis of ideas *(α),* of selecting according to one's interests for one's further usage *(β),* and the parallel *(γ)* that turns up ex post, have as the conditions for their possibility what might be called a common root for the philosophising of the authors in question. Making this explicit by elaborating the details means meeting the claim of reconstruction, which we set ourselves in this essay, viz. the reconstruction of how far the philosophy of Wittgenstein served as a background for the development and formulation of *PTC* by Watzlawick et al.—

Essay II. Skript, Text, Work, Album.
On How To Read Wittgenstein's Way of Writing[clxxxix]

II.I. Prologue

In dealing with the editions of Wittgenstein's Writings, which came to be called his "Works" and whose main part consists of his Nachlass, my colleague, Alois Pichler, based on his own research, was led to four concepts which are to be examined here. My aim is not so much to praise a friend's work – and risk suspicion of being biased – but to concentrate on the *interaction of an editorial-philological point of view with hermeneutical-exegetical perspectives* touched upon and involved in any attempt of a deeper understanding of the application and usage of his four notions.

They are in brief: 'skript', 'text', 'work', 'album'. A document encountered as a piece of writing is *read* as a skript, as a text, as a work, as an album, understood as such, interpreted as such, even edited as such, yet it is also *written* as such, planned or intended as such, the latter aspects being relevant for my and, as I believe, also Pichler's approach to Wittgenstein. Giving definitions of these concepts against a certain so-called 'pragmatological' background and discussing them in their application to our reading of Wittgenstein and of our understanding

---

[clxxxix] To some extent this essay is a translation of Gelbmann 2002a, the first work I wrote after having read Alois Pichler's doctoral dissertation (i.e. Pichler 2001a) during my stay at the Wittgenstein Archives at the University of Bergen in spring 2002, funded by the Norwegian Research Council / Norges Forskningsråd. Yet large parts of Gelbmann 2002a have been revised since they deal too exclusively with Pichler's topics.

Not all of the works relevant for the issues I treat could be covered, partly because it demanded going too far into detail or would have involved other aspects not relevant here, partly because it would have meant learning other languages, like French. In an e-mail from February 2003, Ludovic Soutif pointed out to me that there is a new French publication concerning the problem of the "unachieved/able book in Wittgenstein"; cf. Guest, Gérard (2003): *Wittgenstein et la question du livre. Une phénoménologie de l'extrême. Perspectives critiques*. Paris: PUF. Unfortunately I am not be able to read it, so I hope it will soon be translated into a language I know.

To a large degree I feel indebted to Alois Pichler for his own research in this field. I always tried to make explicit where I relied on Pichler. The originality of my contribution lies more in the conceptual and reconstructive aspects of notions and approaches we share.

of his writing, is one of the purposes of my undertaking. The reader will soon get to know what exactly I mean with this announcement.

It should not be overlooked that in editing somebody's writing the text-ontological questions – i.e. to what textual kind the writing belongs, under which aspect it is to be perceived and, last but not least, to be edited – cannot be avoided, although the temptation to suppress any clear consciousness about them is strong and very inviting. In many cases this does need not rouse pangs of conscience, but I think with Wittgenstein's the case is different. There is an almost moral point involved when being confronted with his writing as a reader, an editor, a researcher, and the relief of finding a solution, or even the "redeeming word", cannot put us to rest with the knowledge of having settled the question once and for all – to rephrase a known Wittgenstein dictum – since there might *not* be any such ultimate solution that clarifies not only the decision about how to read and edit Wittgenstein, but also Wittgenstein's own intentions in these matters.

The phenomenon 'Wittgenstein' has attracted an enormous number of authors, created thousands of books and articles devoted to his thinking, his life, his family, his notes, his peculiarities, his time and its morals. Yet Wittgenstein's style, the way he wrote, and the concept of his writing are not among the main subjects of the publications about him. To my knowledge, it is only more recently that this has become a topic.[cxc] Especially the question *in how far style belongs to a certain written work and is, moreover, not only an aspect of the text but an integral part of the opus*, has seldom been raised. I shall therefore make use of the opportunity to investigate the interweaving of content and form, of the expressed and expression, of style and message, of gestalt and gist, of matter and manner.

I will not conceal that my thoughts are influenced and pre-formed by Alois Pichler's investigations, who already penetrated the problem of how Wittgenstein elaborated the 'album' called "Philosophical Investigations" from the various skripts he prepared, until he achieved those texts that are often seen as fragments of an unfinished *opus*, which, partly incompletely and a bit *ad lib*, were pieced together to edit what was to become a famous and quite influential book.[cxci]

[cxc]   Here I can mention Hintikka 1991, Pichler 1997a, Pichler 1997b, Pichler 2001a, Pichler 2001b, Pichler 2002, Hintikka & Hintikka 2002, Stern 2002.

[cxci]   It is one purpose of my essay to recommend the *publication* of Pichler's dissertation (in a revised version of op. cit.), which seems to be under way.

II.II. Does Wittgenstein Necessarily Intend a Book With What Was Edited as Book?

I think it is a myth that Wittgenstein was not capable of writing any *proper* philosophical work after the booklet called "Tractatus Logico-Philosophicus". This questionable theory can only be defended with regard to the circumstance that the skripts, texts, works Wittgenstein wrote and left to us clearly have not often or not always been rendered in the final printable paper-form of a book, to be published and distributed by publishing houses and book-sellers, to be bought by readers and libraries. He did, so to say, not edit himself very often until the final stage of a work ready for printing.

Yet with what is known as the edition of part I of "Philosophical Investigations" by Anscombe, Rhees, and Wright, Wittgenstein nevertheless presented us with a *work* in which the form of sketches, of fragmentary notes, of fragile un-linearity prevails, a work to which an unfinished state of writing inheres just as much as the impossibility to express any universal and single concept of what it is about. As a book it seems to be incomplete and not quite a book, more a very unconventional way of putting paper together in the form of a book – as a philosophical work it is somewhat resistant to any full understanding, if not entirely unreadable. It seems to be work that can be envisaged or described as an *arrangement*,[cxcii] *collage, puzzle, texture.* Wittgenstein himself finally came to call it an "album".[cxciii] It offers a collection of remarks, not however a stringent line of argumentation or a consistent bundle of arguments.

[cxcii]   The term "arrangement" as describing the production of Wittgensteinian skripts was introduced by Peter Keicher 2003 as a most interesting and pomising device to deal with Wittgenstein's writings and compositions not only from a merely textual point of view but as including activities of drawing and painting, of haptic operations in organizing his texts by putting together various slips of papers produced from his notes, laying them out on a table, gluing them together, gathering them in bundles, etc., similar to what some abstract painters (like the school of Italian Futurism) did, resulting in the skripts we encounter today, and which he himself calls sketches of landscapes and an album (cf. inf. *nota cxciii*). Many thanks to Katalin Neumer from the Institute for Philosophical Research at the Hungarian Acadamy of Sciences, who is going to edit Keicher's article; she made me acquainted with it in summer 2003.

[cxciii]   Cf. "Philosophische Untersuchungen" Vorwort, Wittgenstein 1984, Band 1: 232 ("Preface" in Wittgenstein 1991: vii). The draft of his foreword, in which he first talks about an "Album", is *TS 227*: 2 from Jan. 1944.

So some readers' expectations are not met, and the question may be raised whether Wittgenstein's own expectations were. However, when writing the Preface after part I of "Philosophische Untersuchungen" was finished, he himself admitted being quite content with it. *He disappoints an attitude of expectation on the part of the reader and probably also on the part of the author as to what is to be counted as a philosophical text.* This is probably a result of his attempt to make reading it worth while.[cxciv] This does not comply with the classic characteristics of a book, and some reader might have to overcome a barrier when reading the aphorisms this text consists of.

Yet overcoming a barrier was part of the genesis of this text itself.[cxcv] Wittgenstein was not a philosopher like young Hegel, who produced his work within a couple of weeks, founding what later on was to be raised and praised above all contradictions until finally being resolved. Wittgenstein is not uncritical of himself and his ideas, as his diary and other entries clearly show. Towards the end of his life, which reveals some legendary traits and is often retold as such,[cxcvi] Wittgenstein even seems to have lost *all* certainty, and he comes up with a conceptual work claiming certainty in life to be rooted in a texture of assumptions and a network of tolerated, believed contents, thus (and this goes much further than the practical limitation of Hume's scepticism) *limiting the possibility of doubting with the possibility of knowing.*[cxcvii] Is not exactly this outdated, even if not a Cartesian or Humean type of metaphysics?[cxcviii]

Modernity – in which he got involved as well as we have, although his trips to Norway or Ireland can be seen as attempts to escape it – would prefer to see

---

[cxciv]   I do not say that he originally intended to disappoint a possible reader, yet he realized that a disappointment of the usual attitude to reading books was inevitable.

[cxcv]   Cf. i.a. Schulte & Nyman & Savigny & Wright 2001, but see also biographical accounts, e.g. Monk 1990.

[cxcvi]   To some extent the flourishing of the literature on Wittgenstein is based on being retold over and over again, until a knight for his own cause has become the saint of the cause of others. I don't know how many presentations and narrations of Wittgenstein's life and deeds, work and waggery I have encountered, in articles, booklets, huge volumes, passages, introductions, epilogues, newspaper clips, on-line sites – but I know that I am sick of them.

[cxcvii]   Cf. "Über Gewißheit", Wittgenstein 1984, Band 8. See also Norman Malcolm 1963a, Malcolm 1986: 201 ff., Konstantin Pollok 2001, Avrum Stroll 2002, etc.

[cxcviii]   I am not going to take up the debate about Saul A. Kripke's interpretation given in Kripke 1982.

him running faster through its guts, subjugating him to a division of the labouring of mind to which certain traits in analytic philosophy tend. But instead of making it easy for us to digest him, he approaches with an "album" as the *opus magnum*, which permits many ways of collecting and picturing the same collections and pictures over and over again. And he dares to leave us a Nachlass, unpublished writings, from which a labyrinth of editions has been composed, all of which to quite various extents testifying to his thinking.[cxcix]

In addition, there are all his students, his biographers, acquaintances, his *nimbus* as the genius in liberal Cambridge, so dignified with talents (the same university he fled as a professor), the personal accounts of the man with rough sociability, amazing behaviour and a conduct so straight that an upright friendship must have been a heroic undertaking on the part of the befriended. Wittgenstein's popularity cannot stem from the widespread acquaintance with any depth of his writings, but rather from his strange, marvelled at existence in a certainly not Periclean age. He appears to have been suitable for philosophy because of his appearance and his apt utterances, because of not fitting in or being adapted – the son of Vienna's upper-class who gave away a fortune, volunteered to participate in a gruesome war, sought the remoteness of teaching in a village, and until the very end hid more than ninety percent of his philosophical work from publication during his life-time to let some real or alleged friends decide what was to happen to it. This is the stuff that yields novels and the rumour of fame. Wittgenstein probably deserves the popularity he did not want.

But it is too simple to assume that such a man, whose strangeness and vitality make one allot to him qualities he probably never had, just *could not* write a proper book,[cc] that even "Tractatus" is nothing but a collection of tenets, only better put in order and numbered. It is too easy to say that Wittgenstein's work just mirrors his personality. Trying to avoid any psychologism, one feels prone to assume that a pure text-immanent interpretation would be the best. Then one could avoid studying the Nachlass under the aspect of the genesis of the texts, since "Philosophische Unterschungen" and "Tractatus Logico-Philosophicus" are *the* representative works, sufficient in themselves.

[cxcix]   Thanks to the Bergen Electronic Edition and other, mostly electronic resources, we can find our way through this labyrinth.

[cc]   Hintikka & Hintikka 2002 seem to expect this, and since Wittgenstein did not achieve it, they ascribe to him another 'quality' unheard of before, namely a certain illness making him incapable of writing a proper book. I criticize this inf. *section IV.VIII.*

It is one of the assets of Pichler's investigations that the dismissal of psychologism is not accompanied with the embracement of text-immanent reading. Pichler[cci] understands the *work-character* of "Philosophische Untersuchungen" differently from what one is usually confronted with. Although Pichler does not seem to infer *the non-analyticity of the poetic term 'work' in regard to the term 'book'*, I think that his insight permits this conclusion.[ccii]

When knitting a conception of 'work-character' too closely, lots of philosophers would, so to say, 'lose' their works. Think of Nietzsche, the Pre-Socratics, letter writers like Leibniz, or those who presented us with collections of aphorisms and fragments like Schopenhauer. With at least part of what today is edited in books as their works, they did not aim at any book-character in the academic sense of the word. It cannot, however, seriously be claimed that these works of philosophy should therefore be forgotten.

Hence, *the philosophical relevance of a text is independent from the book-character of this text.* To my mind, this is a philological and hermeneutical principle that should guide us when editing as well as when reading or interpreting such texts. As far as philosophy is concerned with the work-character of texts, philosophy does not necessarily have to end up in a finality and attitude of 'once and for all', which the young Wittgenstein probably adopted with his "Tractatus", when concluding his Preface:

> "[...] the *truth* of the thoughts that are here communicated seems to me unassailable and definitive. I therefore believe myself to have found, on all essential points, the final solutions to the problems. And if I am not mistaken in this belief, then the second thing in which the value of this work consists is that it shows how little is achieved when these problems are solved." ("Tractatus Logico-Philosophicus" Preface, Wittgenstein 1992a: 4; italics original)

"Tractatus" *is* intended as a book, and referred to as a "book" by Wittgenstein himself in his Preface right at its beginning.[cciii] The book-character *here* is the way to make the work-character apparent in the right manner, although as a book "Tractatus" violates academic standards. But at least to (young) Wittgenstein's

---

[cci] Cf. Pichler 2001a and Pichler 2002.

[ccii] Pichler 2002 even sees a certain dramaturgy in "Philosophical Investigations", a further deviation from the standard notion of a philosophical or even academic book.

[cciii] Op. cit., Wittgenstein 1992a: 3.

perception it was a book, much more so than "Philosophical Investigations". Already in this impressive *opus minor*, an attentive reader can sense a distance to other usual statements of finality and definitiveness. Philosophy cannot be coined in currency or achievements.

According to Wittgenstein (loc. cit. sup.), the value of his labour consists in showing how little has been done by solving some philosophical problems. For us this means that *by exhausting the book-character, the work-character does not exhaust philosophising*. Philosophising is, like life itself, more.-

Many people (at least among Austrians, Norwegians, Americans this habit can often be perceived) have photo-albums from their families and their private lives at home, often reaching back over generations with a certain continuity, representing documents for recollection, for construing a personal and familiar history, to show them around in a rite of collective remembering. Now Wittgenstein did not leave us a photo-album but a philosophy-album as his *work*. This is *something different from a definitive, printed, read, written, corrected book*. Here philosophy accords to Life more than a book ever can.

II.III. A Pragmatic Approach to the Nachlass-Edition

Pichler starts his dissertation (whose publication is well under way) by a so-called 'pragmatic approach to interpretation', an approach which *neither strives for an ultimate interpretation, nor for only one result of its undertaking*, and he is aware of *any interpretation being inseparable from the interests and intellectual intentions of the interpreter*.

This approach is not a narrow concept of 'interpretation' aiming at weaving all tenets encountered into one context of truth, and it is not a reading in immanence either, which, for lack of any other sources, is boiled down to a close reading of only that found as written in a text, ignoring contexts or circumstances. At the same time, this somewhat risky notion of pragmatic interpretation does not avoid fundamental questions, even tackles them with frankness and thoroughness other approaches lack, since it would undermine their very fundament.[cciv]

[cciv] A text-immanent approach cannot question what 'text' or the author's 'work' is, it starts off with presupposing this. In this sense, pragmatic approaches can, but need not reach a text-ontologically more fundamental level.

When answering some "methodical questions" in his discussion of Eike von Savigny[ccv] as one of today's foremost representatives of a text-immanent reading and concept of interpretation, Pichler focuses on the simple question:

(Q1)   "What is a work by Wittgenstein?" (sec. Pichler 2001a: 22)[ccvi]

Here one should keep in mind that the textual (or *skriptural*) situation in *Wittgenstein's case does not allow an indubitable, definite answer* to this question, in contrast to the cases of other (known philosophical) authors.[ccvii] When looking at other authors, it is often clearer and easier to say *which of the skripts belongs to which text of which work and is intended to belong to this work in this way.*

Letter and skript, work and text can often easily be determined.[ccviii] But anybody who is only slightly acquainted with Wittgenstein as a (philosophical) writer[ccix] has heard or read about the vast amount of written work unpublished during Wittgenstein's life-time, the Nachlass, *some parts of which were probably never intended to be published* (yet in the light of his last will one can ponder whether the original intention in writing was outdated with his death[ccx]). It is not true that Wittgenstein was convinced that any of these texts contained in the Nachlass were finished or should appear in print.

Schulte's and Pichler's question (Q1), as quoted above, can be reduced to another question with regard to the Nachlass and the problems of editing it, viz.:

[ccv]   Cf. i.a. Savigny 1988, Savigny 1996a.

[ccvi]   By asking this, Pichler refers to Schulte 1989 and Rothhaupt 1996. See also Pichler 1992, Pichler 1993, Pichler 1995.

[ccvii]   Even *opera* of letters, like those of Descartes or Leibniz, are more definite in this regard, in so far as they can be documented and reconstructed, and as far as the skriptural situation is concerned, i.e. the situation on the skript-level. And this holds although, as far as we know today, both writers never intended any book-edition with their letters. They did not intend a work-character in the form of a book, although the work-character of their letters is undeniably a philosophical one and might even contain tenets quite central to their philosophical doctrines.

[ccviii]   As we know, Wittgenstein wrote numerous letters, even more so Bertrand Russell, and in this regard both authors can be compared with Descartes or Leibniz: philosophers write letters and convey parts of their work and doctrine to others, yet do not intend or express the wish that this is ever to be collected and edited in book-form.

[ccix]   Cf. i.a. Pichler 1992, Pichler 1997b, or Ortner 2000.

[ccx]   In the light of *this* one has to admit that any knowledge about such "original intentions" of the writer under consideration are a re-construction, and, moreover, that any ascription of intentions to the writer as warranted by a testament depends on constructions.

(Q2)   "What is a *text* by Wittgenstein?" (sec. Pichler loc. cit.; my emphasis)

By asking in this way, we jump another, systematic question providing the grounds for (Q2), namely:

(Q3)   What, basically, is a 'text'?

There might be no satisfactory and exhaustive answer to (Q3) because of its generality and the lack of any context providing criteria for assessing the correctness and satisfactoriness of any attempted answer.[ccxi] My attempt to answer (Q3) is rather straightforward and clumsy:[ccxii]

(A3)   "A 'text', so one could try to give a definition, is only a text if some other text refers to it. Texts are therefore always located in a texture." (my translation of my own formulation)[ccxiii]

Let aside that this answer (A3) uses "texture" in a metaphorical way, it just shifts the problem to some following or afore going point of reference for this text to be a text, a point of reference which itself can only be a text if there is some other such point of reference for it. This leads to a *regressus in infinitum*.

Practically, this principle of evidence for something to be a text to some degree is fulfilled in the case of Wittgenstein's Nachlass, since there is almost no single entry which has not been revised, i.e. it appears in some other manuscript or typescript, probably a bit changed, probably in a different context, possibly in some skript that got lost. The book-editions of Wittgenstein's writings already available give evidence of these textual occurrences, therefore Pichler 2001a: 23 is right in maintaining that the Nachlass does *not* contain any unknown systematic-philosophical treasures.[ccxiv] Yet the question remains what the original textual

---

[ccxi]   I think a dash of Wittgensteinian method is essential here, viz. the principle of contextuality for any application of criteria.

[ccxii]   Cf. my electronic note Gelbmann 1999 (originating during a summer stay at the Wittgenstein Archives at the University of Bergen in 1998 and the discussions with Alois Pichler, Peter Cripps, Wilhelm Krüger, Franz Hespe and others about the project of the Bergen Electronic Edition, which at that time was still under way).

[ccxiii]   I shall not apply (A3) as a definition for 'text'.

[ccxiv]   It may however be questioned in many cases whether these book-editions, widely available now in several languages, really contain – as so-called 'normalized editions' – the versions of these textual occurrences which were most likely intended by Wittgenstein. It is clear and can hardly be questioned that these versions of works or editions are 'texts' in an

occurrences in Wittgenstein's writings are, and according to which definition they can be regarded as 'text'.

Consequently, my definition (A3) is a bit crude. Yet when looking at Wittgenstein's own (tacit) understanding of 'text', one feels convinced that his way of working reflect his understanding of 'language', especially as 'language' is understood in the "Blue Book": as a tangle, texture of family-resembling structures of references, full of crossings and side-ways, whose overall gestalt does not comply with any common ideal. It is according to Pichler's understanding of the album-character of what Wittgenstein came to perceive as the intended work (at least of "Philosophische Untersuchungen") that these points about 'language' and 'text' are inherent in this peculiar outcome of a 'work'. So one could arrive at the (weird) statement:

(D1)   Language has the character of an album and is (or becomes): *text.*

The definition (D1) has the funny trait that it lets 'language' depend on 'text'.- All these considerations are not to be taken as definite answers, they are rather attempts at finding new aspects of the problem. As unsatisfactory or even crazy they may appear, they bring about some kind of new language-games, outlandish and queer, to tackle a conceptual problem we are still involved in. Their fruitfulness cannot be assessed a priori. If we, in the widest sense, take Wittgenstein as an author, we can define authorship in the following way:

(D2)   An author is somebody who puts writing into action by producing document(s) in written form.[ccxv]

---

everyday-sense of the word, and since there are lots of textual references to them, in citations and writings of other philosophers, (A3) has some practical applicability. It is, indeed, an uncomfortable question, since it is exactly under these ordinary circumstances that nobody would bring up a question for which (A3) could serve as an answer ...

[ccxv]   For this I am also indebted to Alois Pichler (personal communication). I am quite sure that Pichler had the term 'speech-act' (in German 'Sprechakt') in his mind when he introduced the term 'Schreibhandlung'.

In this sense the performance of writing-acts is not necessarily performative in the sense of John L. Austin 1962a, i.e. the performance of writing-acts is not parallel to the realization of performative speech-acts; the latter bring about the *reality of a social situation in an institutional frame*, whereas a *performative writing-act* could be seen on a par with performative speech-acts, yet then the performance of writing-acts is not the same as the performance of performative writing-acts.

This "putting writing into action" – a translation of the German phrase "Schreibhandlungen setzen" – should be taken as a very wide, abundant notion, containing slips of the pen, stains, unique traits of handwriting as well as singular signs or 'tokens' of a unique 'writing-act', as I translate the German term 'Schreibhandlung'. The result of a continuity of such writing-acts can be called 'skript', and a singular occurrence or token of a 'skript' is a unique *document*. Hence we arrive at a further definitional attempt:

> (D3) A skript is the outcome of the writing-acts of an author, set into action with the intention of producing a text.

From the outset we have to state that 'text' signifies something written, just as 'work' does.[ccxvi] This limits the possible cases of application.[ccxvii] It is clear that the concept 'work' will somehow depend on the concept 'text'.

When looking at the text- and work-editions of Wittgenstein's *opus postumus*,[ccxviii] it becomes apparent that most of these book-editions are not directly authorized by Wittgenstein himself, thus not having the advantages of the personal control and care he took concerning a correct edition of "Tractatus Logico-Philosophicus", which he undoubtedly intended to have published.[ccxix] According to Joachim Schulte,[ccxx] there are three criteria for the work-character of a text (with regard to Wittgenstein), which I will render in my own words:

> (C1) We are presented with a work by Wittgenstein, if, firstly, Wittgenstein himself recognizably regarded a text he wrote as an autonomous creation, based on his own skripts.
>
> (C2) Secondly, it must be possible for the reader to trace in the texts a line of argumentation, theses and antitheses, examples included.

[ccxvi] Yet not something *scribed*, if one uses the notion which stems from Ch. S. Peirce: Text is not of the structure of diagrams, but it can be contained in diagrams, can occur in scribing.

[ccxvii] The reason why I add this remark is, that with the debate about 'textuality' and 'intertextuality', the (semiotic) concept of 'text' has become much wider than the way it is dealt with here.

[ccxviii] I am primarily thinking of the "Published Works" at Blackwell or the "Werkausgabe" at Suhrkamp.

[ccxix] Cf. e.g. McGuinness & Schulte 1989 or the letters to Ogden, i.e. Wittgenstein 1973.

[ccxx] Cf. Schulte 1989: 52.

(C3) Thirdly, there has to be a stylistic and formal design of the text which allows talking about it as being completed.[ccxxi] (*sec.* Pichler 2001a: 26)

This list of criteria requires additional comment. Ad (C1): In some form there has to be a *documented and witnessed act of authorization* to justify such an assessment. This can be the performance of a specific speech-act or writing-act under appropriate circumstances, or the documentation of some equivalent in a typographically, audio-visually, or electronically encoded or otherwise conventionally secured form.[ccxxii] To bring a practical counter-example: during Wittgenstein's teaching at Cambridge, some of his 'works' circulated among students, just think of the "Blue Book". Yet these circulating notes, skripts, texts were not authorized by him. We have, in fact, *documents stating his unwillingness to authorize* them, documents which question any authorization of publication and clearly state that this circulation was against his explicit wish.[ccxxiii]

Numerous book-editions of Wittgensteinian skripts are not authorized as works. I shall consequently distinguish between 'work' as a publication authorized by the author, and 'Nachlass-work', done with the authorization of an editor or a

---

[ccxxi] I avoid the term 'completeness' because of its semantic connotations; *a text can be completed in the sense of finished without being complete.* Actually, this is a circumscription of the album-character.

An album as a collection of photographs about the life of family N.N. might be completed in the sense that all the empty pages and spaces are filled with pictures and that the intended period of time in the lives of the human beings constituting this family are covered, yet it will *never* reach the completeness of a documentation of the entire life of all the family members, since much of what they experienced and saw is just not recorded on film or otherwise.

[ccxxii] There have to be institutional conditions to safeguard the verification and justification of such acts. If this framework becomes ineffective, it might happen that an authorization, although once given, is not recognizable any more and hence just ignored. The older a document, the more likely is such an error in the recognition of original intentions. Yet in the case of Wittgenstein this does not play any role.

[ccxxiii] One could investigate whether these circulations did not involve a breach of copyright. Today, many philosophers are grateful for this, since it brought into existence what today is widely regarded as a 'work' of Wittgenstein.

But being an author myself, I cannot agree to this procedure. It is strange that an *illegal act* depriving an author of documents from a certain stage of the development of his thinking produces a 'work', even a book ascribed to him, although he obviously did not want to see it published or edited as a book. Yet Wittgenstein's testament (cf. inf.) justified all this ex post, so if there was a scandal, Wittgenstein's generosity made up for it.

trustee in some way legally entrusted with this task.[ccxxiv] The condition (C1) will then have to be changed to suit the case of what I call 'Nachlass-work':

(C1)[*]   We are presented with a Nachlass-work, if its editor was entrusted by Wittgenstein with the task of editing it, and if this editor recognizably regarded the text of this Nachlass-work as an autonomous creation, based on skripts by Wittgenstein.

Ad (C2): As far as any reading of a *line of argumentation* is concerned, especially with regard to the *conclusiveness of the text*, it is the *semiotic subjectivity of the reader which in reading turns a skript into a comprehensible text*. This point of subjectivity, due to which some philosophers consider, e.g., texts by Heidegger as unreadable, whereas others don't is important. Point (C2) also accounts for the fact that *a work can be one single text.*[ccxxv]

Ad (C3): To my mind, a *stylistic and formal design of the text* (but not necessarily of the skript or work) depends on the question whether the *recipient* who qualifies the text as work *can read a text from the work-skript* in which s/he can recognize a uniform and/or intended gestalt. This stylistic aspect is doubtful as far as Wittgenstein is concerned, since the question must be raised as to when he ever achieved completeness and formal design in his Nachlass-skripts that would give them book-character. One has to concede that our usual habits of reading text can be misleading; Wittgenstein's writing does not comply with the rules of linearity, we have already touched upon in sup. (C2).

On the other hand, *an album can be completed as such*, a *collage* (to use a French term) can be finished as a collage, a fragment can be complete as a fragment in the sense of *it having been intended in exactly this way* by the producer. *The author is the first reader of his/her own work.* Moreover, a reader who is not identical with the author could read a text out of an album-like skript of e.g. Wittgenstein, and such an album-like skript would then be an album-work or

---

[ccxxiv]   The author need not have entrusted the editor with this task, since in case a copyright has expired and an author has been dead for a long time, an *edition* of a Nachlass-work does not seem to be any *legal* problem. The same holds for the publication of a work by this author (and, of course, for the publication of an edition of a Nachlass-work).

[ccxxv]   Points (C1) and (C1)[*] could refer to an autonomous skript, which was authorized as such in some way, either by the author or by some trustee. Then a skript would have been turned into a work or Nachlass-work, without any reference to its text(s). This would identify it as a unique document, like a piece of art or an autograph.

a work which perfects the style of album. This is an even more trivial answer, viz. that *reading something as an album means reproducing a work's album-text,* whatever the writing-acts and skripts were that led to its production.-

According to Pichler 2001a: 26, the work-character of the "Tractatus" is indubitable when applying the criteria (C1)-(C3). Pichler even goes further. He is convinced of the work-character of "Philosophische Untersuchungen" part I. Yet here we have no book-character as definite as in the case of "Tractatus", whose book-character is verified by its edition and justified by the author himself.

Schulte also accepts[ccxxvi] "Philosophische Bemerkungen" as a work. Yet for Schulte authorization seems to be less important, *for him the assessment whether a work has achieved an intended completeness is independent from the author's own assessment.* It is for the reader to decide. In the case of Wittgenstein, Pichler philologically holds against Schulte[ccxxvii] that the draft of the Preface in the skript *MS 109*: 204 ff. (from Nov. 6th 1930) was not necessarily written for "Philosophische Bemerkungen". Hence it was probably Wittgenstein's intention, as well as the reader's idea of Wittgenstein's intention when reading the current edition, that "Philosophische Bemerkungen" be considered a finished work. With this Pichler tacitly seems to link work-character to book-character. And according to Pichler loc. cit., the skript *TS 209*, presenting us with a collection of notes and paperclips, depicts a text at a point before reaching its final stage.

From Pichler's point of view, as I perceive it, one could here insert the reason why *TS 209* is only a text: because *it does not satisfy any book-character.*[ccxxviii] However, this problem might be resolved, if it is resolvable at all in the face of the impossibility of reconstructing all of Wittgenstein's original intentions in his production of writing-acts: Pichler suggests a fourth criterion for the work-character of a text (by Wittgenstein), namely:

(C4)   Only that shall validly be regarded as a work which not only has been accomplished and finished, but for which there are also earlier stages

---

[ccxxvi]   Schulte 1989: 53, sec. Pichler loc. cit.

[ccxxvii]   Pichler 2001a: 26.

[ccxxviii]   If one interprets Pichler so far, our comment above about the connection between book-character and work-character being non-analytic is weakened, and one might sense a certain self-contradiction in Pichler which he was probably not aware of, since he does not discuss the aspect of analyticity in this respect.

    As a typescript, *TS 209* is more than only a skript, i.e. it already represents an intended type and not only an occurrence of a skript.

and traceable preparatory steps.[ccxxix] (*sec.* Pichler 2001a: 27, my re-formulation and translation)

An example of this would be the German translation of what circulated as "Brown Book", i.e. "Eine Philosophische Betrachtung", the second part of *MS 115* from 1936, which nonetheless remains a fragment. Does this now mean that only typescripts can be regarded as (Nachlass-)works of Wittgenstein?

The "Big Typescript" (*TS 213* from Jan. 1932), however, is not at all complete. Even its manuscript-parts and the revisions written by hand have pre-stages.[ccxxx] Yet Wittgenstein himself did *not* authorize the "Big Typescript" as a finished book, and for him it was probably not even a definitive work. (If some testimony or document proving the opposite were found, this would be sensational – and a scandal for Rhees' editorship.)[ccxxxi] Hence we have come across a violation of sup. (C1) or (C1)[*] respectively.-

Here it is worth adding further comments. It can be the case that an author regards something as 'work' which s/he has abandoned without having authorized it as 'definite' or 'finished', or even as 'book' and 'to be published'. I shall call this special case an *opus ad acta*. It depicts a strain or thread of the author's train of thoughts that were not taken up again, probably a document which became alienated from the author him/herself. I think that an author often burns or destroys such a work; some, however, survive because their authors have forgotten them. These *abandoned works* sometimes find their way into the literary heritage of an author, although they were probably never intended to be among the Nachlass. An *opus ad acta* was neither designed as a 'Nachlass-work' nor accomplished as a 'work'. And yet it exists.

If they are authorized ex post by some editor as Nachlass-works, they achieve a status of importance in clear contrast to what the author wished or had in mind. This can even go so far that such an accidental Nachlass-work of an *opus ad acta*

[ccxxix] This is similar to my (A3), if one sees the existence of such earlier stages of a work as texts to which the text of the work in its final stage refers. (D4) When these earlier stages are texts by other authors, the work is an example of intertextuality.

[ccxxx] Cf. Kenny 1976, Krüger 1993.

[ccxxxi] Hintikka 1991 is one more recent example of a scholar who criticizes Rhees' editorial work, especially as far as *TS 213* and "Philosophical Grammar" are concerned, and he does so in the wake of Anthony Kenny.

My account (in German) of this discussion can be found in footnote 13 of Gelbmann 2002a, at *http://h2hobel.phl.univie.ac.at/~yellow/Wittgenstein/Pichler.html#13*.

is edited and published, although the author did not want to see it published. Much of what is called 'diary' or 'personal notes' might be of this character. They survive because the author has forgotten to destroy them or to take care of any regulations concerning their status (I know what I am talking about).

As documents of privacy, of the author's own thoughts, feelings, experiences, hopes, desires, of what he brought to paper for himself, they are problematic cases and are not designed to be read and scrutinized, gossiped about by the *plebs*, and they are not always recognized as *opera ad acta*. This does not mean that every diary is an abandoned work, not at all, but some certainly are, and in the case of Wittgenstein one cannot always be certain.[ccxxxii]

In the case of the 'Big Typescript' we know from Wittgenstein himself that it was not a diary and that it was supposed to become a book. Yet he never developed this work to the stage and maturity of a (proper, printable, finished, linear) book, and so it becomes a difficult question to assess whether *TS 213* was some form of 'work', abandoned or not, or rather some preparatory phase of a later work, which then for different reasons and in different circumstances was not or only partly finished. It is a typescript, but not the type of skript that can be regarded as the draft or final author-skript of a definite work. Was Rush Rhees aware of this intricacy, this complexity?

That the 'Big Typescript' safely reached our days, could be 'blamed' on Wittgenstein's will, which in this case cannot be called his last will, since this *opus* was abandoned years before Wittgenstein's death. But Wittgenstein's testament[ccxxxiii] permitted its publication. So it is probably the Nachlass-edition of some stage of an abandoned work, a *pars opus ad acta*, so to say.

If we go back to Pichler's criterion (C4), we have to note that he loc. cit. pleads taking the content of those skripts not chosen to belong to the 'real works' seriously. In other words, one should not a priori consider a Nachlass-edition as less important than works that have been authorized or even edited by their

---

[ccxxxii] Cf. Wittgenstein 1991, the so-called "secrete diaries" or "coded diaries", which were edited by Wilhelm Baum (in German, as "Geheime Tagebücher").

[ccxxxiii] The essential passage is, e.g., quoted in Hintikka 1996b: 7. Also Nedo 1993: 52 renders this part of Wittgenstein's testament, in which the most important point obviously is that Wittgenstein left the decision about which of his writings should be published entirely to R. Rhees, G. E. M. Anscombe, and G. H. von Wright. Hintikka op. cit. discusses the story of the various edition-projects, which finally ended with the Wittgenstein Archives at the University of Bergen successfully bringing out the Bergen Electronic Edition, which transcribed all of the available Nachlass − including diaries, drawings, and notebooks.

authors themselves. In my opinion, Pichler's comment simply expresses the maxim that documents and writings, skripts of any sort or form, *have to be read*, even if they are not given the epithet 'work'. The problem here is, what kind of 'text' is read as the content of these documents, especially if they are documents written down in longhand, revised, hardly readable or sketchy, etc. In approaching this matter, Pichler suddenly becomes very pragmatic, demanding – what I try to render as our fifth criterion – that:

(C5)   for a skript to be a 'work' it must be a Nachlass-work fit for publishing in *manageable sections*.

So one is implicitly forced to select as Nachlass-work what is suitable for publication, always taking one's bearing along the known production of books. *The elaboration of a complete edition in this understanding only has to edit parts of the Nachlass*, without ever finding a definitive answer to the question about the work-character. That is why Pichler regards the editions of the trustees or those authorized by the trustees as representing 'works' of Wittgenstein in an acceptable form. They enjoy a wide distribution and acceptance among academics, who all seem to use them as sources and quotable references.[ccxxxiv] (C5) can be used as a handy justification for the existing editions exactly because of this criterion's pragmatic practicability.

It is the force of factuality that gives these editions their reputation and usability, yet they are far from a proper, philologically satisfactory edition of a Nachlass.[ccxxxv] If according to criteria like (C5) *recognition of the authorization of a Nachlass-edition becomes a socio-pragmatic matter of a circle of more or less self-named scholars*, it becomes clear that in its last consequence this leads to a conventionalism that completely disregards the author's role in the process of reconstructing or validating an authorization of his/her skripts.

In extreme cases – not, however, with Wittgenstein's Nachlass – this could lead to a skript its author not only abandoned but explicitly wanted to destroy

---

[ccxxxiv]   Hintikka 1996b does not share this opinion.

[ccxxxv]   From personal communication with Edoardo Zamuner (University of Bologna) I know that Anscombe's reaction to Michele Ranchetti's question, why the trustees had not achieved a philologically proper critical edition, was something like: "Who are you?", said in a tone of disdain, measuring a man of aristocratic offspring and scholarship like a freshman or disobedient pupil.

being published as a Nachlass-work, with the implicit indication that this was done according to the author's wishes. Such an unauthorized publication might develop its own its own exegetical influence, causing severe, sometimes even undetectable misinterpretations of the author by being ascribed to him/her as his/her 'work'.- This sounds like an absurd exaggeration, yet we cannot exclude such a case once and for all, i.e. under all circumstances (not to employ the philosophical catch-word 'a priori').

II.IV. **What Is the Text to Be Edited?**

Pichler pinpoints the crucial question about the work-problem as follows:

(Q4)   "Where do we find Wittgenstein's text when faced with the intertextual structure and complexity of his Nachlass?" (sec. Pichler 2001a: 27 f.)

This touches upon the core of the problem, which I shall classify as a semiotic one. Pichler tackles it from the advantaged point of view of the critic by introducing a distinction I will presently place into a larger semiotic or pragmatologic frame. The distinction is about the already used terms 'skript' and 'text', and I shall look upon it as definition:

(D5)   "It is best to see the Nachlass as a *spatial succession of skripts*, and not as text, 'skript' hereby referring to *something written*, whether it is a single letter or a whole book. [Cf. sup. (D3)] [...] The skripts of the Nachlass have been produced by *writing-acts in a certain chronological order* [cf. sup. (D2)], and they present us with spatial succession. [...] The same skripts can be produced by different writing-acts; vice versa, the same writing-act can lead to different skripts. It is often the case that in reading a coherent text from a skript we have to leave the spatial order of the skripts, and this alone makes it impossible to determine the concept of 'work' spatially. It can also be the other way round, viz. that *one* skript serves for the production of more than one text. This point and other issues make it advisable strictly to distinguish 'work' and 'text' from 'skript' as the *bearer of text*. They are mere constructs from the skript-material and have to be dealt with as such." (sec. Pichler 2001a: 28, my translation, my italics)

This invites comment. Firstly, to the issue of spatio-temporal order: It is clear that the temporal sequence of skripts within the Nachlass (the corpus of which should be more than only a sample of documents) contribute to locate 'works', since the chronology of self-sufficient skripts, may their writing-acts be temporally and spatially ever so confusing, will, as the text of his/her work, be more likely to correspond to the text the author intended.

The skripts in spatial order have a typographical and skriptural form. Yet these skripts could themselves have been mapped or represented in some other medium, for example as photographs (facsimile) or transcriptions. In order to model skripts in these forms – to anticipate what is to be discussed later – they have to be *recognized* as skripts. This seems to be the right moment to introduce a further definition:

(D6)   A 'document' shall be defined as either a 'skript' or a 'text'; although according to (D5) skripts are bearers of texts, we shall regard 'mental documents' as texts that have not been made manifest by writing-acts.

This definitional device renders possible observations such as

(O1)   Works are documents.
(O2)   Works are intended as texts documented in the form of skripts.
(O3)   According to the criteria (C1)-(C5), every work has as a forerunner at least one skript, even if no traces have survived of this skript (a case I exclude in the case of Wittgenstein). Such a forerunning skript must at least be documented, e.g. by being mentioned, cited, quoted or used. This implies that a forerunning skript can be the strange case of a *text of a mental document*, which turns mental documents into texts of which there are no skripts in a concrete form.

Although the inference (O3) raises a serious problem – namely the *existence of texts in the form of mental documents without any text-bearing skript* – it also brings the freedom of the editor and (philological) interpreter or exegete into play, because the existence or postulation of such a forerunning skript is a matter of *reconstruction*, and it might be re-produced as a 'proto-work' (in German 'Ur-Werk', what should not be mixed up with the word "Uhrwerk", although as phonemes they identical).[ccxxxvi] A 'proto-work' might, of course, also be edited as a book, and even though Nachlass-editors usually take care of such works, these

---

[ccxxxvi]   In Wittgenstein we have the examples of this in "Proto-Tractatus" and "Proto-Philosophische Untersuchungen".

'proto-works' are not Nachlass-works or *opera ad acta* but belong to a category of their own.

But back to (D5), which was not sufficiently commented upon. Pichler 2001a: 28 adds that *only skripts are "objective", not texts*, to which I remark that works are not objective either.

(Q5) Yet what is meant here by "objective"?

Does it mean "embodied in some physically realized substrate", implemented, encoded in a decipherable way? Or "perceivable as a bearer of text", recognized as such?- There are many possible answers. In (A5) we shall focus on types of answers that verifiably increase their usability for our purpose.

(A5) Hence the sense of 'objectivity of skripts' can be construed as the *starting-point for modelling texts from skripts. Skripts are objective if they serve as so-called 'relative originals' for a text,*[ccxxxvii] which is then "born" by the skript.

Yet the work that is realized in a text read off from a skript is "objective" in *a different understanding* than the skript, even though it claims validity which cannot remain private but asks for intersubjective communicability.

A certain work in full validity as a *mental document in the form of a skriptless text* can be attributed to the author in the stadium before he starts any writing-act, somehow *ante creationem*. In this last sense the text represented in a skript is not the bearer of a work but *the skript is born by the work in the pre-form of a mental document*; the skript enables the existence of the text of the work. This turns the work into what I shall call a "bearer" of skript(s), with the skript(s) being the bearers of text, whereas it would, indeed, be *meaningless* to talk of a bearer of work(s). So from the point of view of the *authority of authorship*, the intended work is skript- and textless, and supports the writing of the skript, which itself allows the text to be read off the writing-acts constituting the skripts.

The interesting point in (Q5) and in the passage above does not so much lie in any quest for "objectivity" but in a strange shift, which sees the beginning of a work in the skriptless text of a mental document. The work-idea of an author or

---

[ccxxxvii] With "relative original" I refer to a term within *GMT*, the "General Model Theory" by H. Stachowiak; see also below *nota ccxxxviii.*

the Nachlass-work-idea of an editor is "objective" in so far as it takes one to the origin of shaping acts, of modelling supposed to represent and develop them.

Is this to be called *a paradox of writing-acts*? Or is it more a pun, a game with words more than a language-game?- It is primarily an attempt *to ascribe to the author some knowledge about the work which is always ahead of any knowledge about the work on the part of the reader or interpreter*, even though the reader and interpreter can be the author him/herself. In any case, this knowledge will contain intentions and will realize intentions, and it will not exhaust all knowledge applied in this field, since in some sense the reader knows more than the author, and the author as his/her own reader might be surprised by his/her own writing.

The notion of 'mental document', which can too easily be dismissed as a form of 'memory' or 'thought', introduces an aspect into the understanding of work-character that has probably been missed out so far, something that should not be neglected. *Writing does not start with piling up ink heaps or pencil-erosions of a certain form on paper.* A writing-act cannot be conceptualised in a positivistic manner, even though the work in book-form is a final outcome of the writing-acts of an author. But isn't the work, as intended by the author, the cause or motive, even reason for each single writing-act?

II.V. Modelling 'Writing'

My own thoughts during the last years have come to resemble what Pichler 2001a: 28 ff. develops, instructively giving examples and always close to the sources. Although I am far from this scholarly devotion, I see my work on the pragmatologic model-Theory of Herbert Stachowiak as resembling Pichler's pragmatic approach.[ccxxxviii] Stachowiak himself talks in German of a "Allgemeine Modelltheorie" (or of "AMT"), which in English can be rendered as "General Model Theory", in short: *GMT*. In order to apply it to our investigation, two concepts and a bit of symbolic formalization have to be introduced.[ccxxxix]

[ccxxxviii] Here I again refer to Stachowiak 1973, Stachowiak 1989b.- I personally am certain that Pichler never read Stachowiak.

[ccxxxix] Readers acquainted with my account of the basics of *GMT* (e.g. from having read Gelbmann 2000c or Gelbmann 2002d) can jump the following points.

The first concept is that of '(pragmatologic) model', in short M, the other that of '(pragmatologic) Theory', abbreviated *Th*.

(1.1) A (pragmatologic)[ccxl] model M is an assemblage or class of attributes, i.e. the elements of the set signified with M are attributes of a thing,[ccxli] and are countable, although there can be infinitely many of them. These attributes of a thing (taken as object to be modelled that itself need not be specified and can be a system of objects as well as a single entity) are (countably) symbolized by A_1, A_2, A_3, A_4, A_5, ..., A_{n-2}, A_{n-1}, A_n, ... Such an attribute can be a property, a quality, a colour, a relation, a relation of predicates, a relation of relations, a state, even a quality of predicates, etc., in a very formal, algebraic understanding of these signs, which are hence variables ranging over a universe of different (sorted) attributes.[ccxlii] Such an attribute may itself be a result of some modelling-Theorizing process. (This will become important for the token/type difference, which has been kept in dark so far.)

(1.2) It must be pointed out that there is no connection between the expression 'model' and what in German is called 'Erfüllbarkeit', which I translate with 'fulfillability' or 'satisfiability'. This would be the approach to the term stemming from the formalistic side of mathematics, a formal-semantic approach, which is merely an equivocal use of the same word. Such a formal-semantic understanding belongs to a *statement-view on theorizing*, taking the second relevant concept in a different reading as well, such that 'model' becomes a semantic interpretation of a deductive, calculus-like theory (i.e. a "theory-in-statement-view"), which makes all the statements of this theory true (provided that the premises, axioms and bases of this theory are expressed in true statements from which all other statements can be deduced). A model in this understanding would be a *truth-maker*, satisfying the corresponding calculus/calculi that serve(s) as their theory/theories.[ccxliii] But in this essay the term 'model' does not belong to any consideration of sentences or

---

[ccxl] There are different readings of the term 'model' from the one I use here, which account for the addition of the qualification "pragmatological". The same can be said about the term 'Theory', which I write with a capital letter in order to distinguish it from other concepts of the same name. This is not the place to enlarge on the differences between these equivocal terms; some explanation is to follow in the text below.

[ccxli] In this paper I do not distinguish between 'class' and 'set'.

[ccxlii] This is my inference from Stachowiak 1973: 134.

[ccxliii] *Sensu* Mulligan & Simons & Smith 1984.

statements in the form of calculi, it refers to a *non-statement-view on theorizing*, its pragmatical touch deriving from 'model' not being an interpretational device.

(1.3) The concept of modelling as applied here simply consists in the *operational picturing of attributes* of a thing or entity, which is then called 'object' or 'original' (in short: O). This picturing is represented by or results in some other entity, called 'model' (in short: M).

(1.4) Here it is necessary to mention auto-modellation, which maps a set of attributes of an entity into itself or into a sub-set of itself: *Skript-production can have the character of auto-modellation.*

(1.5) O and M are just two sets of attributes, in such a way that an operation F transforms a sub-set of O into a sub-set of M.[ccxliv] The sub-set of O is called O_P, the sub-set of M abbreviated with M_E. Then we gain the formula: $M_E = F(O_P)$.

(1.6) An example can easily be given: Let O be $\{B_1, B_2, B_3, \dots B_n\}$, then for producing the aforementioned formula some of the attributes of O have to be left out and are not yielded in $O_P = \{B_2, B_3, \dots B_{n-1}\}$. So O_P neglects certain attributes of O, and the operational function F then takes every element of O_P to map it onto elements of M, but without necessarily letting every element of M refer to one of O_P. Therefore the elements of $M = \{A_1, A_2, A_3, \dots A_m\}$ reached by F normally constitute a selection of M,[ccxlv] called M_E, which in our example shall be the sub-set $\{A_3, \dots A_{m-2}\}$. Those attributes of the original that are not modelled are called 'preterated attributes', those attributes of the model that are not a production of the modelling of the original but are superfluous, are called 'abundant attributes'. *The non-preterated attributes of the original hence correspond to the non-abundant attributes of the model*, the latter attributes also being called the 'essential attributes' of the model.[ccxlvi]

[ccxliv] The so-called ico-structural function of modellation by mapping attributes.

[ccxlv] Note that the indices "$_m$" and "$_n$" need not be identical. Each signifies a natural number.

[ccxlvi] In practice, the sets of attributes M and O will cross and overlap, the same for O_P and M_E. F can but need not 'auto-transform' attributes, in other words, let attributes of O unchanged as attributes of M. In this sense, every physical object models itself completely, one can call it its own document. This is not as trivial as it may seem, because if the physical object serving as an original for modelling is taken as a skript, the skript documents itself. Since (D6) says that a skript is a bearer of a text, its self-documentation is a document of its text. Hence to address something as a skript and as an outcome of writing-acts according to (D3) already means seeing it as a textual document.

(1.7) In most cases of modelling it will hold that neither $O_P = \{\}$ nor $M_E = \{\}$, but also that neither $(O \setminus O_P) = \{\}$ nor $(M \setminus M_E) = M_A = \{\}$.[ccxlvii]

(1.8) It is characteristic of *GMT* that models themselves can be regarded as originals for a modelling of higher order.[ccxlviii] In short: M^2 is the meta-model or second-order model of a model M (or more precisely: M^1), which itself is a model of an object O. So M^1 is the (relative) original for M^2. O as a relative original could be signified M^0.

(1.9) Generally speaking, a model of the order or type *k*, i.e. M^k, is produced from an entity of the order or type *k-1*. What I here called 'orders' or 'types' are countable units and can be taken as 'logical types'[ccxlix] (provided the logical term 'type' is not mixed up with the semiotic term 'type', the latter can be found in the type-token-difference), and such logical types can also be applied to the sign of the operational (ico-structural) function in modelling 'F'.

(2.1) A (pragmatologic) Theory *Th* shall be an ordered relation or tupel of five relata, the so-called 'parameters': $Th = <O, M, k, t, Z>$, making use of the already known concepts of O and M.

(2.2) The sign 'k' refers to an agent that is usually a semiotic subject or person *performing acts of modelling within the frame of a Theory*.[ccl] Please note that in the case of complex structures of theorizing, like Kuhn's paradigms,[ccli] the agent is a social collective, a group of people communicating and cooperating with each other.

(2.3) With 't' we simply signify a span or point of time, depending on the format used for explicating this parameter. Certain Theories will probably want 't' to refer to a qualified time-period like, e.g., the 'era of Charles Magne'. In the case

---

[ccxlvii] The sign '\' abbreviates the operation of substracting the elements of the second set from the elements of the first set, resulting in a set.

[ccxlviii] This does *not* hold for the formal-semantic conception of 'model'. If a model fulfils or satisfies a theory, there is no further model which fulfils the fulfilment of the theory. This is a source of great confusion among philosophers who are confronted with expressions like 'meta-model'.

[ccxlix] Sensu Russell 1908.

[ccl] In our symbolic formalization the term 'frame of a Theory' is the linear assembly of symbols within the brackets '<' and '>'. In words: A Theory's frame consists of the object it models, of the agent performing this modelling process, the time this takes and the purposes, motives, intentions, and targets involved.

[ccli] Cf. Th. S. Kuhn 1962, Kuhn 1965a, Kuhn 1965b, Kuhn 1977, Hoyningen-Huene 1989.

of Wittgenstein, this parameter might find expression in variables like 'the Wittgenstein of the Cambridge lectures'. I can imagine it also implying some scattered references as in 'the Wittgenstein of pictorial thinking',[cclii] covering a range of periods or writing-phases between which, according to the documents available to us, he did not write about these specific issues.

(2.4) 'Z' is the parameter for a certain constellation of interests, for purposes and intentions connected to this frame of theorizing, but also for the targets for a repeated process of modelling within this frame over a defined span of time 't'. The aims will partly be set externally, partly emerge from the involvement of semiotic subjects as agents.

(2.5) According to this exposition, a Theory is far from being a deductive structure of statements, as theorizing was understood by a neo-positivistic statement-view. It is important to notice that in this understanding a Theory is primarily neither hypothetical-deductive nor hypothetical-inductive. In its frame it is just a schematic scheme combining the interaction of the five described parameters in a process that, by feed-back, can be repeated as long as some external or internal mechanism of control allows.

(2.6) Usually the process of this Theory will reach a presentable outcome, or its internally envisaged result of a model of a form or constitution is achieved that satisfies certain limits and targets set in the form of 'Z'.[ccliii] But this is not the only result of a Theory, since *all of the parameters within the frame of Th can be changed* during a longer cybernetic process of such theorizing.

This long list of points is not only to teach us the necessary understanding of *GMT* but also provides us with the means for tackling our problematic notions 'skript', 'text', 'work', 'album' by approaching the textual, semiotic, philological and editorial problem of Wittgenstein's writing or writing as such with these conceptual means.

How can these notions be applied to Pichler's understanding of these terms, in order to explicate them? Pichler's conceptions have a relativistic touch;[ccliv] by

---

[cclii]   I am thinking of K. Nyíri 2001, Nyíri 2002.

[ccliii]   But even the satisfaction of *Th* according to Z is not a fulfilment of *Th* by Z. That the modelling of a beautiful woman as a nude satisfies the painter or sculptor, does not say anything about the modelled woman being a 'truth-maker' for any of the artists statements.

[ccliv]   On another occasion I called Pichler's view on textuality an "algebraic theory of text with a constructivist tinge", as I would translate myself, referring to a passage from Gelbmann 1999. He himself calls his own view a "pragmatic constructivist" approach in Pichler 2000.

analysing them in the way I aim at we may find that this pragmatic relativism is not in the least negative. Firstly, to the term and concept 'skript', which was provisionally defined with sup. (D3).

> (D7)   A certain skript *S* by Wittgenstein can be characterized by a set of attributes whose recognizability depends on perception and training. These attributes of the object 'Wittgensteinian skript' are not exhausted by the characteristics of the language Wittgenstein used. Notably among them are idiosyncrasies of Wittgenstein's way of writing and of his writing-acts that can be perceived and realized by a reader, yet can hardly be described. Some acquaintance with Wittgenstein's writings is therefore a necessary, yet not sufficient condition for regarding any skript *S* as a skript by Wittgenstein.

Among these attributes there will be, to sketch it out roughly, features like "letter in Wittgenstein's handwriting", including the types and tokens of signs, alphanumerical as well as self-designed, and others that Wittgenstein applied, partly relying on his cultural background, partly displaying acquired knowledge, such as the letters and signs from German handwriting and typing at his time, including French, English, Latin, Arab letters, numerals, mathematical and logical, diacritical and punctuation signs.

The matter is not as trivial as it may seem, and certainly *requires a thorough acquaintance with Wittgenstein's modes of writing*, since in the skripts there are also *modifications and alterations of already written signs or of known signs*, including marks of crossing out, scribbling over or underneath, insertions, placing of bookmark-like reminders at the beginning of paragraphs, etc. This acquaintance will train the cognitive abilities of the reader assessing the skript in question. It is important to notice that an exact list of all the elements constituting the set of attributes *S* can hardly be given. The labour of transcription done in producing the Bergen Electronic Edition, to mention this just as an aside, implied an enormous effort of gathering, distinguishing, and organizing all these sign-characters in order to encode them electronically. Probably the *code-book of the Bergen Electronic Edition* (available at the Wittgenstein Archives at the University of Bergen) is *the* resource to consult in order to get such a list of the attributes and characteristics of the Wittgensteinian skripts.

In his Austrian "Diplomarbeit" Pichler has attempted an approach to systematize the Wittgensteinian production of skripts as the remaining and recognizable results of his writing-acts (this, of course, was settled at the level of 'types' and not of 'tokens'), and he refers to the so-called "MECS-WIT Code Book" at the Wittgenstein Archives at the University of Bergen as his main source.[cclv] Pichler distinguishes several kinds of such sign-types, the number of which is certainly finite. Yet estimating their amount is not so easy if one takes into consideration that Wittgenstein had peculiar habits, like marking certain paragraphs, using different forms of emphasis, drawing pictures between the lines or at the margins of pages, etc. It is, for instance, a difficult matter to decide whether such sketches are signs to be understood as letters or alphabetical symbols, hence sign-types. If they are not recognized as such, they will normally not be transcribed but rendered as pictures or graphics. In such a case, the model would take over attributes from the original, and these graphics, pictures etc. would be tokens, not types.[cclvi]

We have frequently made use of the terms 'type' and 'token'.[cclvii] With 'type' I do *not* mean any type-theoretical characterization of the step, level or order of, e.g., modelling; cf. sup. (1.9).

> (D8)   A model of order k, i.e. M^k, is itself a *token*, since it has a unique occurrence.[cclviii] If this model refers to a any chosen object with sign-character, which in its occurrence is itself a token, it might represent a type.

My semiotic approach within the frame of *GMT* is, at least for the time being, that *the term 'sign-types' refers to modellable attributes of signs.*[cclix] So this term does not refer to certain appearances or the phenomena of a single scribed sign, the outcome of a particular writing-act. To illustrate this: Whether Wittgenstein on one occasion writes a hand-written small "a" with a swift hand making a rather

---

[cclv]   Cf. Pichler 1997b: 121.

[cclvi]   I carefully estimate the number of sign-types with at least 200, which is a practical and manageable number of characters or sign-types. This is an estimation of the cardinality of the set of characters or types, a finite set, but one should not forget that each sign-type can practically have countless occurrences in the form of *tokens in scriptu.*

[cclvii]   Cf. also Peirce 2000c: 83 (originally in a manuscript from 1906).

[cclviii]   This concept of 'uniqueness' depends on its localizability within a frame of a Theory.

[cclix]   Cf. sup. *nota lxxxiii.*

large belly out of the lower part of the letter or lets it be set by a type-writer, is completely irrelevant on the level of types – both occurrences or tokens refer to the same type, i.e. an 'a'.[cclx]

From this it follows that looking at skript-elements on the level of types presupposes a modelling of the skript-unit or results of writing-acts in the skript in the original. As a physical document the skript presents us with tokens, yet the skript can only be recognized and dealt with as a skript if the sign-occurrences are understood as signifying or representing the types of these signs, i.e. mainly characters. I have already stated elsewhere that *cognition and perception have a modelling character*[cclxi] (which goes beyond sensual certainty).

This trait, that the perceived is modelled and approached according to a certain attribution, also holds in the case of reading (or writing). By purely semiotic considerations along the token-type-difference, we gain the insight that the attributes of the model as well as those of the original can themselves be results of some modelling operation. That one can recognize a Wittgensteinian "a" as the letter 'a' depends on a culturally preformed gestalt of the type 'a' as a sign-character. That Wittgenstein could write an 'a' and meant to write an 'a' with his "a", depends on the same presupposition.[cclxii]

Let us now begin to characterize[cclxiii] the elements of a skript as the elements of an original that has to be modelled attributionally. We can take our roughly estimated number of sign-types as a first approximation to the number of attributes of the original *S*, cf. sup. (D7). In addition, there will be attributes like 'underlined' and other modifications of types etc., which themselves can be

---

[cclx]   Cf. Hofstadter 1995.

[cclxi]   Gelbmann 2000b: 221 ff.; see also Ernst Cassirer 1938.

[cclxii]   In this sense, writing is not private. And even if, according to the more recent dyslexia-hypothesis of Hintikka & Hintikka 2002, there was a spell on Wittgenstein that rendered him incapable of writing down what he intended, there is no problem, *since the type of the sign in the skript and to be read off an occurrence of the sign in the text are his intentions*, and not the occurrence; even if Wittgenstein failed to write the exact token fit for representing the intended character-type, he intended the type, and the type should be read and understood, not the token.

    The token is only a means of representing the type, and if it fails to do so, the mistake can lie on the part of the writer as well as on that of the reader. I have criticized Hintikka for this elsewhere, cf. inf. *Essay IV*.

[cclxiii]   This word is revealing: we can only characterize in terms of *types* what are the essential and generally describable features of certain occurrences and tokens are to gain insight into the laws according to which they function.

explained via modelling, by reducing them to already existing skript-elements (i.e. sign-tokens *in concreto*, yet sign-types in transcription). With this we again (and this time in application) reach the point interesting for *GMT*, namely that *attributes can themselves be modelled*. It is, however, still not easy to determine in general and in our terms what a skript-sign in Wittgenstein ultimately is.

In our culture letters and all other signs reproducibly produced by writing-acts have to be comprehended in the form of sign-types as attributes of a skript-original *S*. Yet if one understands the concept of 'writing-act' sec. Pichler loc. cit.,[cclxiv] then certain sign-types (and almost any sign-token) will be apprehended as resulting from some modelling or action, especially those signs and drawings, etc. invented by Wittgenstein. Writing-acts would then be conceptually embraced by the pragmatologic notion of modelling within the frame of a Theory.

> (D9) If 'modelling' is thus understood as representing, and theorizing[cclxv] as an operational activity which rests on modelling, *writing-acts will be actions in modelling that result in the production of sign-tokens that as documented results are always intended to represent sign-types* by the operator of such a theorizing, i.e. the semiotic subject called 'author'.

This tentative definition turns a skript or just a 'skript-string' (a term we will soon define) into a mixture of basic or already modelled attributes, of minimal, partial models. We shall hereby distinguish 'string' from the concept 'token':

> (D10) A 'string' is a finite, linear assembly or row of sign-tokens.[cclxvi] If it can be read as a string of a text or 'textual string', it is already taken as a meaningful row of sign-types.

This reveals that *a type is an intended aspect of a token*. The meaningfulness of this aspect is publicly ruled by the pragmatics of language and communication.

> (D11) A 'skript-string' is thus a finite linear order or row of sign-types of a skript,[cclxvii] made manifest in their (bijectively) corresponding tokens.

[cclxiv] Cf. also sup. *nota ccxv*.

[cclxv] *Sensu* "producing Theories".

[cclxvi] This definition allows the occurrence of a linear order of graphems to be called a string.

[cclxvii] The formulation "A 'skript-string' is a finite row of sign-types occurring in a skript" would be wrong, because what *occurs* are the tokens representing the types.

We finally arrive at a textual notion that, as an answer to (Q3), could also be dubbed (A3)[*]:

(D12)   A 'text-string' is a finite row of sign-types of a text.

What is the difference between 'skript-string' and 'text-string'? A text-string is one of the possible readings of a skript-string, and one and the same text-string can be represented by different skript-strings, since 'text' is interpretational in respect to 'skript' (cf. sup. (D5)), and, taken with a grain of salt, this holds for 'text-string' in relation to 'skript-string'.[cclxviii] How a particular token[cclxix] in the co-text of a skript or in the con-text of a reception or interpretation is to be read factually, i.e. as which type it is to be taken, partly depends on what was schematised as 'pragmatologic Theory'.[cclxx] This means that it depends on certain sociological, cultural, conventional conditions for the semiotic subjectivity at work, situated in some historical context within a frame-work of interests and intentions.

A Chinese without any knowledge of the Latin alphabet might read a handwritten "e" in a skript of Wittgenstein as something completely different from what a professor of German in Vienna will, especially if this token is taken in isolation and without a co-text, and by a person who does not have the slightest pre-information about what sort of sign or possible text s/he is confronted with (if s/he pays any attention to it at all). During the work of transcription within the project of the Bergen Electronic Edition there must have been lots of debates focussing on such problems, and I am certain that they were conducted in a *pragmatic and simplified, goal-oriented manner*, since a result had to be produced: an edition of the complete or at least of all the available Nachlass in the form of electronic 'trans-skripts' typifying the text of Wittgenstein's works (without editing some editorially fixed Nachlass-works).

Concerning the pragmatic issues and factors in the editorial master-project of the Bergen Electronic Edition, I can only mention the pressure of time and costs, of contracts to be met with, of the specific sociological and communicational

---

[cclxviii]   The question (Q6) "What is a work-string" could lead to a new quarrel. I shall try an answer (A6) "A work-string is a fragment", it encompasses at least one 'text-string', yet several of such 'text-strings' do not necessarily have a "linear order".

[cclxix]   Such a token will *never* be unique and the only one, i.e. everything regardable as skript or text or work will be manifested in a 'system of tokens'.

[cclxx]   Cf. sup. (1.1.)-(2.6.).

circumstances under which all these "semiotic subjects" laboured, always, at least ideally, striving for the presentation of *documentable* results. These pragmatic factors in such a pragmatologic frame of the Theory manifest in the project of the Bergen Electronic Edition may partly account for transcription mistakes and possible imperfections of the whole Nachlass-edition.[cclxxi] Yet I want to dispel any possible doubts as to the (relative) quality of this edition in comparison with other competing or earlier projects, and I am not alone with this judgement.-[cclxxii]

For a skript S of the (type-theoretical) relative stage n of revising, i.e. S^n, we can write the following recursive scheme, in fact a matrix,[cclxxiii] in which we shall symbolize the sign-types with '$TypZ_i$', the Theory-dependent modelling of strings with 'M_{Th}', for the Theory applying a transcription T the symbol 'Th_T' shall be used, and for sign-tokens we need the symbol '$TokZ_j$'. The semiotic subject involved is to be abbreviated with 'Rez', and 'N' is the (alethic) modal operator for necessity. Else we apply the symbols and notational con-ventions explained above.

This holds for a certain skript S^n (with $n > 0$), which has h partial precursor-skripts up to the order of $n-1$, that themselves have y preliminary or preparatory skripts up to the order of $n-2$ (in which h and y are two natural numbers different from each other). For the case that $n = 1$ we take the skript $S^{n-1}{}_h = S_h$ itself as a non-empty set of sign-tokens of a certain amount, for instance as $TokZ_h$.[cclxxiv]

(L1.i) $S^{n-1}{}_h = \{TypZ_1, TypZ_2, TypZ_3, \ldots, TypZ_i\}$;

(L1.ii) $(x)\ (x = TypZ \longrightarrow x = M_{Th})$,

        with $M_{Th} = F^1{}_{Th}(\{TokZ_1, TokZ_2, TokZ_3, \ldots, TokZ_j\})$;

(L1.iii) $Th_T = \langle\{TokZ_1, TokZ_2, TokZ_3, \ldots, TokZ_j\}, M_{Th}, Rez, t, Z\rangle$;

[cclxxi]   I discuss one such problematic case of transcription in inf. *section IV.III.*

[cclxxii]   Cf. i.a. Hintikka 1996b.

[cclxxiii]   This matrix *(L1.i)-(L1.v)* is merely a sketch. Consisting of five statements or propositions, it deals with incomplete functions and leaves open some question about quantification. But even though this matrix consists of statements, we are not primarily confronted with a statement-view, because the matrix involves (propositions about) elements which are clearly of a *non-statement-view-character*. The matrix is of the form of a statement-view-theory about a non-statement-view-Theory, it involves predicative attributes about elements of non-statement-view-character.

[cclxxiv]   The indices "h", "y", "i", and "j" are natural numbers which can but need not be different from each other, and the indices serve to facilitate distinction between the different semiotic entities of the same kind (of the same sort as well as of the same logical type).- Else I presuppose acquaintance with logical notation of customary prepositional calculi; the sign '$\longrightarrow$' stands for a conditional.

$(L1.iv)$ $S^n = F^2{}_{Th}(\{S^{n-1}{}_1, S^{n-1}{}_2, S^{n-1}{}_3, \ldots, S^{n-1}{}_h\})$;

$(L1.v)$ $\sim N(F^1{}_{Th} = F^2{}_{Th})$.

This certainly is in need of additional comments, best made line by line. Line $(L1.i)$ intends to purport that every partial skript $S^{n-1}{}_h$ at least one type-theoretical step below the skript S^n consists of sign-types. Yet this is a conceptual pre-decision, since why should skripts or strings not simply be read as tokens? To my mind the notion of 'writing-act' is the hindrance, because even though an author commits to paper concrete physical sign-*tokens*, they are always intended as representing sign-types.

The author ordinarily[cclxxv] writes what s/he wants to write, what s/he intends to write. A slip of the pen, although a concrete writing-act, does not refute the author's intention, so even if it does not produce the token of the intended type, the type was nevertheless intended.[cclxxvi] Consequently the author produces a skript via writing-acts according to a mental text,[cclxxvii] hence his/her intentions could be called a 'mental skript of types'; yet the realization of intentions for writing-acts, to enter the metaphysical compartment of the realm of text-ontology, ends up in tokens. A skript is produced by writing-acts, sec. sup. (D3), but what are 'writing-acts'? They ought to have been defined much earlier.

> (D13) 'Writing-acts' produce tokens of signs with the intention of making them readable as representing certain (semantically meaningful) sign-types that serve to constitute the readability of a skript, i.e. they intend (at least one) text.[cclxxviii]

Here I add some observations I believe to be inferable from a sufficiently wide interpretation of (D13):

> (O4) Writing-acts want to make tokens readable as types, which is the very reason why writing-acts produce skripts.

[cclxxv] In this sense 'ordinary' is normative.

[cclxxvi] To my mind, a dyslectic person – such as Wittgenstein is believed to be by J. Hintikka, who is not satisfied with attributing impatience to him, cf. Hintikka & Hintikka 2002 and Hintikka 1996b – would still have clear intentions and intend writing-acts in this ordinary sense, yet would probably fail far more often to realize these intentions, without noticing it.

[cclxxvii] Cf. sup. (D6) and (O3).

[cclxxviii] I hope that an attentive reader has noticed that according to (D13) the concept of 'writing-acts' is partially of the form of a pragmatologic Theory.

(O5) In other words, not every writing-act, accidentally as it may take place, happens to contribute to or produce a skript or string.

(O6) A writing-act that does not intend to realize types (in tokens) and hence the possibility of reading off a text from a skript or some string of a skript, is not a writing-act but can rather be compared to drawing, scribbling, painting, fussing around.[cclxxix]

Now to line *(L1.ii)* of our matrix: this line is an attempt to explicate the fact that when something is a sign-type or suffices to represent a sign-type, it is modelled from sign-tokens in a way that depends on a functional operation of a (relative) first order and on a Theory, i.e. on some background knowledge, cultural heritage, on tradition, practice, customs, also on language and the forming of perception by every aspect and factor just mentioned.

Line *(L1.iii)* explaines the Theory Th_T applied in *(L1.ii)* according to the abilities of the semiotic subject *Rez*, which sees sign-tokens as sign-types within the frame-work of interests and temporal variables characteristics of the operations of Th_T. This Theory Th_T depends on a transcription, yet this way of putting it is somewhat clumsy and does not quite fit, since the semiotic subject *Rez* operating within Th_T can be the author as a reader and writer, only a reader, or the transcriber as a reader and re-writer of what an author has written. *(L1.ii)* together with *(L1.iii)* account for readability in combination with transcribability, i.e. by being realized in tokens, readable types can be transcribed in other tokens of the same types, which themselves are readable.

Line *(L1.iv)* yields the searched for skript S^n as a result of an operation with all or parts of the row of skripts from $S^{n-1}{}_1$ until $S^{n-1}{}_h$ (which could also be re-used in recursion), which, properly speaking, again involves an act of 'pragmatologic Theory' or writing-acts,[cclxxx] which are not expressed in this scheme of a formula, but are implicitly contained in the symbol 'F$^2_{Th}$'. As every modellation, this one also subsists within the frame of pragmatologic Theoreticity.[cclxxxi]

[cclxxix] Probably children, before or when learning how to write, are in a phase of producing certain things with pen or pencil or whatever without the concept of 'writing-act', probably because they have not yet understood that, firstly, they have to intend certain shapes and types, and secondly, that the tokens they produce have to represent what they intend.-
I know, of course, that Wittgenstein was drawing pictures in his skripts, but I do not think that he was fussing around when doing so.

[cclxxx] Cf. sup. *nota cclxxviii*.

[cclxxxi] Cf. sup. (2.2).

It should, however, not be overlooked, to put it cautiously, that line *(L1.v)* states that the two functional operations that on the one hand yield partial skripts or strings according to $F^1{}_{Th}$ and on the other the momentarily or provisionally final skript S'' according to $F^2{}_{Th}$, need not be identical.

Ad *(L1.iii)* it is necessary to state that in the case of a reader or transcriber the point of time t will certainly be after the original writing-act of producing sign-tokens. This could be schematised as: $Th_q = <-, TokZ_q, Au, 0, P>$. Elsewhere[cclxxxii] I call only partially satisfied or partially parametrified pragmatologic Theory-schemata 'simulacra'. This means that a writing-act producing tokens and originating in the author who commences to write is deceptive, as it cannot be determined from where its original form was taken to arrive at a model (or representation). We have already talked about a 'mental text'; a writing-act produces tokens and is in this sense original and not a transformation of attributes any more, yet the intention which sets it into action is dictated by the ideas and imagination of the author, by a 'mental text'.

The sign-use in my last formula still remains to be explained: The subscribed index '$_q$' stands for (the Latin) *'quodlibet'*, i.e. the notion for whatever the author is thinking of. *'Au'* is short for "author", '0' is the birth of writing, the first real writing-act of this writer, whereas *'P'* signifies the situational interests of the semiotic subject 'author' that motivate him/her to write, and might hence stand for 'imagination'. The dash '–' just says that we are confronted with purely mental documents as the "originals" of this writing-act. This presupposes an ability towrite and to think, and this ability comes before any first writing-act. Yet characterizing the attributes of such an ability is far beyond our capacity.[cclxxxiii]

We shall simply start from the idea that somebody who can write can already write *in mente,* without having to use the physical realization of concrete tokens, and that such a person or author has this ability or talent before any concrete writing-act leaves us some tokens that can and are meant to be read as types.-

This long chain of thoughts and their discussion assist us in understanding that the production of a skript by writing-acts involves pragmatic elements of theorizing and interests that, in aspects and processes, determine what sorts, forms and kinds of sign-types can be seen or read from the encountered sign-tokens. I am of the opinion that *the construction or production of a mental skript of types*

[cclxxxii] Cf. Gelbmann 2000c.

[cclxxxiii] I am reluctant to copy B. Russell's 1921 soft spot for mental images.

constitutes the process of reading and precedes any writing-act, at least it is my hope and aim to pave the way for such an understanding of this semiotic situation. It is my conviction that there is no reading without some sort of (inner or mental) transcription. It is furthermore evident that we have come upon a strange circle, viz. that one can hardly transcribe Wittgenstein's writing without having read his texts, without having taken into consideration what he says, e.g., about aspect-seeing and aspect-change.[cclxxxiv]

II.VI. Characterizing 'Text'

The concept of 'text' is now to be dealt with in an analogous manner. The same method will be used, yet in different application. *We presuppose that there are already skripts.* This implies, as the attentive reader might have noticed, that we still owe the reader an explanation of the metaphysical notion 'skriptless text of a mental document', but we shall have paid our metaphysical debts by the end of this essay.

Under the above mentioned circumstances, a 'text' is gained from a set of skripts according to a result of a specific, describable modelling operation, which again is pragmatologically framed by a Theory.[cclxxxv] This is to be schematised in brief with the following abbreviations and symbols:

'TX^c_b' stands for 'text of the reading b' (or for 'texting of b'), in contrast to a reading a, i.e. 'TX^c_a', where the superscribed index ^{c}'just indicates the logical type or order (cf. inf.). The symbols 'S^{c-1}_1', 'S^{c-1}_2', 'S^{c-1}_3', ... 'S^{c-1}_d', are, again, written for parts of skripts (each symbol usually standing for at least one skript-string), in their number countable (from 1 until some natural number d), of the order of $c-1$, i.e. one step lower than the text read off from them. All other symbols are to be understood as before.-

Now we can formulate another list or matrix of schematic formulae, which has to be discussed and commented upon:[cclxxxvi]

[cclxxxiv] Spare me any relevant citations. Cf. in any case V. Ch. Aldrich 1958, J. L. Austin 1962b, M. B. Hintikka & J. Hintikka 1985a, M. ter Hark 1990.

[cclxxxv] Sec. sup.

[cclxxxvi] This matrix *(L2.i)-(L2.iv)* is also a mere sketch. Cf. sup. *nota **cclxxiii**.*

(L2.i) $\quad TX^c{}_b = F^3{}_{Th}(\{S^{c\text{-}1}{}_1, S^{c\text{-}1}{}_2, S^{c\text{-}1}{}_3, \ldots S^{c\text{-}1}{}_d\})$;

(L2.ii) $\quad Th_T = <\{S^{c\text{-}1}{}_1, S^{c\text{-}1}{}_2, S^{c\text{-}1}{}_3, \ldots S^{c\text{-}1}{}_d\}, TX^c{}_b, Rez, t', Z'>$;

(L2.iii) $\quad$ (x) $(x = TX^c{}_b \longrightarrow x = S^c{}_e)$ with $TX^{c\text{-}1} = F'{}_{Th}(\{S^c{}_1, S^c{}_2, S^c{}_3, \ldots S^c{}_e\})$, for which for an arbitrarily chosen skript of this last mentioned set the following condition holds:

(L2.iv) $\quad P(S^{c\text{-}1}{}_q = S^q{}_q)$.

I shall start by commenting *(L2.iii)*: The fact that the logical types of the symbols of functional operations 'F' are given in certain, natural numbers, might be misleading, as these numbers represent only the *relative logical type*, relative in reference to the level or order of modelling in our context.[cclxxxvii] One could try to figure out a better symbolization to avoid this shortcoming. But by introducing variables I hope to have made it sufficiently clear.

There is not much to say ad *(L2.i)* and *(L2.ii)*. These lines simply show that a certain text '$TX^c{}_b$' is constructed from skripts that are at least one step below their order of modelling, whose attributes can truly be taken from the lowest level of a sign-token or from a concrete letter, a skript-string, or some other result of a writing-act respectively, and can also be mapped onto such attributes.

This *texting* is enacted by a recipient (*Rez*) who reads or interprets the skripts. As a semiotic subject, the recipient can, a of course, be the author of the skripts by becoming his/her own reader. Yet a text can (mentally) also be produced by a transcriber, an editor, etc., again by reading from skripts. Any intervention into the skripts, however, when rendering a text in the transcription-process – that leads to another skript – can be such a production of 'text'.

As the point of time t' at which this takes place might not be commensurable with the experienced time of the semiotic subject that functions as author or reader, I choose a typographically deviating form for it. The same holds for the symbol standing for interests, Z'; the interest present when reading and interpreting a text from a skript might be different from that present when a test was laid down in a skript.

The output of *(L2.iii)* is something well-known in Wittgenstein, viz. that a text that is already composed from former skripts again becomes a skript for further writing-acts for some other texting. It is not only the re-writing of the same (mental) text, it is literally the cutting and putting together of skripts to gain new or originally aimed at yet unachieved texts. Here we touch upon something

---

[cclxxxvii] This corresponds to a Russellian observation, cf. Russell 1908: 249.

crucial, which I shall articulate in the form of another leading question (of which not many are to be answered in this essay):

(Q7)   Are textings writing-acts or rather something like reading-acts? Can one write without reading what has been written?

I have no definite answer to this question (Q7), but I will try to make its significance evident. I tend to an affirmative answer to the second half of (Q7), my reason being that,

(A7)   indeed, no skript is producible without the author texting it.

Yet in the consciousness of his/her semiotic subjectivity, the author can know that a parallel or spontaneous texting of his writing-acts and their results, i.e. something like automatic or 'intransitive understanding' (to apply a Wittgensteinian term), is only one of many possible readings of this particular skript, and this awareness can lead to extensions or continuations of the skripts as well as to revisions.

I am of the opinion – here I might depart from Alois Pichler – that *the album-character of Wittgenstein's "Philosophische Untersuchungen" originates from this very insight*: Wittgenstein read himself while writing, he saw the different possibilities of readings and *he did not intend a texting which was exclusively directed towards a non-album-like, linear text* as the right work. To my perception he never pretends to do so, but at the same time *in producing skripts and in writing he wanted to be so perfect stylistically that a final version of the skript could be accepted as 'work' in a definite sense*, which spares the author any further labour, any further acts of writing.[cclxxxviii]

This sounds contradictory. But my reading of Wittgenstein has led me to believe that he wanted to create a finished, rounded-off, complete, definite work containing several partial texts in such a way as to present the text of an album, and from the onset or at least from a certain stage of his work onwards *he did not want to limit the possible ways of reading by composing sections of text in linearity* – so far my hypothetical reconstruction of his attitude(s) to writing.

So the internal connection of content and ideas in his writing, the network of themes he deals with, is mirrored by the gestalt of his work, whose apparent

---

[cclxxxviii] Cf. Janik 2003.

fragmentary character becomes a work-character in the full sense of the term. *There are purposely produced fragments.* In Wittgenstein the collage of texts was intended, *the album was the wanted work that became in a certain sense autonomous*, as he himself ultimately discovered.

Writing in this understanding is a journey, an experiment, influencing one's intentions in its dependence on the reading and texting of one's writing. In this sense I believe – and these are possible answers to (Q1) and (Q2), cf. sup. – that

(A1) & (A2)
> the identity of the album-character of the texts we find in Wittgenstein's Nachlass with the work Wittgenstein intended as his 'mental work' as an idealization of his 'mental texts' – or at least what we find as a Nachlass – is a sufficient approximation of what he intended in his works, viz. sufficient in the way of reaching the limitations of their author's capabilities and capacities.

This suffices for us at least in so far as we are enabled to reconstruct Wittgenstein's intentions and his 'mental work', his *idea of his work*, and I cannot help feeling satisfied with having come so far, even if it might spark off Wittgenstein's protest.-

Let me remind the reader that much of what happens to the attributes produced by writing-acts at skript-level is *incommensurable* and/or abundant with regard to the writing-acts in texting. If, for instance, the idea or presentation of a table or diagram is added to a skript to be edited, as a further explanation or so, it might be relevant for the text hereby produced in the reception of the (relative original) skript, even though it probably did not exist in the *read* skript. I think that in texting and revising his own skripts by adding writing-acts or transcribing in new writing-acts, Wittgenstein was applying something like new writing-acts at the level of tokens, e.g. by scribbling over or inserting by hand in a typescript, by using scissors and by gluing paper-clips of his skripts together, just as one puts photographs into an album.

These actions and materials were necessary media for producing the wished-for skript and work according to his mental modelling of the text, but not all of the measures he took to secure the final state of his work or to get close to it are present in the results we, as readers who do *not* enjoy the privilege of direct acquaintance with his intentions, are confronted with today.-

Line *(L2.iv)* of the matrix deserves a short, final comment before we conclude this section. This line simply denotes that it is possible that some skript, arbitrarily chosen and situated at a level beyond the text we eventually read, is identical with some other skript. This statement only makes sense if one talks about strings in skripts (and of skripts as strings) under the aspect of their being sign-tokens. This means that *in order to text a text, i.e. to read a meaningful text from a skript, use can be made of skripts that have already been employed in other texts and skripts,* or which at any rate are located at a level of writing-acts and acts of modelling far below the level of the current texting.

So *the author has to perform hermeneutical labour in revising already existing skripts,* in order to be able to produce a skript with a proposed text which marks the current state of art, i.e. the work.[cclxxxix] Here we have reached the point where *one learns to see 'skript' and 'text' as procedural aspects of what I shall call "working-acts" or 'creatio',* which follow and accompany each other. An 'interpreted work' itself will thus not be a mere aspect of a text, but *one* text of a final and whole skript, to which work-character must duly be ascribed. Isn't it interesting how deep the hermeneutical level is rooted?

II.VII. On the Task of Interpretation

Interpreting a work may reveal new or astonishing aspects of the text read from the work's final appearance in skript (or print), but at the moment of a consistent interpretation, a work cannot contain more than one text at the same time for the recipient. As recipient of the final script, the reader can once read it under the aspect of one text, another time under the aspect of another text, and in this sense the interpretation will be aspective.- I shall discuss this by starting with two further definitions, followed by some observations:

(D14)   From the point of view of an interpreter or recipient, i.e. of a reader, a 'text' is an aspect of a skript.

(D15)   From the point of view of an interpreter or recipient, i.e. of a reader, a 'work' is an interpreted text of a final skript.

(O7)   A 'work' is hence an aspect of a final skript.

[cclxxxix]   In this the mental text or the understanding in reading which the author gains from this last stage of the skript-process need not be the only text corresponding to this skript.

(O8)   An aspect of a work would then be an aspect of an aspect of a final skript, which is a semiotic absurdity.[ccxc]

(O8) reveals that the mode of talking about 'aspects of a work' is metaphorical; it just means 'another reading of the same (final) skript' or 'an alternatively construed text'.

This can be illustrated by an example, e.g. 'the' Bible (i.e. the canonical edition without the apocryphic parts). The Bible can be read as a theological treatise combined with religious elements such as praying and the narrative aspect of legends; or it can be seen as a compilation of skripts and texts into a network, presenting us with historical material for historiographical studies.

The skript will be the same, the text will not, and the interpretation of the text one reads from the skript will be decisive for one's assessment and estimation of the Bible, of the way one deals with it: with devotion and the attitude of belief, or with a critical and exegetical eye. Depending on the texts one reads from or into the Bible, one will have different concepts of the work "Bible".

(Q8)   One could now ask if there is no entire or whole or compound character of the work containing all the possible texts read from or into it, embracing all the texts allowed for by the final skript; so to say, is there, so to say, a "Bible of the Bible(s)"?

Yet this exactly would exactly be the mistake of misunderstanding "objective", cf. sup. (A5), namely as *dependening on a construction and not as something given*!

(A8)   'Work' is essentially *open* for a plurality of interpretations.[ccxci]

The reason for this is that a single semiotic subject, an individual person as interpreter, has no method of deciding whether s/he has considered all the aspects of the text of a skript and hence whether s/he has read all the possible texts. *The possibilities of readings depend on semiotic subjectivity*. It is a society or

---

[ccxc]   There are no higher-order aspects, i.e. the concept 'aspect' knows of no hierarchy of logical types (perhaps this is the core of Wittgenstein's stance against Russell's logic). *There are no aspects of aspects*. Cf. Gelbmann 2002b: 27 f.

[ccxci]   Umberto Eco wrote a book whose title reveals this insight. Similar thoughts can be found in Eco 1977, Eco 1991, Eco 1994a, Eco 1995.

community of semiotic subjects that enforces a faithful, binding, obliging reading of works, by practice and conventions, and *this lets the final interpretative character of the work depend on the form of life of the interpreter.*

A written work that is not only mental any more, enjoys some kind of life of its own: it grows like a child and becomes independent from the author and from the interpreter. It can be relatively external to the modelling and Theory-loaded succession of skripting and texting.

Explicating the concept of 'work', however, cannot avoid one central question in this respect:

(Q9) Does 'work' concern (μ) a *specific action* (e.g. writing-acts, performation of mental texting or something like that), or (ν) the *representation of its reproducible results*, i.e. the outcomes of (μ)?

In the light of what has been said from the point of view of the interpreting reader, the character of 'work' is, under certain circumstances, *relatively alien or external to the writing-acts*, reading-acts, skripting and texting, thus making it lean towards option (ν). The semiotic subject as author might in the course of writing not be able to objectify and judge whether the eventual compilation in one skript comes up to the wished-for text of a final skript and is in fact the 'work', and whether the labour of writing has hence come to an end (which, of course, says nothing about the labour of reading).[ccxcii]

Yet if a semiotic subject other than the author objectifies an encountered skript regarded as final as 'work' – for instance if an editor ascribes work-character (or Nachlass-work-character) to this skript – and if this person then produces an edition, the act of ascribing work-character is definitely alienated from the original and authorized activity of writing. This can go so far as to actually finalize skripts as texts of works that are sanctioned by the editor as "works", printed and published, without the author verifiably having written them as a text or with the intention of producing a work or of seeing it published.

In my eyes the representation of work-acts, sec. sup. (ν), will always be a *mental but semiotic situation.* But, and this point is important, especially when dealing with Wittgenstein, this does not purport to say that they must be private and could not be comprehended and con-strued by others. A book, as *opus*, is not

---

[ccxcii] By reading him/herself, the author might feel induced to produce further writing-acts, different from the work just read, leading to a new creation.

something physical, it is *not* a skript, but *it is the text to be read, the text asking to be read as a work*, it is the text of what is to be regarded as the final skript of the author that expresses the intentions of the author (or the editor) sufficiently. *The text is something mental and construed*, but this does not make it "private" or "subjective" or even "solipsistic", because the rules these mental constructions have to observe are not private or purely subjective.

The mind implied here is *the essence of semiotic subjectivity*, which in its activities and actions is bound by social, linguistic, and communicative conditions, it is situated in language-games and has a form of life. *Reading is a practical activity, not a theoretical one.* It consists in following rules under certain circumstances, and it presupposes a shared form of life, viz. shared with others, in so far as something has to be gained from the skript that can be decoded in a way that conforms to established codes.

'Work' can therefore only be oriented towards a public, as the understanding of written language is bound to the public character of language and other sign-systems. *A skript is only published under the (often tacit) assumption that it has work-character (or Nachlass-work-character)* and that it can hence be *one text* in its entirety.

II.VIII. On the Character of Wittgenstein's Works

As stated above, Joachim Schulte and Alois Pichler formulate certain criteria for the work-character of Wittgenstein's writings.[ccxciii] These criteria will not be repeated here but will just be summarized and concluded:

The condition (C1) that Wittgenstein (or an editor authorized by him) regarded his texts as autonomous creations based upon his own skripts, is *not* satisfied in many of the edited and compiled manu- and typescripts. Thus it is only with certain reservations that they can be regarded as 'works'. We consequently talked about 'Nachlass-works', which dispenses us from (C1), and modified this criterion to (C1)[*].

It is commonly known that many of Wittgenstein's skripts are not recognizably authorized by himself as 'final skripts'; the documented expressions of dissatisfaction with his own writings are by contrast quite frequent. So if this

---

[ccxciii]   Cf. sup. (C1)-(C5), including (C1)[*].

criterion is understood narrow enough, the book "Philosophische Unter-suchungen" or "Philosophical Investigations", as we know it,[ccxciv] edited by the trustees of the first hour, Anscombe, Rhees, and Wright (besides some interventions on the part of Geach), *is not a work* but only a Nachlass-work. It could by the same rights have been edited differently, i.e. a different edition of material contained or partly contained in this edition could, with the same justification, bear this title. The same is true for Rhees' edition of "Philosophical Grammar", which also only has the character of a Nachlass-work.

Kenny's laments that the "Big Typescript" was not published as it was left,[ccxcv] are unfounded, because it was not a work authorized by Wittgenstein, but *was left unfinished* (without being an *opus ad acta* either). Hence any edition of the material contained in these skripts would have been a Nachlass-work, be it in the form of Rhees' "Philosophical Grammar" or in some other form. That Rhees more or less claimed to have finished Wittgenstein's work, is a different matter altogether. Dewi Zephaniah Phillips comments on this discussion some years after Rhees' death, by editing a letter of defence (about whose addressee we are not informed) by Rhees, in which he admits that

> "[it] cannot be sustained that there is only one conception of editing" (Rhees 1977 in Phillips 1996: 57),

the elementary requirements of which Rhees, however, ignored, according to Phillips loc. cit. Yet Rhees writes that *he did not have any editorial policy* (loc. cit.), his edition was, so to say, done more by rule of thumb:

> "In any editing I have done I hqave asked again and again what Wittgenstein would have wanted." (Rhees 1977 sec. Phillips 1996: 56)

This stems from his *belief of being privileged.* It must be respected that Wittgenstein's testament is evidence of his trust in his literary executors, in this sense Rhees is legally covered. Yet this confidence on the part of Wittgenstein does not give Rhees the right to believe to be in possession of privileged insight into Wittgenstein's wishes concerning the edition of a *Nachlass*-work, since this is based on a *contradictio in adiecto.* Rhees might have (justifiable) subjective reasons for his belief that he was nearer to knowing Wittgenstein's (possible)

[ccxciv]   Cf. Wittgenstein 1953.

[ccxcv]   Cf. Kenny 1976: 46.

wishes than anybody else, yet *the intention to regard this as a relevant basis for a Nachlass-edition was Rhees', it was not backed by any decision Wittgenstein could ever have made.* Rhees did make editorial decisions, consciously or not, and the conviction of truthfully and conscientously fulfilling a last will does not spare one from taking such decisions. Rhees made such decisions, but does not justify or explicate or explain them.

He is right, however, in pointing out that the coherence of a stage in Wittgenstein's life can hardly be said to be represented by the "Big Typescript". So *what Rhees was editing were the Nachlass-works documenting a certain, relatively coherent stage or phase in Wittgenstein's creative life,* reflecting the work-intentions Wittgenstein had *at that time.*[ccxcvi] The old fellow Rush Rhees was probably the best man for *this* job, "best" in the sense that there was no alternative for Rhees as the editor of "Philosophical Grammar", where "editor" now is to be read in the sense of an 'edition' being advocated by *the friend entrusted with a self-defined task.*-

Criterion (C2) is met with, at least in most of the cases of what has been edited and published. The reader can, as required, trace argumentations in the works as well as in the Nachlass-works, although there might not be common agreement on details.-[ccxcvii]

Criterion (C3) seems to be a somewhat unfortunate formulation from a current point of view, since a formal design of the 'text' cannot render a final stage of a 'skript'. The *text is a hermeneutical and mental product of the reception of skripts.* So I would say that the editors of Wittgenstein's skripts have striven for final skripts, and that from Wittgenstein's utterances about himself and his writing we can infer that he at least sometimes tried to achieve such (editable) final skripts. But the final stage of skripts in their edition as works and Nachlass-works was seldom if ever reached by Wittgenstein himself.-

Criterion (C4) has become trivial, since to every publication there are skripts that precede it – at least in the case of Wittgenstein and to my limited knowledge – and were already text for the author before they were any text for a

---

[ccxcvi] So one could produced time-indexed editions, probably a further task for the Wittgenstein-community ...

[ccxcvii] The ascription of some mental defect or disability like dyslexia would give reasons to doubt (C2) in the case of Wittgenstein. That Hintikka & Hintikka 2002 come up with such an ugly hypothesis, might satisfy certain scholars' need for sarcastic irony, yet it cannot be taken seriously by me.

reader other than the author. *The representation of works* sec. sup. (v) *is a task of the community of reader and author*, and in this sense it involves many semiotic subjects and their socio-semiotic history.-

Criterion (C5) is more a practical point, on which I do not want to comment any further here.- One question might remain when examining (the edition of) "Philosophische Untersuchungen" and the fact that Wittgenstein, at least during a certain decisive phase of his life, wanted to achieve a 'final skript' and 'work':

(Q10)   Who is entitled to judge whether Wittgenstein had this work-intention?

To which I retort:

(A10)   It is *primarily the author or editor who has to judge*, and of course anybody fairly acquainted with Wittgenstein's writings, i.e. *any competent reader*.

Nothing turns a work-skript into something special, different from other results of writing-acts, than the final satisfaction of the semiotic subject that believes to have discerned in it – to a certain degree – a final stage. *The perfection or definiteness and the finality of writing do not mean that the result cannot be a fragment, since a fragment might be the desired appearance of a work.* There might be perfection in fragmentation ...

In the same sense – even harder to swallow and for most people not immediately evident, yet just as viable as the rest of my considerations – *an author might intend the character of Nachlass-works for his writings.* It is possible that an author performs writing-acts and produces skripts with the explicit or growing interest that these writings should *not* be published during his/her lifetime, or even with the testamentarily announced and regulated desire that these skripts be published as Nachlass. I think, *diaries can have this character*; some of Wittgenstein's notebooks and writings certainly have.

The character of 'diary' does not belong to the sort of character of 'work' almost analytically tied up with the notion of being publishable. Nevertheless, the Bergen Electronic Edition (and other editions) have published Wittgenstein's notebooks and diaries, certainly to great advantage for scholars like e.g. Jaakko Hintikka, who are able to follow the development of Wittgenstein's thinking much more closely and better than with the help of any other source.

However, in the case of such writings not explicitly written with the intention of having them published, the intentions of the Nachlass-editors have got the upper hand. I am not against Nachlass-editions of letters of Wittgenstein, if legally possible – yet I am reluctant to ascribe to them the work-character that ought to be seen as the character the author intended with his other writings.

II.IX. Epilogue

I plead for reading Wittgenstein in such a way that his manner of writing does not make him a hero, but that any sense for the peculiarities of his style do not get lost either. The uniqueness of his writing cannot be expressed in a simple label one can tag to it, like the slips of paper glued on books in libraries, giving the number of the shelf they belong to. There are new demands on the reader as there were on the writer, and, last but not least, we should realize that our understanding of how a text becomes a work should be completely different from our reception of books and editions.

The philosophical work of a thinker does not just consist of the sum or product of his books, and is not only a result of proper editions. Even if Wittgenstein were his own editor, thus liberating us from the weight of his Nachlass, his philosophical labour would not be exhausted thereby. *Texts are not just the nutshells of thinking from which the tree of knowledge grows.—*

Essay III. Recollection of References. With Wittgenstein on the Language-Games of Remembering[ccxcviii]

III.I. Solely on Wittgensteinian Grounds

"It's a confusion of the time of the film strip with the time of the picture it projects. For »time« has one meaning when we regard memory as the source of time, and another when we regard it as a picture preserved from a past event. [...] [S]peaking of memory as a picture is only a metaphor [...] We know what a picture is, but images are surely no kind of picture at all. [...] We have just used a metaphor and now the metaphor tyrannizes us. [...] If memory is *no* kind of seeing into the past, how do we know at all that it is taken as referring to the past?" ("Philosophical Remarks" V §§ 49 f., Wittgenstein 1990a: 81 f.)[ccxcix]

In his half-forgotten book *Memory and Mind*,[ccc] Norman Malcolm gives a startling answer to a question which seems to be directed against what might be

---

[ccxcviii] This essay was mainly written at the Wittgenstein Archives at the University of Bergen in Norway, where I again spent a fruitful time in early 2003, funded by the European Union's Commission's 5th Framework Programme *Improving the Human Research Potential and the Socio-economic Base: Access to Research Infrastructures (ARI)*. The databases of the Bergen Electronic Edition, the on-line access to the *PastMasters series of the InteLex Corporation* and *JSTOR* were useful tools (and I largely relied on the first in dating certain sources). Both institutions, the Wittgenstein Archives at the University of Bergen as well as the *EU*, shall be acknowledged with the best wishes for a prosperous future and a furthered cooperation.

My project's roots lie in several conversations I had with Thomas Ballhausen in Vienna, to whom I owe a lot for his steadfast belief in the path my life has taken, devoted to Writing and Philosophy, a belief whose strength often outlived my own.

[ccxcix] Cf. *MS 108*: 33 ff. from Dec. 23rd 1929 and *TS 209*: 18 from Jan. 1930 (so the entries are preliminary to the preparations leading to "Philosophical Investigations"); the German edition renders this passage in "Philosophische Bemerkungen" V §§ 49 f., Wittgenstein 1984, Band 2: 81 f.-

Cf. to this passage Kristóf Nyíri 2001 and Nyíri 2002, who interprets the post-tractarian Wittgenstein as developing a philosophy of (cinematographic) pictures not unconnected to "Tractatus Logico-Philosophicus".

[ccc] I.e. Malcolm 1977, which is anticipated by Malcolm 1970; Hacker 1996: 480 ff. has the honesty to admit that he is indebted to Malcolm 1977, whereas Schulte 1987 lacks any substantial recognition of Malcolm, and Evans 1982 does not even mention him.

called 'the essence of memory': *Memory does not consist in anything;*[ccci] it has, so to speak, no substance!-

Isn't this contrary to *any* expectation of what a philosopher is supposed to propose when scrutinizing 'memory'? The manner of inquiring along the lines of questions like "What is memory?", "What, at it's conceptual core, does it mean to remember something?", or "Which feature is basic in (talking about) remembering?" hereby clearly is rebuffed.

Although Malcolm's book, to my personal taste, is not among the best of his writings,[cccii] and only one among many works written on the theme 'memory' or 'remembering' in the last decades,[ccciii] it yet stands in a specific close connection to not so much a methodical or historical investigation of Wittgenstein's philosophy but to *Wittgenstein's way of reasoning itself* by serving the purpose to criticize

---

[ccci] Hacker 1996: 486 ascribes this view to Wolfgang Köhler, and Hacker 1996: 496 aligns it to Wittgenstein saying the same about 'to mean' in "Zettel" § 16, Wittgenstein 1984, Band 8: 268.

Remembering also has no 'experiential content', cf. H.-J. Glock 2000: 242 and "Philosophische Untersuchungen" II xiii, Wittgenstein 1984, Band 1: 579, i.e. "Philosophical Investigations" II xiii, Wittgenstein 1991: 231. Wittgenstein turns here against Russell's "Analysis of Mind" (cf. Russell 1921), who characterizes remembering as consisting of a feeling of familiarity and pastness. Wittgenstein stresses that *memory-experiences merely are accompaniments of remembering.*

Moreover, the idea of a content of recalling stems from the comparison of psychological concepts, and finally Wittgenstein thinks that recognizing a feeling about something as remembering something because of it being past is only possible because the *concepts of pastness and familiarity depend on memory (and recognition)* or reflect them, and not the other way round.

[cccii] I personally prefer Malcolm's mature "Wittgenstein: Nothing Is Hidden" (Malcolm 1986).

[ccciii] Various reviewers of Malcolm 1977 notice that it is mainly destructive and mostly a critique of former views, cf. e.g. E. W. Averill 1978, R. Brandt 1979, or G. Vesey 1978. The longest review by R. Amundson 1981: 101 especially remarks the book's first part to be "carefully thought out", whereas most of the critics, unlike D. Locke 1978, do not prefer the second part to the first.-

Malcolm's "Knowledge and Certainty" (Malcolm 1963a) is, philosophically assessed, his best contribution on the theme in question, gathering the same lectures on which Malcolm 1977 is based. I also remind the reader of other articles or sections in books on (or around) the themes of 'memory' and 'remembering' (but not necessarily in a Wittgensteinian context) like B. S. Benjamin 1956, Evans 1995b, Glock 2000: 241 ff., Hacker 1996: 480-512, ter Hark 1990: 96-111, Hintikka 1996j, Hintikka 1996k, Martin & Deutscher 1966, Russell 1921, Schulte 1995b, Wrinch 1920, just to name a few.

Malcolm 1977 untiringly cites and reviews a lot of other works, even back to the contributions of classics like Aristotle, John Locke, David Hume, or Thomas Reid, but he does not always get this attention he would deserve.

quite established ways of conceptualising the functioning of *sememes* like 'memory' or 'remembering' in our natural language,[ccciv] viz. as phenomena[cccv] which serve as *units for common reference in our culture*. This reasoning, which is partly deconstructive, offers insights combined by taking one through a certain drama, ending and entertaining a conceptual *katharsis*, a cure or purification.

In an earlier attempt of Norman Malcolm, viz. in "A Definition of Factual Memory"[cccvi] (Malcolm 1963c), he defines an *often occurring form of memory*, namely of 'remembering that *p*', where *p* is a fact, namely a fact in the sense that a past state of affairs is referred to in past tense,[cccvii] whereas an actual state of affairs simply is referred to in present tense. Yet it (eternally or timelessly) *holds*, that there *was* a friendship between Frank Plumpton Ramsay and Ludwig Wittgenstein. So *factuality, even if temporally indexed, as a concept is not itself dependent on temporal states.*

We have to labour with terminology and make our language use precise without becoming too artificial. What is a 'fact' here, and how are facts expressed in statements with a temporal extension?- To say

(A)   "It *is* a fact that it rained in Bergen on the evening of the 17th of January in 2003"

or to utter (e.g. in a trial)

(A*)   "Rain in Bergen on the evening of the 17th of January in 2003 *was* the case"

comes up to the same fact in so far *both judgements refer to one and the same (past) state of affairs*, independent from when they are uttered or written down[cccviii] (or thought). Remembering this fact then could be called a 'factual

---

[ccciv]   My reservations towards the term 'ordinary language' have been explicated in Gelbmann 2002b and Gelbmann 2002e; cf. inf. *nota* **ccclxxii**.

[cccv]   I take here the term 'phenomena' in the wide sense for "everything which comes before the mind", according to Ch. S. Peirce 2000b: 132.

[cccvi]   If it sounds appropriate, I might use for "factual memory" equivalent expressions or circumscriptions like "factual remembrance", "true recollection", "factually recalling".

[cccvii]   Or through equivalent or comparable grammatical devices and constructions.

[cccviii]   As long as (A) or (A*) are stated at a point of time after the date mentioned in (A) or (A*). As Deirdre Smith pointed out to me, to say as (A) or (A*) in autumn 2002 would *not* state a fact but somehow absurdly talk about something which could not have taken place (since it

memory' of (A) or, equivalently, of (A*). To state

(M^A)   "I remember that it rained in Bergen on the evening of the 17th of January in 2003"[cccix]

or something like

(M^{A*})   "The rain in Bergen on the evening of the 17th of January in 2003 is remembered"

can simply be taken as a statement about or a description of recalling the fact signified by '(A)' or '(A*)', respectively.[cccx] Then the factuality of our memory, i.e.

---

might depict a future state of affairs) in a way as if it had taken place. This presupposition is hardly ever made explicit.

[cccix]   Here the first-person-usage in memory expressions does not make a vital difference; cf. inf. *sections III.III* f. and *section III.VI*.

[cccx]   "Facts cannot be named", as Wittgenstein states in his "Notes on Logic" (Wittgenstein 1979b: 96, translated by J. Schulte in Wittgenstein 1984, Band 1: 192, in Costello's edition of Russell's preparations of these notes it appears in Wittgenstein 1957: 232; i.e. *TS 201*: 7 from Sept. 1913), and it reoccurs in "Tractatus Logico-Philosophicus" § 3.144, Wittgenstein 1984, Band 1: 19 as "Sachlagen kann man beschreiben, nicht *benennen*".
This should make us think about revising our talk about facts being signified by our notation. But since *we talk here not about the naming of facts but about the naming of devices* (in other words: sentences) *expressing facts*, which themselves are facts (cf. "[...] facts are symbolized by facts", in "Notes on Logic", Wittgenstein 1979b: 96, cf. with "Tractatus" § 3.14, Wittgenstein 1984, Band 1: 18), I have decided to leave this formulation as it is.-
A relevant difference between the assertion/expression/statement of the sentences tagged with '(A)' and '(A*)' is, that (A) explicitly attributes this recollection to the one who says (A), whereas (A*) leaves it open whom this remembrance belongs to. Yet *this* difference can be neglected if one concentrates not on the (situational) fact who remembers the state of affairs expressed by (A) or (A*), but on the brute fact of this state of affairs itself, viz. of rain at a specific place on a specific day.
With Herbert Stachowiak's 'General Model Theory' (in brief: *GMT*; cf. inf. *nota* **cdxvii**), one could here say that in this modelling of expressive or predicative facts (sentences) the *situational aspect is preterated*, whereas the *statement of a state of affairs is taken as corresponding to essential predicative attributes*. So the fact which is expressed by '(A)' or '(A*)', if taken as independent from the situational aspect of who the utterer of the fact corresponding to (A) or (A*) actually is, is nothing but a *description of a selective representation* according to propositionally standardized interests in the *attitude of a pure statement-view*. So whether we take '(A)' as propositionally equivalent with '(A*)', depends on our attitude.
Cf. thereto a remark in "Letzte Schriften über die Philosophie der Psychologie" I § 670, Wittgenstein 1990b: 85; originally only noted in *MS 137*: 141 from Jan. 5th 1949.

(M^A) or (M^{A*}), tells us that (A) or (A*) *are* past. To say that they were past would most likely refer to their utterance being past, so one would then talk about them as acts of expression and not as statements about whose content we care; that the utterance of a sentence might be past does not entail that the fact the sentence is about is past! Here we take

"[m]emory as a source teaches us what is past" (Schulte 1995b: 100),

as Schulte puts it, in due reference to "Bemerkungen über die Philosophie der Psychologie" II §§ 592 f., Wittgenstein 1998b: 103,[cccxi] where Wittgenstein compares 'remembering' with "a seeing into the past", which could be called 'dreaming'.

Alas, as he adds, "still it takes remembering to tell us that this is past", whereas memory "does not show us the past" (loc. cit.).[cccxii] This is directed against that memory *must* present us with (mental) images (or representations) of the past, while memory can function <μ> as a *source of the concept of 'the past'* and at the same time as <ν> a *checking instance for what is past.*[cccxiii] Compare this to famed passages in "Philosophische Untersuchungen" II xiii, Wittgenstein

---

[cccxi]   Again in "Zettel" §§ 662 f., Wittgenstein 1984, Band 8: 430 f.

[cccxii]   Cf. *TS 232*: 747 f., entry probably from early 1948 into a typescript which is based on *MS 135* to *MS 137* which were written from July 1947 until Jan. 1949 sec. Bergen Electronic Edition.

[cccxiii]   Here I depart from the translation given by Raymond Hargreaves and Roger White in "Philosophical Remarks" II § 19, Wittgenstein 1990a: 62. Cf. *MS 107*: 242 and *TS 209*: 7, i.e. "Philosophische Bemerkungen" II § 19, Wittgenstein 1984, Band 2: 62 (these entries are older, from Jan. 1930).

J. Hintikka 1996j: 215 ff. draws the reader's attention to Wittgenstein's thinking about time in his middle periode and to the contrast he sees between "memory time" and "information time", referring also to *TS 213*: 517-522 and to "Philosophical Remarks" V §§ 49-53. Hintikka terms these two concepts of time "phenomenological time" and "physical time", and he interprets Wittgenstein as having taken a development from a phenomenological starting-point to a physicalist language. Especially the completeness of the picture theory presupposes the primacy of (phenomenological) memory-time (cf. Hintikka 1996k: 257), and this leads to the (actually Augustinian) problem *whether there is a factual past independent from anybody recalling it.*

I agree to Hintikka's account, also of Wittgenstein's later development towards physicalism (very much in the sense of a Rudolf Carnap), although I ask myself why Hintikka never quotes Malcolm, at least not in respect to 'memory'.

1984, Band 1: 579,[cccxiv] where Wittgenstein i.a. says that <o> *one learns the concept of 'the past' by remembering*, or see the variant edited in "Letzte Schriften über die Philosophie der Psychologie" I § 837, Wittgenstein 1990b: 107,[cccxv] where Wittgenstein calls <π> 'remembering' a "criterion for the past".

The aspects or moments <μ> and <o> are akin to each other, as well as <ν> to <π>, since the source for a concept (*genuinely*) lies in learning, and a criterion is a checking instance. Although the philological evidence provides us with variants, we can identify aspect <μ> with aspect <o>, and moment <ν> with moment <π>, without losing anything of Wittgenstein's (documented and inferable) intentions.[cccxvi]

So in important issues, especially as far as Wittgen-stein's steadfast *opposition to the image-theory as giving essential characteristics of the concept of 'memory' or its correctness* are concerned[cccxvii] and in taking memory-expressions as a (grammatical) *measurement for pastness*, Wittgenstein *continuously* held and developed his position in remarks through a long period which begins before the "Brown Book" (*D 310*) was dictated and reaches well into the late fragments put into the composition of the second part of "Philosophische Untersuchungen".[cccxviii]

(M^A)'s truth as an expression of 'factual memory' (necessarily[cccxix]) depends on the truth of (A), but the fact signified by or through (A) *alone* is not sufficient for the establishment of the truth of what is expressed by (M^A), since it might be wrong that the rain in Bergen on the aforementioned day is recalled, although it took place, and analogically for (M^{A*}) and (A*), because I could *pretend* to

---

[cccxiv]   Cf. *MS 144*: 89, dated by the Bergen Electronic Edition with Jan. 1949.

[cccxv]   Cf. *MS 138*: 16b from Feb. 1949.

[cccxvi]   I would even say that the philological detectable variants scattered over different sources and skripts support our philosophical conclusions because of their semantic and terminological kinship (cf. inf. *nota cccliii*).-
Here the words 'aspect' and 'moment' are interchangeably used, what lacks an accuracy a reader schooled in Peircean thoroughness ought to crave.

[cccxvii]   Cf. i.a. "Philosophische Untersuchungen" I § 258, Wittgenstein 1984, Band 1: 361 f. and Ayer 1985: 75 ff., Schulte 1995b: 97 ff., ter Hark 1990: 98.

[cccxviii]   This is partly paralleling the edition of "Letzte Schriften über die Philosophie der Psychologie", cf. Wright's and Nyman's preface in Wittgenstein 1990b.- Cf. inf. *section III.II.*

[cccxix]   I.e. under all (conceivable) circumstances.

remember or even deceive others in overtly claiming memory about what is a known fact without *really* remembering it.[cccxx]

Even though I might not deceive others[cccxxi] and although others would sometimes probably have reliable means to be able to decide whether I am right in my claim of recollection,[cccxxii] or although some Norwegians might be less forgetful about the weather than others, *the truth of judgements about claimed memory does not only and automatically depend on the factuality of what is recalled.* (A) could be true without entailing (M^A);[cccxxiii] yet the truth of (M^A)

[cccxx]   Let's imagine that no Norwegian recalls this boring incident, used to rain as they are.

[cccxxi]   Let alone the case that I might not deceive myself.

[cccxxii]   A documentation of weather forecasts and meteorological data could aid us in independently deciding the correctness of such a claim.

[cccxxiii]   This does not hold for all sentences, the scope of the *variable* (S), and neither for all the statements of the corresponding variable for memory-expressions (M^S), which has then to be read as containing the past tense of (S): If (S) itself is already a memory-expression like
(L)   "I remember having been to the island Osterøy in my youth",
then it *almost analytically entails*
(M^L) "I remember that I remembered having been to the island Osterøy in my youth".
From this I induce a rule: *First-person-statements containing memory-expressions entail their memory-self-reference in this sense,* I would venture to state, and they do so in virtue of first-person-factual-memory-of-experiences being *indubitable in the actuality of their occurrence*: I cannot doubt that I factually remember that I remembered something, although I can actually remember that I doubted having correctly remembered something before. The tinge of reflectivity in "I remember to have remembered *Y*" does not imply that one recalls *Y* now but that one *regained* what one once *retained*, that one is now again able or enabled of memory acts one could not access or perform in the meantime.-
Please do not mix up grammatical reflexivity of, e.g., pronouns in "He knows himself" with logical reflectivity as a sort of repetitiveness and self-reference like in "He knows that he knows"; even if one knows something in the sense that one knows that one knows, one does not necessarily know oneself! (And if I hurt myself, I do not hurt my hurting.) It certainly is the case that both are often confounded, and the mixed orthography to be found in application to both terms does not safe us from this menace.
Some of these iterative and self-referential cases might have to do with 'factual memory', so to remember that one had remembered could mean that one knows now again that one once had factual memory of something *Y*, yet from this it does *not* follow that one has now this factual memory of *Y* again. If I remember that I have remembered *Y* before, I (believe to) know now that I knew *Y*, but I do not then necessarily know *Y* now. To know that one has known has a similar structure, and hence the reflective cases of memory-expressions resemble the reflective cases of epistemic expressions (and cognitive expressions like "I see that I saw" turn into epistemic expressions by iteration).
Georg Meggle 1991 writes on the concept of reflectivity, as I call it, but unfortunately his article is in German and uses the German word "Reflexivität" for what I dubbed 'reflectivity'. Meggle's definition is from the onset that a case ("Sachverhalt") is *reflective if*

should imply the truth of (A), provided that (M^A) represents a case of 'factual memory'!

Obviously one has rightly to believe in oneself remembering the fact in question, viz. in a sense that one was *(a)* acquainted with this fact *before* and moreover *(b)* is *now* aware of that former acquaintance with it in order to *(c)* be justified in claiming a factual remembrance of it.[cccxxiv] So the interesting point about factual remembering has to be sought in *some contribution from the side of the personal subject who is actually remembering*, in this subject's attitudes *complex relations* towards the content of her/his memory.

According to Malcolm 1970: 64 and to J. Schulte there is no essential connection between 'content' and 'remembering';

"a content which we have in mind *may* coincide with what we remember, but that is by no means *necessary*" (Schulte 1995b: 105; italics original; G.G.).

Do we have an objection to this strictness Schulte applies, a restriction not to the loosening of the link between 'content' and 'memory', but to the imposed clarity of the usage of 'to remember'?- We start with an example, Schulte 1995b loc. cit. brings himself:

The vivid, almost cinematographic remembrance of my being to London,[cccxxv] this so-called "inner film" before my "mental eye", is then – to comment Schulte – actually not 'factual memory' of a sojourn in London I had, accompanied with Bertrand Russell's feeling of pastness or familiarity,[cccxxvi] but *the ability in my imagination to reproduce an animating chain of pictures I am acquainted with* due to my growing up in a Western Society, due to my having been to the cinema or having seen broadcasts on television, read books by Agatha Christie or Arthur Conan Doyle, listened to Ralph Jewell's stories, presenting me with impressions of how, generally or even archetypically, it would look, feel, be like to travel or stay or stalk in London!

So could I mistake imagination for 'factual memory'? That is absurd. Yet nevertheless I might express myself in an awkward context of story-telling with a sentence like "I remember London". Yet by saying "I remember London" in a

---

and only if under the necessary and non-trivial conditions for it there is at least one which refers to the case itself.

[cccxxiv]   Cf. inf. *section III.IV.*

[cccxxv]   Where I, G.G., until May 2003 *never* have been to.

[cccxxvi]   Cf. Russell 1921: 168 ff.

somehow casual and elliptical way, what is not too far off the ordinariness of everyday language use, I might have intended to say something like "I can imagine how it would be like if one were in London (because then I could remember"). So, to rephrase myself, *I could imagine my memory* and remember *that*, an expression supplemented by the description of exactly what one *usually remembers* if one had been in London (as a tourist, for instance).

My imagination could go as far as to let me fancy how my memory would be, and fill it with an 'experiential content' which has no clear or direct reference to my personal experience, in a way which probably is not only undetectable for others (which would be a case of deception), but in a way where it *simply is not important to know that it was not my personal factual memory*, rooted in my experience. If the language-game of telling stories requires, for instance, to produce descriptions of imagined contents of experiences, the expression "I recall my last sojourn to London" does make sense (and be it lying – lying then is another language-game).

So the generality, with which Schulte sticks to a certain meaning of 'to remember', can be attacked on the same grounds on which his attack against 'content' rests: *The variety of possible language uses produces a variety of possible meanings*, and keeping this in mind is, in fact, a marker of a capability or even talent which became interesting or even indispensable among philosophers since a guy called Wittgenstein started with *construing contexts* to show the manifoldness of meaningful language usage. Don't forget to remember that in my reading of Wittgenstein's philosophising about memory, 'factual memory' is *not* the only or the vital meaning of 'to remember'.-[cccxxvii]

We have been talking about that factual remembering requires a personal subject who is actually remembering. At the moment I am not thinking of memory being made up by the remembering subject, but of the person's propositional attitude towards the so-called 'content' of its memory.

It is *not* enough to maintain: "My memory has a content Y"[cccxxviii] or "I vividly/really *do* remember (that) Y", in order to have a *sound reason* to claim 'factual memory of Y', even though one might be able to give a correct descriptive or narrative account of Y; *one also has to believe or even better: to be certain that*

[cccxxvii] The last sentence is in itself a performative verification thereof; for the term 'performative' cf. inf. *nota cccxciii*.

[cccxxviii] Let 'Y' represent a state of affairs.

one knows (about) Y now what one knew (about) Y then, whence 'factual memory' contains temporally indexed 'propositional attitudes' or 'epistemic operators' (and this, indeed, does not supply enough reasons for others to believe in what one maintains).

So the (isolated or even private) justification of one's memory-claims lies in justifying the identification of one's current knowledge about something with one's former knowledge about the same thing.- Let's dwell a bit further on clarification, before we enter deeper into Wittgenstein's philosophising connected to this: If one *remembers* a state of affairs in the meaning of 'factual memory' (involving knowledge),[cccxxix] it normally is tacitly presupposed that this is a past state of affairs or a former *situation*,[cccxxx] otherwise we would talk about 'awareness' or

---

[cccxxix] Cases like "I remember how to do it", even though they might express a fact, are not instances of 'factual memory', they are not even what Dorothy Wrinch 1920 calls a 'memory act' or 'dispositional memory'. They say something about me being (or becoming) aware of a capability, which I notice and of which I give notice to others. So here I am not factually remembering a former, but actual ability *in making use of my retention of practical knowledge*.

My playful nature induces me now to inquire about the example "I remember how to remember"; what could *that* mean? Can this be seen as a case of knowing how to do something, viz. how to use one's memory? In Wittgensteinian manner we might find a context fitting to this case, it reminds me of one of Hitchcock's films where somebody "lost his memory", as people say, so he has probably forgotten how to remember or forgotten how to play the language-games of remembering, and when regaining this important ability by overcoming the psychological hindrances or neurological blocking or trauma, he exclaims, with delight and with the same playfulness I exhibited above: "Now I remember how to remember!"

[cccxxx] For my usage of the term 'situation' (in contrast to 'constellation') confer footnote 54 in Gelbmann 2002b: 40; *situations essentially involve persons, constellations don't* (and now I feel inclined to take the expression 'state of affairs' as the over-all-concept). Wittgenstein's term 'Konfiguration' does not make this difference (cf. i.a. "Tractatus Logico-Philosophicus" § 2.0272 *et* § 3.21, Wittgenstein 1984, Band 1: 14 *et* 19; cf. N. Malcolm 1986: 1 ff. *et* 40 ff.).

Wittgenstein's term 'Lage' (Pears and McGuinness translate it with "position", cf. "Tractatus" § 5.551, Wittgenstein 1984, Band 1: 65 and Wittgenstein 1961a: 111) is a quite different one. It is distinguished from Popper's 'Situationsanalyse' (cf. i.a. Popper 1965, Popper 1984: 96 ff., Popper 1995, Lenk & Maring 1987) as well as from the term applied here. When Wittgenstein talks of 'Sachlage', he does not use this German term in my sense of the English 'situation', at least I could not find a single occurrence; yet to translate 'Sachlage' with 'situation' (as Pears and McGuinness do with "Tractatus" § 4.032 in Wittgenstein 1961a: 43), is an admissible compromise. In "Philosophische Untersuchungen" the usage of the German term 'Situation' is broader, more colloquial and closer to everyday language, yet in "Philosophische Untersuchungen" I § 337, Wittgenstein 1984, Band 1: 386 (cf. inf. *section III.III*), there is a talk about *intentions being embedded*

'personal experience' of e.g. me currently writing; and future states of affairs might be intended or wished, even hoped for, or taken care of, or longed for, but are *not* subject to memory in the usual and intelligible sense, for a mere phenomenological reason: *they have not yet been subjected to experience, they even have not yet become phenomena or constituents in any constellation.*[cccxxxi]

We simply do not experience 'the future' (or 'the past' in its entirety or abstractness) as we experience the weather, a sense impression, an adventure, the taste of bread, falling in love, fancying, a fragrant smell of decay, or dreaming.[cccxxxii] Experience is something performed at present, necessarily *connected to phenomena*, and stated as acquired in past times or as having been or as having taken place.[cccxxxiii]

Wittgenstein draws on exactly this last observation in "Eine Philosophische Betrachtung" ad exemplum 60: "Perhaps one could say", Wittgenstein writes,

> "»What has this to do with grammar? We do not *recall* the future!« Well, it depends how one uses the word 'to recall'. In our *ordinary* language it does not make *sense* to say: »I clearly remember that which will happen tomorrow«, – not even then if I am a prophet. (Here it is useful to think of the words, »that a human being that thinks of the past turns his eyes to the ground; but the human being, who thinks of the future, turns them upwards«. Because if you think yourself remembering and predicting, you will see that it contains some truth.) In so far as the *facts of experience* determine those concepts of time – they are, so to speak, the units in measurement according to which we measure those – thereof later. One could characterize our concepts of time through the sentence: »The past yet at least has already been here, but the future not at all«." (Wittgenstein 1984, Band 5: 159, i.e. *MS 115*: 176 f. from Aug. 1936, my

---

in situations, furthermore in habits and in institutions which comes relatively close to my terminology (cf. G. E. M. Anscombe's translation in Wittgenstein 1991: 108; but Anscombe is *not* always a reliable translator, cf. e.g. the critique in Candlish 2002).

[cccxxxi] Memory would, of course, be no help to distinguish between presence and future; yet having a memory of something might become a present constituent of a constellation.-

[cccxxxii] I do not want to discuss the differences in meaning of all these usages of 'to experience'; it lies beyond doubt that 'to experience a dream' is quite different from 'to experience a new acquaintance', and I am aware of the oddity of both examples.

[cccxxxiii] It does not just happen, but one might happen to have an unpleasant experience, which later on turns into a memorable incident or becomes just one of many recollections.

translation, italics for the original underlining, one insertion of single inverted commas marking a lexem; punctuation original; G.G.)[cccxxxiv]

Before I philosophically comment on this passage within the course of our unfolding discussion, I want to have a look in the following section on the philological side which is noteworthy in itself;[cccxxxv] however, I have to state in advance that I most probably am *not the first one* to have noticed its peculiarity, yet it is worth recalling it.[cccxxxvi]

III.II. Sources and Situations

"The language-games are rather set up as *objects of comparison*[,] which are meant to throw light on the facts of our language by way not only of similarities, but also of dissimilarities." ("Philosophical Investigations" I § 130, Wittgenstein 1991: 50)[cccxxxvii]

"Eine Philosophische Betrachtung", as the editor, Rush Rhees, explains in the "Vorbemerkungen des Herausgebers" from 1969, has its original sources in Wittgenstein's dictating in English to his class in the Cambridge session of 1933-1934 and to Francis Skinner and Alice Ambrose during 1934-1935.[cccxxxviii] In his memoir Wittgenstein's acquaintance and student, Theodore Redpath, mentions

---

[cccxxxiv] Neither the English edition of the "Brown Book" (Wittgenstein 2000: 109) nor the source *D 310* render or translate this passage.- The last part in quotation marks could be taken from Augustine or Aristotle (and Wittgenstein himself maybe was not aware of this).

[cccxxxv] That Wittgenstein enters this passage of "recalling the future" in overworking the "Brown Book" is significant of its relevance for him, and hence important for us. I think his thinking on this range of subjects is mirrored in the development of his writing, and later entries reveal some results or intermediate steps of consequential force.

[cccxxxvi] Alois Pichler might have been, besides the editor Rush Rhees himself.

[cccxxxvii] Correction of punctuation in quotation by G.G.- Cf. to this locus *MS 142*: 120 § 133 from Nov. 1936 and *TS 220*: 92 § 115 from Jan. 1937; furthermore *TS 238*: 15 § 145 and *TS 239*: 86 § 145, both from Jan. 1942; *TS 227*: 89, already as § 130, from Jan. 1945; the German edition renders this passage in "Philosophische Untersuchungen" I § 130, Wittgenstein 1984, Band 1: 304. The translation into English is from G. E. M. Anscombe.

[cccxxxviii] Cf. Ambrose 1972, Ambrose in Wittgenstein 1982a: vii ff., Rhees' "Preface" from 1958 in Wittgenstein 2000: v, Rhees' "Vorbemerkungen" in Wittgenstein 1984, Band 5: 9-14, Malcolm 1984: 13 f., Ayer 1985: 51, etc.

that there might have been four dictates, but we know of only two:[cccxxxix] one was the so-called "Blue Book", the other, due to its brown binding, in which it circulated among students and friends (like the "Blue Book" did), was dubbed the "Brown Book". The latter's final and typed version, a nonetheless fragmentary dictate, is called *D 310*, the first's is called *D 309*, according to G. H. von Wright's estimable catalogue. There is no English manuscript of the "Brown Book", and it *was* designed for publication, yet not in English, as Rhees loc. cit. presumes.[cccxl] According to R. Rhees[cccxli] it was in August 1936 that Wittgenstein titled an overworking of *D 310* in German with

"Philosophische Untersuchungen. Versuch einer Umarbeitung";

this German manuscript begins at *MS 115*: 118 and ends at *MS 115*: 292 with declaring this attempt as worthless towards the end of Aug. 1936 (Rhees loc. cit.).

But that was not the first attempt of a revision of *a German version of D 310*; the attempt of 1936, i.e. *MS 115*, was (sec. Rhees loc. cit.) the *last* one, probably also based on *MS 152* or some lost skripts;[cccxlii] yet the Bergen Electronic Edition gives for the origin of *MS 115* as well as for *MS 152* the date "August 1936", so *Wittgenstein could have written these skripts simultaneously* or in very close, even overlapping intervals of working periods. This, by the way, also holds for other stuff, see for instance the discussion around the edition of "Philosophische

---

[cccxxxix] Cf. Redpath 1990: 74 f.- To complicate the matter even more, von Wright 1986: 70 says about *D 311*, the so-called "Yellow Book", of word-by-word notes by Margaret Masterman, Alice Ambrose and Francis Skinner in 1933-1934 (partially edited by Alice Ambrose, cf. Wittgenstein 1979a), that it is *not clear whether it should be put among the other dictates or among the notes about conversations and lectures taken later on.* Could then this variant or other variants in *D 310* (and in *D 309*) hint to these notes of the "Yellow Book" or some previous version?- Obviously we cannot answer all these philological questions, and the citation of such variants should not lead us astray from our subject.

[cccxl] The dictate *D 310* was obviously not copied and bound into one of the Cornell volumes, although it is a typescript, a copy of which the Wittgenstein Archives at the University of Bergen had obtained from the Trustees for the purpose of transcription during the Norwegian editorial project of the Bergen Electronic Edition.

[cccxli] In Wittgenstein 2000: v and in Wittgenstein 1984, Band 5: 10; Redpath loc. cit. points to von Wright.

[cccxlii] My source for this assertion is a personal conversation with Pichler in Jan. 2003. The Bergen Electronic Edition in its released form dates the whole item *MS 152* with Aug. 1st 1936 as the *earliest possible date*.

Grammatik", its relation to the prestigious "Big Typescript" from Jan. 1932, i.e. *TS 213*, and its continuity with "Philosophische Untersuchungen".[cccxliii]

However, the dating of the skripts, even in the Bergen Electronic Edition, is not always completely reliable, hence it is highly recommended that specialists check the Bergen Electronic Edition for these and other, minor errors.[cccxliv] If an accurate dating is manageable, the questions about gaps in our *reconstruction* of Wittgenstein's writing process might come nearer to being settled for good.- In editing "Eine Philosophische Betrachtung (Das Braune Buch)", i.e. Wittgenstein 1984, Band 5, R. Rhees took already in 1969 the first part of the title from a manuscript-binding from June 1931, *MS 110*: 214, where it says:

"Mein Buch kann/soll heißen: Eine Philosophische Betrachtung",

whereas the title of *MS 115* at that time, when Rhees' editorial undertakings began, had already been used for Rhees' and Anscombe's edition of the praised "Philosophical Investigations" (i.e. Wittgenstein 1953), which were partly based on *MS 142* (viz. "Philosophische Untersuchungen" I §§ 1-188, probably compiled in Nov. 1936), a manuscript which itself was based on *MS 115*.[cccxlv] I regard this as an editorial misfortune.[cccxlvi] Rhees does not fail to point out that his edition in German, titled

"Eine Philosophische Betrachtung (Das Braune Buch)" (cf. Wittgenstein 1984, Band 5),

significantly differs from the "Brown Book" (i.e. Wittgenstein 1958b or *D 310*); in the German "Vorbemerkungen" we find his comment about these changes:

"Besonders wichtig ist hier der lange Kommentar zu Beispiel 60, wo Wittgenstein einen kritischen Gedanken einführt, den er in den *Untersuchungen* weiter entwickelt und der im *Brown Book* [zum Beispiel 56; G.G.] kein Gegenstück hat" (so Rhees in Wittgenstein 1984, Band 5: 11),

---

[cccxliii] Cf. i.a. Anthony Kenny 1976.

[cccxliv] I am thinking of Alois Pichler or Wilhelm Krüger, who both are well acquainted with the sources from the times of the editorial project of the Bergen Electronic Edition.

[cccxlv] Cf. Pichler 2001a: 188; here I have to thank Pichler once more for many hints, for the preparation of sources, and for his own precise research, all of which enabled me especially to enter these remarks.

[cccxlvi] Cf. also Hintikka 1991 for a criticism of Rhees' editorial work.

but *this* is about the Nothung-passage refusing a primitive conception of a word-object-correspondence[cccxlvii] and *not* about the passage I encountered at *MS 115*: 276 f.!

Strangely enough, Rhees' changing the title of *MS 115* may not have been entirely arbitrary. In this he could have been guided by *considerations fit for a publisher but not for a scientific editor*, in a way resembling what he already had done in the edition of "Philosophische Grammatik", whose title in a similar mode was taken from *MS 110*: 254, a manuscript, which, like *MS 110*, stems from 1931 (as Kenny 1976: 42 criticizes).

In addition to that, Rhees left it uncommented that "Das Braune Buch" as a subtitle in parenthesis to "Eine Philosophische Betrachtung" (cf. Wittgenstein 1984, Band 5) is *misleading*, since it brings with it a propensity for any layman reader, unarmed with a professional scepticism towards the edition, to believe that "Eine Philosophische Betrachtung" was a translation of the edition of the "Brown Book", i.e. Wittgenstein 1958b. This is rather misleading, although I am quite aware of the fact that Rhees did not do this on purpose; it is what one could call "careless".

Although *MS 115* is to a large extent a translation of *D 310*, i.e. of the "Brown Book", produced by Wittgenstein himself, it is striking that the passage I translated from "Eine Philosophische Betrachtung",[cccxlviii] placed in *MS 115*: 176 f., is *unique in Wittgenstein's whole Nachlass*; even more so I feel tempted to reproach Rhees with not having commented more explicitly what he left out from *D 310* in the "Brown Book" as well as in "Eine Philosophische Betrachtung" in his "Preface" or "Vorbemerkungen"!

The passage (*MS 115*: 176 f.) I above have translated into English appears in the (physical) original in a form *untainted by any improvements*, completely free from any crossing out or the usual scribbling over we so often encounter in Wittgenstein's writings, it only presents some underlined textual strings[cccxlix] (I *had* a thorough look at *MS 115*: 176 f., Cornell copy Vol. 17).

This now gives us some reason to conjecture that this passage in *MS 115 was taken over from some other source hitherto (and still) unknown to us*, since it

---

[cccxlvii] Cf. "Eine Philosophische Betrachtung" ad exempl. 60, Wittgenstein 1984, Band 5: 158.

[cccxlviii] Loc. cit. sup. in *section III.1*.

[cccxlix] In "Eine Philosophische Betrachtung", Wittgenstein 1984, Band 5: 159, underlining is rendered in italics.

looks as if Wittgenstein just copied it from some draft, note or skript, without trying to alter or improve it. This unknown skript then could easily be dated between 1935[cccl] and 1936.[cccli] This is a *philological conjecture* whose credibility depends on the probability of the dating of the skripts concerned.-[ccclii]

Let's again take up our discussion of the puzzling 'remembrance of the future', which will not entail leaving the philological track pursued so far since our philosophical debate will interact with our philological investigation:[cccliii] That we

---

[cccl]   That is, after *D 310* was finished, cf. von Wright 1986: 70.

[cccli]   I.e., when *MS 115* presumably was written, a date about which we can be relatively certain since Wittgenstein himself entered "Ende August 36" at *MS 115*: 118.

[ccclii]   In addition it depends on the assumption that Wittgenstein did not take this passage from a source much earlier than the dictates, or parallel to them, probably from one of the other two of the four dictates Redpath 1990: 74 f. mentions (cf. sup., another riddle in itself).

[cccliii]   The inseparability of these two aspects, the philological and the philosophical, in scientific research on Wittgenstein's Writings and Philosophy is comparable to the inseparability of History of Science and Philosophy of Science I tried to argue for in the fourth chapter of Gelbmann 2000b by a still unrecognized argument.

As the historical investigations might offer the richness of material on attempts and paths of reasoning already taken from which methodological systems can arise, *the philological material is in need of a formation in the light of an understanding of the ideas and conditions which produced, altered and left it.*

How Wittgenstein's thinking developed, as far as this can be re-construed, might provide us with insights into his philosophical intentions and into the course his reasoning took in order to arrive at them or to alter them, and it may allow assumptions about the final opinions he reached with certain documented formulations. *But a formulation he in the end left without revision does not allow for the immediate conclusion that it definitely states his view,* since the achievement of real 'texts' as finished and completed or intended works is rather rare in Wittgenstein's case.

Much of what we have of his writings was put together by editors who tried to keep to his intentions, as perceived by them, or to document the different stages of his work according to their opinion about his philosophical development; so we have on pure philological and editorial grounds to differ between "Nachlaßwerk" and "Werk", to say it in German terms I introduced in Gelbmann 2002a.

As far as our ascriptions of opinions to Wittgenstein himself are covered by philology, we might interpret any such edition or collection as representative for his philosophical point of view and opinions emerging from that. Yet the intertwining of philosophy and philology cannot be avoided, since the philological interests are influenced by philosophical intentions, and vice versa, and *what finally guides us in the produced selections of skripts and opera for our reading, editing, interpreting has in itself not a degree of definiteness which justifies an interpretation on pure philological grounds.*

On pure philosophical grounds, i.e. without any philological hindsight, we would arrive at a crude immanentism which would go much further than Eike von Savigny ever did (for instance with Savigny 1996a), who is a parading example for relying on the so-called "text alone" and leaving aside any contextual factors of life, social, cultural and historical

do not use the verb 'to remember' with expressions of future events or future states of affairs (or future situations) reveals a *grammatical feature* of our usage of the concept of '(factual) memory'. That this term is not applied to future facts is a conceptual fact and essential for it.

This 'temporal asymmetry' concerns the 'grammar of memory expressions' insofar as it depicts features of the use of the concepts 'memory', 'remembering', etc. Before this passage I above have translated from *MS 115*: 176 f., the corresponding passage in the earlier "Brown Book" ad exempl. 56 yields:

"The idea of a proposition saying something about what will happen in the future is even more liable to puzzle us than the idea of a proposition about the past. For comparing future events with past events, one may almost be inclined to say that though the past events do not really exist in the full light of day, they exist in an underworld into which they have passed out of the real life; whereas the future events do not even have this shadowy existence. We could, of course, imagine a realm of the unborn [*sic*; G.G.], future events, whence they come into reality and pass into the realm of the past; and, if we think in terms of this metaphor, we may be surprised that the future should appear less existent than the past. Remember, however, that the grammar of our temporal expressions is not symmetrical with respect to an origin corresponding with the present moment. Thus the grammar of the expressions relating to memory does not appear »with opposite sign« in the grammar of the future tense." (Wittgenstein 2000: 109; i.e. *D 310*: 50 f.)

Isn't this utmost anti-platonic, expressing the future impossibility of *anamnesis* due to conceptual Grammar?- Now *another deviation* of the editions from the Nachlass originals can be detected:

In the typescript of the "Brown Book", i.e. *D 310*,[ccliv] there subsequently follow two further sentences, which are not printed in Rhees' editions, since they seem to depict a variant to the immediate foregoing sentence, and Rush Rhees, with the freedom of the Nachlass editor in producing his version of a very normalized edition, chose to leave out these lines. They are about a 'temporal

---

circumstances which so brilliantly were taken care of by Janik & Toulmin 1973. Yet Savigny, a philologist of outstanding quality, from my point of view *cannot draw a line separating philological interests and factors on the one side and contextual interests and factors on the other side as the basis of the documented text alone.*

[ccliv]   It is an unfortunate mistake in the Bergen Electronic Edition transcription of *D 310*: 51 that the normalized transcription as well as the diplomatic transcription render this variant.

asymmetry' concerning the 'grammar of memory expressions' insofar as it depicts features of the use of the concepts 'memory', 'remembering', etc.:[ccclv]

> "//Thus there is nothing in the grammar of the future tense corresponding to the grammar of the word »memory«. This part of the grammar of the past tense does not recur »with its sign changed« on the future side.//" (G.G.'s diplomatic rendering of *D 310*: 51; double slashes original; G.G.)

Can we infer from this the absurdity that the notion of 'fact' depends on '(factual) recallability', so that if we don't remember something, it could never become a fact?[ccclvi] Wittgenstein does not go into this idealistic trap, which is too

---

[ccclv] These two sentences can neither be found in Rhees' English edition of the "Brown Book", i.e. Wittgenstein 1958b (cf. Wittgenstein 2000: 109), nor in *MS 115* or in the supposedly earlier *MS 152* or in any other skript transcribed for the Bergen Electronic Edition, and Rhees' German edition "Eine Philosophische Betrachtung", Wittgenstein 1984, Band 5, shows as well not the slightest trace of them!-
That this deviation is a variant, indicated by slashes like "//", and that therefore Rhees was justified in applying some editorial liberty, can be supported by i.a. J. C. Klagge's and A. Nordmann's comment in Wittgenstein 1993a: xv. Pichler 2001a: 331 and Pichler 2002 argues that from 1934 onwards, firstly, Wittgenstein produced variants at large scale in his own skripts, secondly, that these variants were often marked in manuscripts as well as in typescripts with double slashes, thirdly, that this marking of variants should in Pichler's (normalized) edition of such passages not be printed since they belong to what Pichler calls "Skriptniveau" in contrast to "Textniveau".
Pichler's editorial suggestion is a defence of the Bergen Electronic Edition's diplomatic transcription of this passage at *D 310*: 51 without a direct attack on Rhees. So the Bergen Electronic Edition's diplomatic transcription of loc. cit. hence differs from the normalized edition *only* in regard to the slashes "//" and in nothing else, but the normalized as well as the diplomatic version of the Bergen Electronic Edition render the lines between the two slashes at the beginning and the end of loc. cit., whereas Rhees *left out the complete text between the slashes*. What I call "G.G.'s diplomatic rendering" differs from the Bergen Electronic Edition's diplomatic rendering only in applying two times different quotation marks within quotation marks, i.e. the inverted commas '»' and '«'.-
An impression of Rhees' view of his editorial work, in a different context, gives his angry reaction to the criticism of i.a. Kenny 1976 in a letter which was edited by Dewi Zephaniah Phillips in 1996. Here, Rhees 1977 as well as Kenny 1976 (who wanted to edit the so-called "Big Typescript", *TS 213*, "as such", which is untenable due to the impossibility of giving a normalized edition of *TS 213*) seem to overlook that it "cannot be sustained that there is only one conception of editing", and Rhees "ignored its elementary requirements" (no italics rendered; G.G.), as Phillips 1996: 57 comments *with my full consent* (I have commented this discussion in Gelbmann 2002a). But this does by no means imply that I consent to Pichler saving Rhees any criticism.- For philological debates about the dictates of this time see sup. *nota cccxxxix*.

[ccclvi] I am less prone to call the dependency of factuality on representability an absurdity.

obvious, since some facts simply might not be a matter of recollection or memory at all.[ccclvii]

The *grammatical facts ruling the expressions or phenomena of 'factual memory'* themselves are the best example for this, their factuality cannot itself depend on factual memory if they shall concern the grammar of expressing or executing factual memory. There are *grammatical facts about memory* which themselves are not a question of 'factual memory' but of practical knowledge, of abilities in performing 'language' (and remembering *them* is then a case of 'remember how to follow a rule').

Instead, Wittgenstein draws our attention to another point; so-called 'future facts' are not inconceivable because factuality depends on the possibility of a memory, but *because true propositions about future states of affairs or situations would express factuality independent from anybody knowing, anticipating them or otherwise relating to them*. That's what a true proposition is, the expression of a fact; facts are time-independent truth-makers (cf. Mulligan & Simons & Smith 1984).[ccclviii] The *grammatical fact* that words like 'memory' or 'to remember' are *not* applied to 'future states of affairs' or 'states of the future' reveals *nothing* about 'the future' or the notion of 'fact', it shows something about our language and about the linguistic fact how we use these words! One could attempt an objection by bringing the example:

(B)   "After having finished writing this essay, I will have recalled a lot of quotations from Wittgenstein's Nachlass."

Yet does the phrase (B) present us with a case of 'factual memory', even though it talks about 'recalling'? Does this example of a rare grammatical form, which in Latin is called *futurum exactum* and implies to talk about a 'future past', really express a fact about a *future* event which is *recollected*? Not at all, *it is an (epistemic) anticipation*, an *assumption about future memory*, not about a factual

---

[ccclvii]   Besides, Savigny 1991 points out that one does not have to be able to express (or make explicit) a rule in order to be able to follow it. Parallel to that I would say: One does not have to explicitly recall a grammatical rule in order to be able to follow it. Especially the grammatical devices organizing our language about 'memory', our speech-acts and language-games involving the word 'to remember' etc., do not comply us to explicitly recall their rules; we just apply these grammatical tools in our daily practice, they are part of our 'tacit knowledge'.

[ccclviii]   From *GMT*'s pragmatological standpoint I would here add "in a statement-view".

memory of 'the (past) future'! In our formalism, as sketched out with the foregoing examples, the sign '(M^B)' should mean something else,[ccclix] namely:

(M^B)   "Somebody remembers that after having finished writing this essay, I will have recalled a lot of quotations from Wittgenstein's Nachlass".

In our example the formulation '(M^B)' is *supposed* to signify some 'conditional memory' about that what is expressed by (B); '(M^B)' expresses an *imagination of a factual condition for memory*, it expresses no memory itself.[ccclx] '(M^B)' is *not* supposed to denote the expression of some act of memory (or representation of memory) somehow contained in the sentence (B).

So (B) *tacitly* expresses *a propositional attitude towards a description of a possible future memory*, and not any factual memory itself. Yet (B) can be read as intended to factually perform a propositional attitude towards a description of a possible future memory, and if one's linguistic taste tells one that *this* performance succeeded, then (B) expresses the fact of this success!

But this, however, does not tell us anything about the truth value of (B), even if we have one for (M^B)! The truth value of (B) can hardly be determined, it is kind of epistemically inaccessible, the more so holds for (M^B). They are difficult to assess just to the same degree as 'the future' is not knowable, it in principle cannot be known.[ccclxi] This does not carry any enlightening information about 'future facts' or the 'factuality of future'!-

If one looks now at the etymological background of the Latin word 'fact' in 'facere' (i.e. to do, to make) and in 'factum' (i.e. done, made), then one might come

---

[ccclix]   With acute thoroughness any talk about a sign shall typographically be distinguished from the sign or what it represents. This semiotic principle shall also guide us here.

[ccclx]   It is vital to understand this! The usage of the word 'to remember' in examples (M^B) and (M^{B*}) is idle and superfluous, cf. inf. It is comparable to a mechanism to which some extra wheel is attached which does not drive anything (at best an ornament or spare wheel):
Cf. "Philosophische Untersuchungen" I § 271, Wittgenstein 1984, Band 1: 366; first appearance of this metaphor of an "idle wheele in the machine of language" in *D 302*: 29 from Jan. 1932, then in almost the same words as in the final edition it was entered into *MS 241*: 11 in Jan. 1944, taken over into *MS 124*: 271 in July 1944, to be written down again into *MS 129*:48 in Aug. 1944.

[ccclxi]   Wittgenstein noticed this already in April 1915, cf. "Tagebücher 1914 - 1916", Wittgenstein 1984, Band 1: 134 and takes this as the reason for the freedom of the will; this entry reoccurs in "Tractatus Logico-Philosophicus" § 5.1362, Wittgenstein 1984, Band 1: 48.

to speculate about the relationship of 'future' and 'facts' not in terms of 'future pasts' as *all that which at a certain point of time will have been the case* but in terms of 'past futures' as *all that which at a certain point of time would have been the case.*[ccclxii]

> (B*)   "Had I finished writing this essay by January 2003, I would recall a lot of quotations from Wittgenstein's Nachlass in May 2003."

Even though I, as a matter of fact, have not finished this essay with January 2003 (and not even with October 2003), nevertheless recall a lot of Wittgenstein quotations now in May 2003; so what one sees as the *consequence of a counterfactual antecedent might be the case anyway*. The 'past future', i.e. my future knowledge of certain lines of Wittgenstein as something which *was* in the *future* some time ago, *can* be present or past *now*. Ergo, (B*) does *not* say that my essay being completed by January is the (only) *cause* for my assumed acquaintance with Wittgenstein's writings.

In (B*) there could be sensed something like a 'counterfactual memory', since the grammatical subjunctive expression, that somebody *would* recall something, is *not the expression of an actually given memory of what is a fact* (or about what was the case) but the *actual expression of a possible or assumed memory of a state of affairs*. Then, '(M^{B*})' signifies not the factual memory of a '(future) past' but clearly *refers to a counterfactual conditional*:

> (M^{B*})   "Somebody remembers that if I had finished writing this essay by January 2003, I would recall a lot of quotations from Wittgenstein's Nachlass in May 2003."

Here I would like to comment the same I have already commented above, regarding '(M^B)': The example '(M^{B*})' also expresses a sort of 'conditional memory',[ccclxiii] yet here as an *imagination of a counterfactual condition for memory*. '(M^{B*})' is about some probably memory, memory, that probably would exist, if this or that were the case. '(M^{B*})' is *not* supposed to denote the expression

---

[ccclxii]   Cf. Wright 1983: 58; 'future pasts' are then connected counterfactual conditionals, and the latter are retrospective (see (B*)), whereas sentences about 'past futures' like (B) are prospective.

[ccclxiii]   This notion should not be mixed up with a behaviouristically "conditioned memory".

of some act of memory (or representation of memory) somehow contained in the sentence (B*).[ccclxiv]

(B*) tacitly expresses a propositional attitude towards a description of an imaginable memory of something which was not the case (it is a fact that this essay was not finished in January 2003, whereas I can pretend or imagine that it were the case), and not any factual memory itself. (B*) can be read as intended to factually perform a propositional attitude towards a description of a possibly, yet not actually present memory of the past, and if one's linguistic taste tells one that this performance succeeded, then (B*) expresses the fact of this success! But this, however, does not tell us anything about the truth value of (B*), even if we have one for ($\mathbf{M}^{B^*}$)!

But what do (M^B) and (M^{B^*}) perform as speech-acts? To remember 'future past' of someone's memory or to remember the 'past future' of someone's memory is *no* 'factual memory' or 'memory' in the so-called ordinary sense at all, as our analysis has revealed! To express 'conditional memory' in stating factual or counterfactual conditions of memory is something like a *remark*. So why should we not formulate these two statements, (M^B) and (M^{B^*}), without using *any* memory-expression about the memory expression contained in (B) or (B*), respectively? This would yield:

(M^B)*   "Somebody remarks that after having finished writing this essay, I will have recalled a lot of quotations from Wittgenstein's Nachlass".

and

(M^{B^*})*   "Somebody remarks that if I had finished writing this essay by January 2003, I would recall a lot of quotations from Wittgenstein's Nachlass in May 2003."

[ccclxiv]   In analogy to '(M^B)' and (B).- And what about the truth value of (B*)? It is just the truth value of conditionals, whether the antecedent is true or false, as long as the consequent is true, the whole proposition (or better: statement) is true.

But since it is February 2003 while I am this writing, we cannot determine whether I still recall Wittgenstein quotations in May 2003 or not! We can believe in the truth of this, anticipate the future to a certain degree and likelihood, but we cannot be assured in any certainty of such knowledge.

As locutions, '$(M^B)^*$' and '$(M^{B^*})^*$' syntactically and semantically differ from '(M^B)' and '(M^{B^*})', but this is just the surface-grammar of their textual or phonetic appearance. To *remember* a 'past future' of memory or a 'future past' of memory is in the light of our investigation no proper memory, so the memory-expression, even if belonging to an over-stretched language-game of remembering, could be easily *exchanged with something which has the illocutionary force of statements about memory-expressions or 'conditional memory' without making any memory of themselves impossible.*

The verb 'to remark'[ccclxv] seems to match these conditions, since by remarking via $(M^B)^*$ and $(M^{B^*})^*$ what (B) and (B*) purport about 'conditional memory' of factual/counterfactual sorts, one can refer to 'future pasts' and 'past futures' in connection to memory-expressions *without pretending that this reference illogically involves memory itself.* The performance of commenting on the imagination about memory and its time-relation(s) remains as the tacitly intended invariant. And the principle, that *grammatical facts about memory-expressions reveal nothing about 'the future', 'factuality', 'factuality of future' or 'future factuality'*, is still valid.[ccclxvi]

We should keep in mind that Wittgenstein explicitly warns against drawing conclusions about some essential traits of the future from grammatical observations. Let's look at how the passage cited above goes on:

"This is the reason why it has been said that propositions concerning future events are not really propositions. And to say this[,] is all right as long as it isn't meant to be more than a decision about the use of the term »proposition«; a decision which, though not agreeing with the common usage of the word »proposition«, may come natural to human beings under certain circumstances. If a philosopher says that propositions about the future are not real propositions, it is because he has been struck by the asymmetry in the grammar of temporal expressions. The danger is, however, that he imagines he has made a kind of scientific statement about »the nature of the future«." (Wittgenstein 2000: 109; i.e. *D 310*: 51)

There are no scientific statements about 'the future' inferable from a grammatical insight! (The same holds for 'the past'.[ccclxvii]) To give it a note of

---

[ccclxv] There might be others, think of 'to comment' or 'to observe'.

[ccclxvi] As suggested by common sense.

[ccclxvii] There is also no logical inference leading from some remembrance to true sentences about the past, unless one really has the claimed 'factual memory'.

conventionalism,[ccclxviii] I would rather say that the expressions 'the future', 'the past', 'the present' have no direct reference to an objectively given temporality, except the one semantically emerging in our socio-semiotic collective: *This is how our culture semantically is organized by grammar*, we indicate temporality by grammatical devices in the common belief that time has a structure comparable to a line along which our now-experience runs.[ccclxix] This shows itself in such grammatical devices of our language as the future tense, the past tense, etc.

We can feel secure about our usage of these devices since we rely on *a social organisation of our semantic universe*[ccclxx] in our daily language-games, in our practices; we have not only learned a language, this has co-formed our temporal ontology. We grew up in a common semantic universe, *inevitably biasing us towards the possibility of any common sense.* Here I understand under the Ecoan term of 'semantic universe' *the totality of language-games subsisting in a culture* (or other linguistically organized community), which should not be mixed up with

---

Yet how could one, in a pragmatic communication situation, *prove* that one has performed the utterance of 'factual memory' and that therefore things were really as described? The fact that somebody claims 'factual memory', is no evidence. The question is, by which criteria and (social) facts one could support one's rightful claim of 'factual memory' to depict 'factual knowledge'! (I do *not* deny that there exist devices and means to settle this question; a lot in Searle 1995 is actually about *that*.) Cf. inf. *section III.VI.*

[ccclxviii] Wittgenstein's latest phase definitely had conventionalistic tendencies, I think of "Über Gewißheit", cf. Wittgenstein 1984, Band 8. See also K. Pollok 2001 and A. Stroll 2002.

[ccclxix] Cf. i.a. *MS 105*: 86 from Feb. 1929, *TS 209*: 19 from Jan. 1930, edited in "Philosophische Bemerkungen" V § 51, Wittgenstein 1984, Band 2: 83.
Cf. also Wittgenstein's comments on the pictorial comparisons of time with a landscape and the flowing of a river, where our thinking is taken prison by analogies, and the remark on the "jetzt" as "Zeitzeichen" ("now" as the "time-indicator" in my translation) in "Eine Philosophische Betrachtung" ad exempl. 60, Wittgenstein 1984, Band 5: 156 f.:
Originally this famous remark appears in the German translation and overworking of the "Brown Book" in *MS 115*: 173, dated with Aug. 25th 1936, but the German formulation "Zeitzeichen" in combination with "jetzt" has a yearlong history: It can already be traced way back to Sept. 14th 1930 in *MS 109*: 141, followed by a note in *TS 211*: 372 f. from Sept. 1931, which is taken over into *TS 212*: 1379 f., *TS 213*: 527, and again to be found in *MS 156*: 13r, all the last three entries from about early Jan. 1932, and it finally occurs in *TS 219*: 19 in Jan. 1933. Then in the "Brown Book", Wittgenstein 2000: 108 f. there is the English version of a temptation to call the "now" the "name for an instant of time", originally in *D 310*: 50 from Jan. 1934, from where Wittgenstein translates it back into the former German terms of "Zeitzeichen" in what was unfortunately called "Braunes Buch" (*MS 115*, loc. cit. sup.).

[ccclxx] Cf. also Savigny 1991, Savigny 1996b; compare this with Eco 1976 or Gelbmann 1998.

the 'semantic memory'[ccclxxi] of an individual person socialized in this social system as a (highly dynamic) sector of this (relative stable) semantic universe, since a single person does not take part in all the language-games actually played or 'playable' in this community. Certain language-games arc obviously shared by all who share a language.[ccclxxii]

The agreement in language is, according to Wittgenstein, preformed by an agreement in form of life.[ccclxxiii] 'My semantic memory'[ccclxxiv] has this as a background, containing the richness of all "cultural units" or *sememes* (as Eco 1976 calls them), which are, in fact, *all (semantically) recallable phenomena*, everything of which a memory is possible or to which language-games enact references.

That my memory is reliable depends then on my capability and possibility of expression being organized in this social way, because then it is reliable for

---

[ccclxxi]   This notion of 'semantic memory' is *not* the one Hintikka 1996k: 269 refers to, who thinks it is the "public memory" with unclearly grounding in some neuroscientific evidence. The term I use originally stems from Quillian 1968 and Eco 1976.

[ccclxxii]   In the notation of Stachowiak's *GMT* (cf. i.a. inf. *nota cdxvii*) these language-games, common for all personal 'semantic memories', would then depict the non-abundance of any representation of the collection of language-games in the semantic universe (also called 'essence'). The language-game(s) of remembering are for any representation within the frame of *GMT* to be regarded as not to be neglected (non-preterable).

The abstract notion of 'language' in the sense of 'ordinary language' or better: 'natural and actually used language' is then always already *a representation or pragmatic model of semantic memories or an idea of their contribution to a totality of language-games in a semantic universe*. And that means that it requires a Theory. Within its frame, such a model selects certain features and traits of what is phenomenologically and empirically encountered in order to depict its idea about language by the means of functionally mapping and mirroring these essential attributes, but also by adding certain attributes of the model in the theorizing activity and outcome of representing and depicting. So the notion of 'ordinary language' is the outcome of a conceptualisation.

As side remark I want to draw the reader's attention to Wittgenstein writing of "die tatsächliche Sprache", "actual language", in contrast to an ideal language in e.g. "Philosophische Untersuchungen" I § 107, Wittgenstein 1984, Band 1: 297, see in the English translation "Philosophical Investigations" I § 107, Wittgenstein 1991: 46. I fear that a lot of what is written about 'ordinary language' is in danger of idealizing actual language. Cf. also Gelbmann 2002b: 93 ff.

[ccclxxiii]   Cf. "Philosophische Untersuchungen" I § 241, Wittgenstein 1984, Band 1: 356.

[ccclxxiv]   Cf. Quillian 1968 on which Eco 1976 with his idea of a 'Model Q' draws. I have described and criticized Eco's conception of reference (which is closer to John Stuart Mill's notion of the difference between denotation/connotation than to Gottlob Frege's conception of the difference 'Sinn/Bedeutung') in Gelbmann 1998.

(potential) others in keeping their references invariant to counter-check mine; the language-game of remembering cannot be played alone (as it, by the way, holds for all language-games). The world would be weird, if somebody could virtually[ccclxxv] recall the future (or have the doubtful gift of clairvoyance), not because it is impossible per se, but because nobody would understand him/her, since nobody could know what exactly s/he refers to!-

The terminological decision about how to use the word 'proposition' (which hardly can be seen as an everyday language word) mirrors the impossibility to decide the truth value of statements about the future; in this understanding the Greek oracle did *not* mumble just any propositions. So I take Wittgenstein's remark as a remark about *empirical statements being a posteriori*, whereas *logical, grammatical or a priori statements (or dispositional statements) are not temporal at all.*[ccclxxvi]

III.III. Social Facts Revisited

"An intention is embedded in its situation, in human customs and institutions." ("Philosophical Investigations" I § 337, Ludwig Wittgenstein 1991: 108)[ccclxxvii]

Now I would like to go over to another, yet connected line of thought, linked to the theme of 'future facts and grammar' like, if I might bring a picture, a single woollen fibre belongs to a woollen yard.[ccclxxviii] At face-value this side-remark does not seem to have much in common with the theme of this essay, namely the language-games of remembering, because all instances of formulating a 'factual memory' (i.e. something of the form '$(M^@)$') of what is expressed in the following

---

[ccclxxv] In other words: We just cannot say that we can recall the future without running against the limits of language as if we were running into a wall.

[ccclxxvi] The question, whether this distinction between a posteriori statements and a priori statements is exhaustive, is another, conceptual, but not grammatical problem, and my remark does not have a bearing of transcendental weight upon Wittgenstein's philosophy.

[ccclxxvii] Cf. *MS 129*: 103 from Aug. 1944 and *TS 227*: 201, already as § 337, from Jan. 1945; moreover *TS 228*: 70 § 241, June 1945 and *TS 230*: 118 § 418, from Aug. 1945; the German edition renders this passage in "Philosophische Untersuchungen" I § 337, Wittgenstein 1984, Band 1: 386.

[ccclxxviii] Not every allusion to known sayings by Wittgenstein shall be accompanied by a verification of the citation.

statements *fail to have the intended meaning in everyday language use*, viz. that the statement labelled with '(@)' really *is exclusively used* to express a fact.[ccclxxix]

In phrases using the futurum exactum one might come pretty close to encountering 'pretty certain statements' about (e.g. institutional or physiological) future states of affairs. Think of

(C)   "By May 2003 I shall have delivered my correctly issued application form E104, to be obtained from the Norwegian National Insurance, to the Austrian Social Insurance Office" (if one keeps in mind that (C) was written in Jan. 2003),[ccclxx]

which is not that indubitable as

(D)   "At the end of this millennium I will have been dead for a long time" (by the same reservation applied to (C)).

Here the reliability is not that of 'causal knowledge'[ccclxxxi] but lies in our *attitude to propositional descriptions of a 'future past'*. Under more or less ordinary, i.e. expected and even customary, institutional and hence, for our knowledge about the interaction of social and physiological states quite *constitutive* circumstances[ccclxxxii] a statement might nevertheless be understood as a locution about an 'anticipated future fact'. At a dentist's, a sentence like

(E)   "This will cause pain",

mumbled by the dentist to reassure, not to scare, the patient before commencing his treatment, is based on common knowledge about the physiology of human jaws and the pain-receptiveness of their inmates (i.e. teeth coming in contact with cold metal, acid, fast rotating tiny needle-like drills and other surgical instruments). This is *knowledge about consequences whose (immediate) future*

[ccclxxix]   The sign '@' shall algebraically denote the specific name of the assertion, statement, locution, sentence or phrase in question; it therefore serves as a variable for truth-makers.

[ccclxx]   Cf. also my reaction to Hrachovec 1994 in Gelbmann 2000a.

[ccclxxxi]   Cf. Wright 1983.

[ccclxxxii]   Cf. Anscombe 1976, Bloor 1996, Nientied 2001; but Anscombe 1976 was not the first speculation on 'linguistic idealism'. The early constructivists of the Cybernetic Revolution anticipated this already in their socio-psychological works, especially Ruesch & Bateson 1951 deserve being acknowledged.

realization is not logically forced upon us with the cruel inevitability of kismet
(since we might jerk away from the dentist's tools or just not go there[ccclxxxiii]).

    (F)   "This causes pain"

comes pretty close to stating a fact which holds for almost *any* time of attending a
dentist, presupposed that one has urgent reason's to make and meet such an
appointment (like a suspected cavity in a tooth),[ccclxxxiv] and might also hold for the
future, like a Law of Nature, as long as one has teeth (and even longer).

    Yet all these cases (C)-(F) depend on some more or less *tacit propositional
attitudes*, on cognitive and epistemic presuppositions, which themselves are of
logical contingency and not necessarily expressible by the speaker or receiver of
such locutions: I might not in May do as I have steadfastly announced to do today
(cf. (C)); I might, without my knowing, enjoy the ability of eternal life (cf. (D));
the dentist might be wrong about his patient's neurological receptiveness to his
drilling tools (cf. (E)), which also applies to the last example (cf. (F)). I am afraid
to say *that empirical statements about the so-called future all carry a likelihood of
our knowledge, yet not the certainty of knowing facts.*[ccclxxxv]

    Even if it are, in the last consequence, Laws of Nature on that we build our
empirical predictions, *our knowledge of them might be fallible;*[ccclxxxvi] we do not
live in a calculable world, at least we cannot be certain that we do, and hence this
sort of certainty or uncertainty always bears some metaphysical weight, destroying
any clarity or pureness of any knowledge attached to it. *We do not really know any
Laws of Nature*, although we, as a matter of fact, have a concept of them. This
concept of 'Laws of Nature' consists therein that *we know with certainty that if we
knew the Laws of Nature, we could be certain about (some)*[ccclxxxvii] *future
experiences under certain circumstances, because they would be future facts.*-

---

[ccclxxxiii] So the freedom of choice presupposes the ability to imagine counterfactual situations or to
anticipate alternative options.

[ccclxxxiv] In defence of dentists I have to admit that attending a dentist can and shall help to avoid the
suffering of pain in the future.

[ccclxxxv] Cf. also the difference between senses of 'certainty' Malcolm 1942 draws.

[ccclxxxvi] I am not ashamed to declare myself as a Popperian in this point; cf. i.a. Popper 1963.

[ccclxxxvii] This restriction is necessary since there could be among the Laws of Nature one stating that
there is, to a certain degree, a principal unpredictability (think of Chaos Theory, cf. Gleick
1987, Fjelland 1999, etc., or of Quantum Theory).

The memory-expression of these sentences are easy to discuss: (M^C) resembles the case of futurum exactum and subjunctive that were already discussed above, cf. the cases (M^B) and (M^{B*}), and I do not have to formulate (M^C) in order to show that it is nonsense or at least weird and far from 'ordinary' or intelligible (independently from how well Norwegian bureaucracy works). It is constructible for philosophers,[ccclxxxviii] so to say, but does not exist in wild language life out there. This does not say anything about the sense a sentence (I) makes, when this sentence reads

(I)   "I remind you that [you maintained/promised/announced/speculated/ hoped for that] by May 2003 you shall have delivered your correctly issued application form E104, to be obtained from the Norwegian National Insurance, to the Austrian Social Insurance Office".

For example (I) a reasonable context can be easily imagined, ready to establish a meaning and usage for it. Yet (I) talks about a speech-act or a propositional attitude towards an anticipated state of affairs, confer the last part of (I), which itself depicts a partial sentence (I*) about the delivery of some form to some branch of bureaucracy. Since (Austrian) bureaucracy is reliably involved, there is an institutional fact detectable on which the reasonability of (I*) rests (my personal attitude towards Norwegian bureaucracy, feeding on my memory of experiences with it, prevents me from transferring my assessed reliance from Austrian to Norwegian circumstances).-

(D) does not so much concern a fact but a common and tacit assumption (whose existence is a fact itself), viz. the finitude of all human life being limited to, say, less than one hundred twenty years (which seems to me to depict the current upper limit of human life-expectation); since I am now 34 years old, I am supposed to live not longer than until about the year 2089. What then shall it mean to recall this biological knowledge?

If one says (D), we nowadays might interpret it on the background of this common assumption, but probably the speaker of (D) has the knowledge of biological facts we do not have, about what until today only is a speculation,

---

[ccclxxxviii] I do not want to enter the debate about 'possible languages'. Here we use, in good Wittgensteinian manner, *the actual language as a measurement of what is conceivable.*

But then there cannot fall language itself under that what is conceivable (and this *is* a weakness of Wittgenstein's philosophy, but not only of his philosophy, of many strains and grains of Analytic Philosophy and Ordinary Language Philosophy as well).

namely that with proper, say, bio-genetic treatment the biological life of human beings would in principle be practically unlimited or at least cover a much longer time span, for instance 3000 years.

Then (D) would have a different meaning and probably imply a planned death of the speaker of (D), and (M^D) then could mean that this speaker *remembers his plan*. But this is a *speculation* that better fits into a science fiction novel than into a philosophical essay, since we can always imagine a possible world counterfactual to ours, and here I take 'counterfactual' in the understanding of it being *in contrast to our current knowledge of facts*, or in contrast to our common assumption about what is the fact.

If we stick to the currently most likely reading of (D), (M^D) expresses the memory-reference to an empirical fact with empirical certainty, at least within our culture and Weltanschauung. However, what does it purport to say that I *remember* that I will have been dead for a long time until the year 3000? Can I remember a 'future past'?[ccclxxxix] This is queer, since the first person, who is to remember *now*, will at that time no longer be an object for linguistic reference any more. I cannot bring myself to call (M^D) an example of factual memory, not because I doubt this sort of finitude of my life but because *I cannot imagine any actually possible context* in which a locution or representation of (M^D) factually makes sense! (Unless I lose myself in wild speculations which give reasons for doubting what we recognize as common knowledge about biological facts.)-

(M^E) can stand for 'remembering a warning', yet then it is not a case of remembering a *fait accompli* but has its residue in (E) being a speech-act;[cccxc]

[ccclxxxix] No, I can't, and nobody can. Cf. the foregoing discussion in *section III.II* at (B).

[cccxc] Sec. Austin 1962a.- One should not overlook that (E) need not talk about physiological states or body-feelings; the word 'pain' in this context could have a much wider meaning, think of a political discussion about taxes as the frame within which somebody comes up with a remark like (E). Yet isn't it interesting that the same frame hardly can match the utterance of
(K)   "This will cause memory"?
To my feeling, (K) is absurd, and (M^K) even more so. I locate the absurdity in a *wrong attribution of causality to memory*; that we can state that somebody has a remembrance of a fact does not purport that the fact or its expression caused the memory of it, unless it is a *grammatical causality* of memory being caused by the *experience of the remembered* thing or event (cf. Glock 2000: 243, loc. cit. inf. *section III.V*). This insight goes deeper than just making a philosophical point against the still popular theory of memory-traces (against which i.a. Malcolm 1977 argues, without citing Foerster 1963 as a remarkable quantum-theoritical and informational approach to memory-theories which does not resort in any physicalism of traces) and a simplified picture of the correlation or even isomorphism of

thus, by uttering (M^E) there is an *emphasis on a speech-act performing a warning*, yet this emphasis itself takes away the speech-act's immediate reference to a current situation and brings it over to a more general statement, a maxim or rule for conduct, or an anticipation of a future state of affairs or situations which are supposed to be caused by some measurements. Then my memory in producing (M^E) *factually draws on my grammatical and pragmatic knowledge about warning as a speech-act*, but does not draw on the prediction of pain or the state of affairs corresponding to this.

Even though speech-acts of warning can have an *imperative character*, the memory of them does not. Just think of a military situation and a yelled

(L_1)   "Be cautious!" or (L_2) "Head down!",

and then look how similar they are to military commands and strict orders like

(L_3)   "Stand still!" or a sheriff's (L_4) "Hands up!".

---

brain and mind or brain and memory.

His admirable knowledge of Wittgenstein's Nachlass has led Michel ter Hark 1995b: 128 to the valuable observation of an unpublished remark he traces back as fitting into "Bemerkungen über die Philosophie der Psychologie" I between § 907 and § 908, cf. Wittgenstein 1998a: 160 ff., where Wittgenstein recommends to

"throw away the old prejudices about causality" (cf. *MS 134*: 102 f., as Michel ter Hark loc. cit. translates the German Nachlass original which is dated with April 4th 1947; ter Hark cites *MS 134*: 104-105; his as well as Bergen Electronic Edition's pagination have to be scrutinized on the basis of the double-sheet's pagination in the original with "52", cf. Cornell copy Vol. 36).-

There is a location in "Zettel" where Wittgenstein clearly takes a stance against any trace-theory of memory, and I shall only give the German citation (the English can be found at loc. cit. Wittgenstein 1998c: 105):

"Ich habe diesen Mann vor Jahren gesehen; nun sehe ich ihn wieder, erkenne ihn, erinnere mich seines Namens. Und warum muß es nun für dies Erinnern eine Ursache in meinem Nervensystem geben? Warum muß irgend etwas, was immer, *in irgendeiner Form* dort aufgespeichert worden sein? Warum *muß* er eine Spur hinterlassen haben? Warum soll es keine psychologische Gesetzmäßigkeit geben, der keine physiologische entspricht? Wenn das unsere Begriffe von der Kausalität umstößt, dann ist es Zeit, daß sie umgestoßen werden." ("Zettel" § 610, Wittgenstein 1984, Band 8: 417; i.e. "Bemerkungen über die Philosophie der Psychologie" I § 905, Wittgenstein 1998a: 160; italics original; G.G.).

Here the estimated reader might forgive me for not translating this passage, but Anscombe's translation is quite okay and easy to check.

But *to remember an order* can be expressed by a statement of factual memory of the form (M^L_3) or (M^L_4), and *here one recalls not only the disposition of obeying the order but really of how to obey it*. This makes sense, in contrast to a formalisation (M^L_1) and (M^L_2), because what does it mean to say

(M^L_1)　　"He remembers to be cautious" or (M^L_2) "She recalls to keep her head down"

in the meaning of 'factual memory' and *not* of dispositional memory or of remembering a speech-act of warning, if (L_1) and (L_2) are not some past events s/he has a memory of? If I *describe somebody's behaviour*, say on a battle-field with the sentences (M^L_1) or (M^L_2), I do not say anything about this soldier's retention of facts but about her/his appropriately following an advice or warning that probably was clothed in the tone of a military command or a yelled shout.

That's why I tend to see '(M^L_1)', and '(M^L_2)' respectively, if taken as an abbreviation of memory-expressions containing the phrases (L_1) or (L_2), *not* as examples for 'factual memory' but as paradigms for the *rehearsal of a maxim, rule, recommendation, etc. for one's conduct and behaviour, referring to a situation and not to a constellation*: What here is remembered is not a past event of, e.g. putting one's head down, but *the past command or warning* telling one to put one's head down, and the *recollection refers to the speech-act of warning and a prescription of behaviour and not to a statement about a state of affairs or situation as a constellation of things or cases*!-[cccxci] Yet in another context, one could say

(L_5)　　"Then, as he stood with his whiskey in front of the mirror at the bar, gazing at the girls on the dance floor, he was told to put his hands up",

which is the context of story-telling, and here one factually recalls the story and a narrative succession of events by giving a discription. But in (L_5), uttered in a recollection of a narration of the form '(M^L_5)', *a memory-expression need not be mentioned*, it is superfluous, because the context itself informs one already that (L_5) is uttered as '(M^L_5)': So (M^L_5) without cutting out redundancies comes up to $(M^L_5)^*$ which could read as:

[cccxci]　In so far as it refers to a speech-act, it refers to a social situation.-

$(M^L_5)^*$ "Then – I vividly recall the scene -, as he stood with his whiskey in front of the mirror at the bar, he was told to put his hands up",

and this is propositionally and situationally equivalent to (L_5), tacitly being identified with (M^L_5).-[cccxcii]

The event itself, the putting up of one's hands in surrender or the occasion of being told to do so, is *fictional*, ergo: there could in principle be no factual memory of that (it is something else to remember the fact that this was fiction); *there is or was nobody actually participating "in the scene" who is giving an account of his memory by narrating the movie's scene*! Even an actor would not be "in the scene" in the sense of the fictive persons the scene is about; and if 'in the scene' one of the main figures expresses her/his memory about the very scene, this report is only 'factually relative to the fiction', hence 'relative factual', and the memory-report would convey 'relatively factual memory', equalling 'factual memory in the scene' as 'acting as if having factual memory'.

So the expression of a factual memory of a scene in a film is just the same as the expression of a narration of the film-scene, and this comes up to a performance, viz. actually narrating a part of the film; to everybody who narrates a film we attribute that s/he accurately and factually recalls the film, unless we have a reason to doubt her/his words, due to being able to give a better report: And a better report is possible because our factual recollection of the scene to be told is more accurate then hers/his, and this would lead to changing the narrative element (L_5) into some other, let's say (L_6), but it would not change anything about the relation of (M^L_5) to (L_5) or of (M^L_6) to (L_6).-

This discussion of the relationship of memory-expressions to speech-acts, think of case (E) and (M^E), seems to end up in a terminological question, viz. if we should widen our (still not yet defined) concept of 'factual memory' to cover this case, since *to retain the function of speech-acts for a performative usage in memory-expressions draws on the social factuality of speech-acts.*[cccxciii] We could

---

[cccxcii]   So $(M^L_5) = (M^L_5)^* = (L_5)$.

[cccxciii]   Cf. e.g. Searle 1995.- It is worth noticing that Jaakko Hintikka 1962: 12 ff. prefers the term "performatory" to "performative", but loc. cit. he seems to have in mind the same or something very close to it. About the "performatory" character of statements he says:
"It depends on an act or »performance«, namely on a certain person's act of uttering a sentence (or of otherwise making a statement); it does not depend solely on the means used for the purpose, that is, on the sentence which is being uttered." (Hintikka 1962: 12; order of punctuation signs corrected and the latter changed; G.G.)
I agree with this as a definition of "linguistic performativity". Yet *the question remains*

grant this; but keep the differences in mind: To factually remember a warning falls then under remembering a (social) situation in which *a possible anticipation of a state of affairs was indirectly subjected to a speech-act* or hinted at thereby.

Yet then, as the wits of language will, to remind somebody of particular consequences of one's doings, and particularly to remind somebody via the anticipation of a physiological state of affairs of certain experiences and sensations can be the speech-act of a warning itself! So the difference between 'to remember something' and 'to remind somebody of something' can mirror the difference between 'being warned' and 'actually warning somebody'.-

---

whether there are other sorts of performances in thinking and communication, and at least since Gelbmann 2002c I count "attitude(s)" among the latter. What I do not agree on with Hintikka is that he does not mention anything about the rhetorical dimension, namely *towards whom the statement is made*, i.e. in which frame performativity in this understanding has to take place. My reply to him is, that it can only be a social frame, involving others as communicants. *It would not be a statement if only uttered by a solipsist towards himself.*

Now the interesting point is, that a marvellous paper, Hintikka 1962, is about Descartes and the Cartesian "cogito ergo sum" or "sum res cogitans" (cf. Descartes 1637 and Descartes 1641), and that Hintikka loc. cit. says that Descartes' famed dictum *is* a performative statement. To this I consent, in admiration for Hintikka's analysis and learnedness, *but* if Descartes' known statement is performative, Descartes cannot be thought of as a solipsist any more in the course of his meditations, and *he cannot think of himself as a solipsist any more* at this stage of his argument (so the genius malignus becomes a possible partner of communication, what is inconsistent with its concept). The reason why Descartes in a certain sense discovered a truth lies in his discovery that *any* statement, and the more so his self-certifying statement, as a speech-act presupposes the possible existence of communicants.

So if "cogito ergo sum" shall be a statement and not only a sentence, hence if there is a first-person-speaker uttering this sentence and thus committing a speech act, then performatives presuppose a social frame and in their conceptualisation are *pragmatic* in my sense, i.e. in the sense of Morris 1938: they involve *a three-fold relation* of signs, meaning, sign-use by a community of communicants. *For the sole and lonesome speaker no sentence s/he puts forth can be a statement, even if it asserts the existence of the speaker.*

Therefore Descartes' deeper problem, of which he was not clearly aware, was the proper recognition and acknowledgement of a concept of 'mind' that as the *res cogitans unica* could not exist, *because it could not state or express anything*. The malignity of the invented genius malignus lies in it being a product of a solipsist; but along with this goes already the impossibility of it. That the thinker and ego discovers the idea of God in its own mind, is nothing else but the discovery of *the necessity of a res cogitans altera* (and this is a *necessitas de re*, not only a *necessitas de dicto*). So Descartes' mindful God actually is the first communicant, penetrating the unity of a dangerously solipsistic view.

Language is clever enough to mark a certain difference lexically, namely *whose memory shall be affected by a certain memory-phrase* from the phrase expressing the activation or constitution of retention and recollection. To say to a person

(P)   "Remember to take an umbrella",

what under circumstances in Western Norway is a smart precaution, means to remind the addressed person of taking his/her umbrella, so somebody else's memory is affected. The polite "Let me remind you to take an umbrella" is, putting aside it's politeness as a perlocution, just the same performance. But it would be weird to say this to oneself, or to narrate about having said so to oneself.- From this should be distinguished the cases

(Q)   "Æ remembers to remind Ø to bring an umbrella"

as Æ's recollection about having to bring about that somebody else, viz. Ø, recalls to do something, and

(R)   "Æ reminds Á to remind Ø to bring an umbrella"

as the situation of Æ reminding somebody that s/he should make Ø remember the damned umbrella, so Æ shoves the responsibility on somebody else. (Q) could be reformulated into

(Q*)   "Æ reminds Ø to bring an umbrella"

by getting rid of some syntactic-semantic redundancy without any loss of performative information,[cccxciv] whereas for (R) there is the reformulation

(R*)   "Æ reminds Á to remember to remind Ø to bring an umbrella"

which adds redundancy and is hardly ever applied.- The reader can run through examples using "forget" and "not to forget" in combinations with memory-phrases

---

[cccxciv]   I owe to Deirdre Smith the final example:
(Q**)   "Æ reminds himself to remember to remind Ø to bring an umbrella",
which just adds syntactic-semantic redundancy.

and will soon discover that for the difference between 'to remind somebody of something' and 'to remember something' there cannot be construed an equivalent difference with applying the lexem 'to forget' or 'not to forget'. The expressions for affecting somebody else's memory are lexically only provided for positive constitution of retention, for the negative effect we have to apply circumscriptions like "to make somebody forget something", what hardly can be a warning.-

If we go back to our discussion of the relationship between memory-expressions and speech-acts, we should notice that we arrive at the absurdity that (E) *and* (M^E) could *both* be translated as speech-acts of warning (or some other language-game applying speech-acts). Such an absurdity does *not* lie in the *manifold functionality of linguistic expressions* in daily life observable at this occasion, but in the problem that *our initial (tacit) assumption, that the notion of 'factual memory' is unequivocally definable and unambiguously restricted to clear cases which either fall under its concept or not, has to be given up!*

If (E) and (M^E) made us think that cases with no 'factual memory' involved were clear cut, then the next example[cccxcv]

(M^N)   "You will remember my words!"

is even more spurious if taken as connected to 'factual memory'. The strangeness lies therein, that (M^N), firstly, uses the future tense of a memory-verb and looks like a prediction, secondly has no explicit factual statement (N) as its origin contained in (M^N) but only some joker-reference to what could have been said before (M^N) was uttered. What does, in general, the phrase "my words" refer to, to which state of affairs or situation?

Obviously a foregoing situation yields the necessary context, but this context is only referred to by *a phrase which works like a variable*; and (M^N) can then be rephrased as the prediction of the addressed person recalling the fact that (N) was said, including what (N) was about, but by hearing (M^N) alone, isolated from this situational context, we just don't get it as a case of recollection.

All other reference-statements (@) of memory-expressions ($M^@$) could be reformulated as statements about facts, so, e.g., "We remember your name" could be seen as being a memory-expression of

---

[cccxcv]   I owe it to joking with Edoardo Zamuner and Luis Serrano Fernandez, both were in winter 2003 research colleagues in Bergen, Norway.

"It is a fact that your name is Gerhard"

or of

"[We know that] [Y]ou have a name".

What does '(M^N)' depict, if not 'factual memory', *which it cannot depict because how should one know now about one's future memory?*- '(M^N)' should have received an asterisk, just to indicate how *inappropriate* it would be to take it as a case of 'factual memory' or as a 'prediction of factual memory': $(M^N) = (M^N)*$, so my interpretation of $(M^N)*$ then is that it is a speech act, *performing or displaying the authority of the speaker* who thereby denotes or employs some advice, warning, command, prescription, with "my words" referring to (N), i.e. words the speaker has already given before $(M^N)*$ is uttered. By putting it all in future tense, stress is put on what is stated or prescribed or commanded or warned about by (N), since *by giving the impression of being able to predict the future of the other's memory one's authority gets more weight.*

So the speaker is *self-certifying his/her authority* by applying a memory-phrase in the future tense towards another person, and the frame of reference for $(M^N)*$ is the *situation where this power can be experienced*, the same presence in which $(M^N)*$ is uttered.- From this the first-person-case has to be distinguished

(M^O): "I shall remember your words" or "I shall keep in mind your words", but not "Your words shall be kept in mind";

although (O) here is referred to by "my words", whatever speech-act these words set into action, (M^O) can express *accepting the authority of the person addressed by the first-person-speaker*. The frame of reference for (M^O) is then the very situation of a state of affairs, hence a *social fact*, which turned (O) into the speech-act it was.

This is related to swearing (an oath) and to avowing. A lot of what happens in court is, by the way, an *institutional preparation of a context by rituals* to which such speech-acts can properly refer, *intended to secure that the usage of memory-phrases really are cases of 'factual memory'*. After having sworn the oath to "tell the truth and nothing but the truth" in the presence of an authority of the court and the judge(s), any phrase containing a memory-expression is supposed to be understood as 'factual memory' (and the court has the right to use such utterances as evidence against the person uttering them); and if one gives an account by using memory-phrases as a witness in court,[cccxcvi] i.e in the situation of a trial, s/he is either lying or presenting expressions of 'factual memory' and hence 'the truth'. But even if s/he lies about his/her memory, s/he plays the language-game of factually remembering by pretending to remember correctly.

So the *ritual of swearing an oath on the Bible just marks a context*, and the socio-linguistic institutions hereby upheld and activated bring about the conventions the language-games in courts rely on. *To these very conventions the word 'forget' does not apply*, and violating them either leads to punishment (for contempt of the court or for lying) or to one's sane reason being seriously doubted, hence to one not being regarded as a reliable witness any longer. So here we have, indeed, *a case where factuality depends on recallability*, or better: where *the givenness of an institution relies on a restriction of memory-expressions to the language-game of 'factual memory'*.

In court, one cannot reasonably say "I have forgotten the oath I have sworn", and then go on by exploiting memory-phrases without any hindsight to an intended application of the concept of 'factual memory', because any context which might give sense to *this* phrase of a failing memory is ruled out in such a situation! If one has sworn the oath, presupposed that one was regarded as mentally sane while doing it, one has entered the language-game of 'factual memory in court'; there is no escape one can be reminded of, except certain rights like 'the right to be silent in order not to incriminate oneself' or, most certainly an excuse often used, the known "I cannot remember", thrown into the inquirer's face. But to pretend in court that somebody cannot remember is either a statement of a fact about one's memory, hence admissible, or a lie and therefore a possible reason for one's punishment if the lie is discovered, since lying is against the oath sworn in court. *The conventionalistic traits of such memory-situations are rooted in institutionality.-*

Last but not least, let's look at the case (F), which clearly is *empirical knowledge about experiencing sensations* under certain circumstances. If I say:[cccxcvii]

(**M**^F)   "I remember that this causes pain" or

[cccxcvi]   Cf. inf. *section III.VI.*

[cccxcvii]   Here the sign '(**M**^F)' is misused.

$$(\boldsymbol{M}^{F^*}) \quad \text{"She remembers that this causes pain",}$$

we seem to have an expression of 'factual memory' presented to us, used to go to the dentist's as we all are. Yet can we not imagine cases where these statements are used to assure somebody (like the dentist) of somebody's preparedness,[cccxcviii] to describe a person's *presumed* state, without intending to say anything about this person's memory? I at least feel that other meanings and usages resonate with the 'factuality of memory' involved in $(\boldsymbol{M}^F)$ and $(\boldsymbol{M}^{F^*})$.

I do not intend to exhaustively list all examples[cccxcix] (this actually is principally impossible), because I partly have already made my point. Yet I want to reflect once more on the discussion of 'future facts' with a sentence like

---

[cccxcviii] Imagine that $(\boldsymbol{M}^F)$ is said by the patient to the doctor who wants to inform him/her, and that $(\boldsymbol{M}^{F^*})$ is said by a mother accompanying her child to the dentist's as a reply to the doctor's questioning glance cast in the worry that the child might start screaming and be not prepared at all.

[cccxcix] That one remembers a person when being re-introduced to him/her, is properly called a case of *recognition*, where the memory involved can be characterized with a certain 'factuality', yet is *not* about state of affairs (whether past or not), but about persons or individuals (cf. Hacker 1996: 482 ff.). This "I remember you" is of the form of "I know now again that I knew you before", which is not that far from the definition Malcolm 1963c: 236 gives (cf. inf. *section III.IV*).

But even if we could remember having recognized somebody, say at the party last Saturday where I talked with a common acquaintance of a classmate of mine, it is hardly ever said that one recognizes a memory or recollection or remembrance, unless the words 'memory', 'recollection', 'remembrance' are used in a secondary meaning, signifying a representation or exemplar of something (for instance one could recognize a book which *is* a recollection).-

Hacker loc. cit. rightfully points out that remembering a person is not connected to any pastness of the action involved (yet with Russell we could talk about 'familiarity' here), it is more like *an expression of re-encountering an object or human being*, that is present, although it once also *was* present when one firstly encountered it. Yet in expressing the recognition and *awareness of re-encountering*, one hints at the past occasion and *therefore* applies a memory-expression, i.e. exclaims:

"Ah, I remember you, weren't you the lady-friend of so-and-so at the time I was at the army, down there in far Eastern Austria towards the border of Hungary, we met each other at this lousy mess hall on the farewell evening, and I was completely drunk?"

I don't think that in saying so one has an image or picture of the person in one's mind, vividly in front of one's inner eye, so to say. Rather, one in remembering re-establishes a link to a (causal) chain of references, thus enhancing this reference-chain to the current moment of which one hence is aware, a chain which connects other events with the current event. *The case of re-encountering and recognizing is a case of re-collection of semantic references* (and Plato's notion of *anamnesis* is therefore a notion of semantic memory, serving as a model for knowledge).

(G)   "There is a future",

taken as even

(G*)   "The future exists",

which is a bit off the mark in everyday language use; what these statements express is a *social fact with conceptual certainty* which does not tell us anything about what comes into being or shall happen. And then to say

(M^{G*})   "He remembers that the future exists", or

(M^{G})   "I remember that there is a future"

is just equivalent to saying one knows that there is a future, a rhetorical phrase at the most, and nothing more. So (M^{G}) and (M^{G*}) are not cases of 'factual memory'. Here a test could be (to write in Wittgensteinian style) to show, by adding modifiers, that neither

"I have a faint memory of the existence of a future" nor

"He has a faint memory of the future"

makes any sense at all, whereas 'factual memory' could be qualified by degrees of its intensity. But even though some of the language-games one can play with 'memory' and 'remembering' resemble those with 'pain', the expression

"I almost have a pain"

can make sense, one just has to construe a fitting context. In merry lunch talks[cd] in winter 2003 in Bergen, I once described such a possible situation where this statement would make sense: Imagine a child pinching her uncle, just to test when he would react to the pain, and he takes part in the game of testing practical hypotheses by giving her feedback in this way, instead of jumping away from her or scolding her.- But what could the sentence

---

[cd]   With Luis Serrano Fernandez and Richard Sørli, the first a student in the science of translation at the Universidad de León in Spain, devoted to his research on film-dubbing, the second a scholarly learned analytic philosopher from Tromsø in Northern Norway, who always had borrowed and kept the books I needed.

(U)   "I almost remember"

correspond to? It is important that one sees the contrast between (U) and (V):

(V)   "I almost remember*ed*",

because (V) is a report on (the past of) a failing memory, and as that (V) makes sense, whereas the vacillating example (U) as a first-person-statement only reveals uncertainty on behalf of the speaker. There are situations when one says,

(W)   "Ah, I just can't recall it, it lies on the tip of my tongue".

But *this* is an expression of a certain *inability in expressing*, somebody not being able to say what one knows one can, and the form of a first-person-statement excludes the possibility of doubting the propositional content of (W). (W) *does not purport a failing memory or even forgetting*, yet since there is an apparent lack of ability to express one's memory, one might quite *imprecisely* speak of a faint memory, of a low degree of recollection.[cdi] Wittgenstein[cdii] uses

---

[cdi]   But how can one have a faint factual memory? Either one does recall a fact or one does not. There is no in between. The fact, that somebody has a memory of something, can also not be "faint". There is an all-or-nothing-principle at work, isn't it?

[cdii]   Philologically seen, this remark from *D 310*: 62 goes back to Jan. 1934, reoccurs in Wittgenstein's own German translation in the phrase "»es liegt ihm auf der Zunge«" in "Eine Philosophische Betrachtung" ad exempl. 68, Wittgenstein 1984, Band 5: 168, i.e. *MS 115*: 189 from Aug. 25th 1936. But a similar and in German quite colloquial expression can already earlier be found in his diaries from the First World War, look at *MS 101*: 44v from Oct. 18th 1914 (and again in Nov. 1914 in *MS 102*: 24v ff.; cf. Janik 1999), where Wittgenstein, in desperately looking for a "redeeming word" (das "erlösende Wort"), observes that the solution to a problem lies on the tip of his tongue.
Already in *MS 142*: 109 f. § 121 from Nov.1936 we find this search for the "redeeming word" again, this time in comparing the inexpressible word or the expression one looks for with a "hair on one's tongue", which again occurs in *TS 220*: 83 § 106 in Jan. 1937, *TS 238*: 11 § 139 in Jan. 1942 and *TS 239*: 84 § 139 in Jan. 1942. He asks what is going on in one's (burdened) consciousness when one says that a word is lying on the tip of one's tongue in "Philosophische Untersuchungen" II xi, Wittgenstein 1984, Band 1: 561 f. (also edited in "Letzte Schriften über die Philosophie der Psychologie" I § 828, Wittgenstein 1990a: 106), which dates already with *MS 142*: 109 f. § 121 from Nov. 1936, *TS 220*: 83 § 105 in Jan. 1937.
This was taken over into *TS 238*: 11 § 139 and into *TS 239*: 84 § 139, both from Jan. 1942, further in *MS 130*: 63 from May 26th 1946, where Wittgenstein explicitly inquires after the meaning of "an expression lies on the tip of my tongue", to again come to think about this theme in *MS 131*: 53 on Aug 16th 1946, in *TS 245*: 182 § 920 in Jan. 1947, in *TS 229*: 250

the example of a third-person-expression in the "Brown Book" ad exempl. 64, Wittgenstein 2000: 116,

"It lies »on the tip of his tongue«"

to illustrate forgetting, in which I just cannot follow him! At the most this version of (W) shows a failure in reproducing a certain memory.

Saying (W) in the descriptive third-person-form, one knows about somebody that this somebody knew what s/he cannot express right now; so it is not so much a question of 'factual memory' but of somebody's metaphorical statement about his/her own practical (in)ability in expressing his/her remembrance of which s/he might be certain, but not the speaker of (W).-

Confronted with this mass of philological material I go even further: Wittgenstein used such phrases not about failing retention or a shortcoming of recollection but about an *incapability to express a cognitive achievement*, which in the case of the young Wittgenstein was connected to a personal search with a religious touch, whereas the elderly Wittgenstein's thinking turned completely to the meaning and use of such phrases.-[cdiii] For an example of 'factual memory' being qualified according to its intensity, look at:

"I have a clear memory of my first mountain tour in Norway"

or a phrase which could appear in a novel:

(X)   "He unfortunately had only faintly kept in mind the looks of the lady he had met eleven years ago in a tiny hotel in Vienna and whom he was to re-encounter at the tiny airport of Ocaloosa County in May 2001."-

Let's go back to the consideration of *how propositional attitudes are linked with 'factual memory'*, and let's transfer it to another well-known case. To

---

§ 920 in Sept. 1947 (the last three entries are published as "Bemerkungen über die Philosophie der Psychologie" I § 254, Wittgenstein 1998a: 52), see also *MS 134*: 41 from mid-March 1947.

The last entries on this subject are to be found in *MS 144*: 85 f. and *MS 169*: 69*v* f., both from Jan. 1949, and in *MS 138*: 15 ff. from Feb. 1949, edited as "Letzte Schriften über die Philosophie der Psychologie" I § 841 f., Wittgenstein 1990a: 107.

[cdiii]   This hints, by the way, in the direction of Wittgenstein's dyslexia as probably not so much a cause, but interesting personal feature giving rise to his philosophising, cf. Hintikka & Hintikka 2002 and my criticism in *Essay IV*.

complete the row of riddles, we could think of *predictions of a destiny* like the oracle's mysterious pronouncement:

(H)   "Oedipus is bound to kill his father and marry his mother".

The plain people of the ancient or legendary Greek society are said to have *believed* that *only* the oracle knew the future (by excluding any doubt in this belief), whereas the oracle's institutional reliability depended on it being commonly supposed to know the future.[cdiv] *Describing this situation cannot be managed without applying propositional attitudes as constituents of the situation.*

Since we are all in our acting and demeanour governed by propositional attitudes, these people in the *mythos of Οιδιποσ*[cdv] are thus *setting into action* a chain of events which finally let (H) come true and established poor Oedipus' fate.[cdvi] This story, if I recall it correctly, its main traits can be told as follows:

As a child Oidipos was left abandoned in a wild wood, doomed to death, because the oracle predicted a terrible future (cf. (H)). But a shepherd finds him and raises him as his own son. Years later the grown up and unusually strong Oidipos comes to quarrel with a traveller at a crossing, to proud a man to show patience and give way to others, and in this quarrel Oidipos kills the stranger. In continuing his trip he arrives at a city, where he settles and marries the queen, a widow. Some time after these events he has to learn that the queen was not only the wife of the man he slew in this quarrel, but is in fact is own mother!

So destiny fulfils it horrible course not only by lifting the veil over the dark offspring of this poor man and his tragic entanglement into events the people of his home town originally wanted to avoid, but it also reaches its utmost horror when the desperate Oedipus blinds himself in seeing that he carried out the fate predicted by the oracle.-

Imagine, that these people would not have had such a good memory to rely on an oracle's sinister warning (yet *it is hard to compel one to forget*, especially under mythological circumstances ...). Here these people might have (M^H) as a memory

---

[cdiv]   A classical case of linguistic idealism; cf. sup. *nota ccclxxxii.*

[cdv]   In Latin letters the Greek name is transcribed as "Oidipos"; the version "Oedipus" is already transferred into Latin.

[cdvi]   We know this as 'self-fulfilling prophecies'; cf. i.a. Ruesch & Bateson 1987: 217 ff., Watzlawick 1981b (in English Watzlawick 1984b), Gelbmann 2000b. Popper 1957 calls it the "Oedipus effect".

about '(H)',[cdvii] yet this does not mean that (H) expressed a fact already at the time when the oracle announced it, then it would have been a 'future fact' that was known to certainly come true by the oracle, although it was only through the oracle's *intervention* (by its so-called 'prediction'), so to say, which proved the oracle's mastery of clairvoyance![cdviii]

Obviously some language-games of pronouncing induce us to recall something,[cdix] which furthermore could lead to this pronouncement coming true. In a certain sense we can call some of these language-games 'performative speech-acts', and they would not work without memory, even though this type of remembering is not a pure case of 'factual memory'.[cdx]

Well, we should advance to the seemingly unsafe ground of the definitional problem. Claiming the applicability of a particular concept has already brought about a *profound doubt whether a definitional approach, in tackling the concept of 'memory' as unambiguous and univocally definable, is liable to provide any general solution.*[cdxi] In walking there, Wittgenstein's method (if one could name it thereby) is a good stick we can hold on to when our attempts to achieve a clear, perspicuous view cannot penetrate the fog covering our path of philosophical striving.

[cdvii]   Be careful, "memory about '(H)'" is to be distinguished from 'memory about (H)'; by the first token the memory is kind of meta-linguistic, by the second it is about the state of affairs expressed by (H).

[cdviii]   Oracles might have a bad memory about their predictions, because otherwise how could they bear to know the future?

[cdix]   Semiotically seen announcements or pronouncements primarily are *indices*, they attract attention to a thematic object, and that to which one is attentive easier enters one's memory. So *pronouncements master to summon retention.*

[cdx]   How can somebody (i.e. the oracle) sensibly be said to recall something that at the time of such a prediction (and summoning of presupposed recollection) has not yet taken place? The only way out seems to be the *belief in fate*, so *fate functions as an explanation!*

[cdxi]   This is one of the many occasions where one has a chance to lose one's confidence in the logical-analytical methods Philosophy of Language still advocates.

III.IV. **Walking with Wittgenstein's Stick**[cdxii]

"One ought to ask [...] how the word 'memory' is used." (Peter Michael Stephan Hacker 1996: 492)

We have already come quite close to suspecting that the various ways of expressing oneself by applying phrases containing words like 'to remember ...', 'to recall ...', 'to recollect ...', 'to have a memory of ...', 'to retain ...' etc., can be a *kind of an extension of our means of expression* in daily intercourse by everyday language means. Nevertheless, in good old logical-analytical tradition, we should tackle the task of clarifying the relation between 'memory' and 'facts' and the problem of defining 'factual memory'.

Let me start with the question of the relation of 'fact' to 'memory' and what one sensibly could predicate about it: we may talk about

{i}   a 'memory of facts', a 'correct recollection', i.e. about 'factually remembering', or of 'remembering that so-and-so was the case';

or we may talk about

{ii}   the 'fact of (having) a(n) (accurate or inaccurate) memory about something', the case or fact or situation 'of (truly or falsely) remembering that ...'.

[cdxii]   Cf. *MS 109*: 38, *MS 110*: 274 f., *TS 211*: 293 f., *MS 114*: 136 f., *MS 156a*: 44r, *TS 212*: 612, *TS 212*: 1022, *TS 213*: 367 f., *MS 116*: 241, *MS 119*: 140 *et* 119v f., all of these citations in Wittgenstein's writings (mainly from the thirties) show that he had a walking stick.

The last citation concerns an incident with Anna Rebni in Skjolden from Sept. 1937 or earlier; she must have felt threatened by Wittgenstein's stick (cf. the allusion in McGuinness 1988b: 298), with which he jokingly or "caressingly" played around in a manner she was not used to. To use his stick as an extension of his means of impression was a kind of personal rite of himself, cf. "Remarks on Frazer's *Golden Bough*", Wittgenstein 1993b: 137.

Perhaps it was the same habit of playing with objects when at a Cambridge occasion he seemed to have shaken the famous poker towards Karl Popper. Yet the poker he surely did not use as a support in walking. (Cf. Edmonds & Eidinow 2001; I have to thank Ralph Jewell and Deirdre Smith for having drawn my attention to this journalistic piece).

The usage {ii} can be addressed as a situation whose specific circumstances might vary from case to case in communication, when one tries to make *true statements about somebody's memory* or just *to describe or qualify somebody's memory*;[cdxiii] for the occurrence of memory-expressions a la {i} we can, more narrowly, use the term 'factual memory'. The aim is, of course, *to discern and determine whether in making statements of the sort* {ii} *one could infer statements of the form* {i}, viz. if we can conclude from the statement about somebody or oneself 'having a memory of ...' that somebody or oneself has 'factual memory', i.e. that somebody or oneself really and truly recalls a fact. The difficulty lies in

{iii}   the possibility of 'false memory', i.e. in a state of affairs or situation where somebody has a recollection of something which was not the case or was not the case in the way s/he describes her/his own recollection of it, so that his/her statements of the form {ii} can be true as descriptions of him/herself subjectively having some memory, whereas any statement of the form {i} is not clearly and reliably fulfilled. So s/he can be ascribed to subjectively believe in recalling something, whereas s/he factually does not.

We have to admit that {iii} is a case frequently experienced in communication with others, but also in observing oneself: We somehow know or believe that we remember according to {ii}, yet what we remember is doubtful, hazy, unclear in its status and relevance sec. {i}. Let's discuss this a bit, by using the formalism already introduced:

Case {i} *presupposes just a description of a state of affairs*, (S), which is *truly or correctly recalled*, (M^S). So here we start with the truth of (S), (S) states a fact. Hence in stating what is signified by '(M^S)' as a claim of 'factual memory' one would also assert the truth of (M^S).- Here arises a meta-logical problem of signification, aporetic and enigmatic: Shall we write

"we express/state (M^S)"

or shall we write

"we express/state '(M^S)'"?

[cdxiii]   So we need memory-expressions of the sort {ii} to attribute 'factual memory' to somebody in statements of the sort {i}.

The single inverted commas usually indicate that one talks about the sign for that what is thus signified. So if I talk about '@' I do not talk about what @ stands for but about what this sign signifies!

Yet '(M^S)' deputizes for a statement of 'factual memory' of (S). The sign '(S)' denotes a true statement (that was a requirement of {i} above), which is recalled by asserting (M^S). By asserting (M^S) one does *not* talk about '(M^S)', and by talking about '(M^S)', one does not assert (M^S). Yet by expressing that what is signified by '(M^S)', one states or asserts (M^S). If then '(M^S)' denotes the expression of a fact (of the kind called 'factual memory'), then (M^S) itself just expresses this fact, which comes up to assert 'factual memory'. So *the expression of 'factual memory' is a fact*, and ergo (M^S) is a fact *because* '(M^S)' denotes it, which is a completely absurd consequence. *An expression of memory is not therefore 'factual memory' because it is called 'factual memory'.*

The semiotic problem condenses to the question with what right one applies the name of 'factual memory' if confronted with some memory-expression. {i} holds that (S) must be true in order to call '(M^S)' the sign for 'factual memory', in other words, (M^S) signifies only then 'factual memory' if (S) expresses a fact of which '(M^S)' expresses veridical memory. So to state '(M^S)' is completely different from stating (M^S).

If (M^S) *is* a statement, we can assert its truth. But '(M^S)' *signifies* a statement, and *it is senseless to talk about the truth of a signification*, unless the sign applied is a symbol of the form of a statement,[cdxiv] but '(M^S)' does *not* refer to a statement, it still *indicates a sign for a statement.*

One should for the following discussion keep in mind that *memory-expressions do not represent or signify what they are about*; to say that somebody remembers some state of affairs does not depict a memory which refers to a sentence expressing this state of affairs. (M^S) does *not* signify (S), whereas '(M^S)' signifies (M^S).- The signification of (M^S) shall also be written as M(M^S), so the sign 'M(M^S)' equals in this regard '(M^S)'. And this, in all its brevity, anticipates already the answer to our question raised in inf. {v}: To say that M(M^S) is true talks about the justification of applying the signifier '(M^S)', and the claim of (M^S) is justified if (S) is true.-

In case {ii} a sentence (Σ) might be about a memory (of a statement) of a fact, i.e. *about* (M^S), and putting aside the question of how to determine (Σ)'s truth and

---

[cdxiv]   Ch S. Peirce would have called it a legi-sign, I suppose, but this is leading us astray.

what criteria one might have in doing so, we shall read (Σ) as *a statement about the presumed fact that somebody remembers something*, accompanied by a description of this memory-situation.[cdxv] Then '(Σ)' deputizes an expression of something of the form 'M(M^S)', to say it in German: "die Darstellung der Erinnerung von (S)". (Σ) is then to be addressed as something like a/n picture/ image/documentation/expression/representation/model/[cdxvi] of (a/n assertion/ documentation/description/occurrence of) a certain memory-act. If I am allowed to display a formalism which rests on Herbert Stachowiak's 'General Model Theory' (in short: *GMT*).[cdxvii]

In case {i} we just stick to our symbolism as applied above, so '(M^S)' signifies that one really remembers what is expressed by (S), so one has a memory about (S). Shall we then see the form '(M^S)' as standing in lieu of 'factual memory',[cdxviii] as being the first step of its conceptual analysis?- Let's require that

$$\{iv\} \quad \sim((\Sigma) = (S)).$$

Shouldn't a sentence describing the memory of somebody be distinguished from a statement of a memory? Here the paradox arises by asking: Is then M(M^S) the same as (M^S) or not? In substituting 'M(M^S)' for (Σ), we arrive at formula {v} which shall be read as a question whether the first disjunct (a negated molecular statement) or the second disjunct holds, i.e.:

$$\{v\} \quad \sim(M(M^S) = (M^S)) \vee (M(M^S) = (M^S)) ?$$

In other words, *would then the statement about the (factual) memory of (the statement of) a fact*, taken in some semantic system as representing the fact of a

---

memory of a fact, *coincide with simply remembering that very fact?*[cdxix] Is there a difference between talking about having a memory of some thing and about actually remembering this thing?

If the condition {iv} is not complied with, the syntactico-semantic *representation of the factuality of memory could be identified with actually expressing memory*. So to talk about someone remembering something would be the same as giving an expression of really remembering something (granted that it is always the same thing which is said to be remembered). One might then inquire if there would be any reasonable talk of *inexpressible remembering.*[cdxx] So far, so good.- But now I reach up with my crucial, devastating, confusing query:

{vi}   What could a symbol $'(M^\Sigma)'$ mean, if $'(\Sigma)'$ is defined as $'M(M^S)'$?[cdxxi]

This seems to lead to a conceptual collapse; remembering the true statement (Σ), which itself semantically represents the documented or expressed 'factual memory' of a statement (S), would *then*[cdxxii] just be a *claim of a factual memory of something which itself is the actual memory of something*. This now can be *misread* as a Wittgensteinian answer, dependent on his refusal of {iv}.

Does, then, Wittgenstein mind identifying the representation of the memory of a fact with the expression of 'factual memory'?- Yes, he does; memory-expressions occurring within language-games of remembering do *not exclusively* represent 'factual memory', as we have seen (we play other games with them, too; they are quite versatile).

From this one could immediately infer the uselessness of any neatly circumscribed out-line and definitional capturing of 'factual memory', without

---

[cdxix]   In Peircean terms one could ask if memory-expressions are self-indicating, like (physical) objects (of perception) are, if taken as indices. I ask myself if Wittgenstein's view on first-person psychological statements grants an answer in the affirmative to this.

[cdxx]   Is it then the inexpressible memory thereof one has to be silent? Or is it the unconsciousness of psycho-analysis, which then works its way up to outward behaviour in Freudian slips of the tongue?- One has to feel the tension produced by advocating too much explicitism in order to grasp the radical approach involved!

[cdxxi]   I do not want to suggest a "theory of memory-levels", analogical to Russell's logical Theory of Types (cf. i.a. Russell 1908). A memory of the expression of remembering a fact is *not* the memory of this fact but of another fact, namely of having expressed a memory of this fact; cf. sup. *nota* **cccxxiii**.

[cdxxii]   Provided that {iv} does *not* hold, hence (Σ) = (S).

running through all these long-winded natural language counter-examples the smart reader is so easily fed up with. It seems to look like a *reductio ad absurdum*, whose outcome we have already anticipated before starting off with this logical strategy, whereas it is a historical fact that Norman Malcolm, the Wittgensteinian scholar, former student and friend of Wittgenstein, rose and dealt with the problem of 'factual memory', yet without maintaining that it exclusively represents the core of memory-expressions.-

We have now kind of shaken Wittgenstein's stick long enough in ironical attempts to frighten the representatives of a logical-analytical approach to 'factual memory'.

III.V. Memory as Attitude to Knowledge

"The capacity to retain information is memory." (G. Evans 1995b: 235 f.)[cdxxiii]

Well, Eddy M. Zemach 1968 critically refers to Malcolm's explication of a concept of 'factual memory' *without giving up the claim that such a definition can be achieved.* We shall, in brief, have a look at both. Malcolm 1963c: 236 cryptically states, a

"person, B, remembers that p from a time, t, if and only if B knows that p, *and* B knew that p at t, *and* if B had not known at t that p[,] he would not now know that p" (italics sec. Zemach 1968: 526 f.; correction of punctuation by G.G.),

which Zemach tries to refine, {1} by drawing our attention to the circumstance of one sometimes forgetting previous knowledge and being reminded of it, hence

"a definition which makes it impossible for us to distinguish between cases in which one learns something entirely new and cases in which one comes to remember things known previously, cannot be an adequate definition [of 'factual memory'; G.G.]" (Zemach 1968: 527),

---

[cdxxiii] Evans' definition is quite empty, besides one aspect of interest, namely the practical aspect of 'capacity'. If "information" here shall be expressible in statements of facts, then we can redefine Evans' attempt by: "The capacity to retain expressible knowledge about facts is *memory*", and this capacity presupposes the capacity to express knowledge, hence language.

and {2} by accurately pointing out that someone might *believe* that s/he is *not* remembering anything, so his/her knowledge of a fact *p* might not be called 'memory knowledge' at all (op. cit. 528).[cdxxiv] This in its entirety is a profound criticism and improvement of Malcolm to which I wholeheartedly agree.

Zemach then proceeds with his own intricate definition, which involves the application of operators of propositional attitudes[cdxxv] to sentences already containing such operators.[cdxxvi] I comment this version (slightly altering it):

> "*B* [factually] remembers *p* iff *(1)* *B* believes *p*; and *(2)* if *B* believes *p*, then *B* knows that *p*; and *(3)* if *B* knows *p*, then *B* knew that *p* in the past; and *(4)* *B* believes that s/he knew that *p* in the past" (sec. Zemach 1968: 529).[cdxxvii]

For Zemach the antecedent in (3) implies p, so from knowing the fact asserted by (T) one can safely infer the truth of this sentence (T),[cdxxviii] whereas the whole condition (3) is to purport that if there is a (personal) knowledge of a fact now, then there must have been some past getting to know this fact.[cdxxix] Thus, I do not read Zemach as intending to say that "p was the case in the past", but as stressing with condition (3) that

---

[cdxxiv] This rules out any conception of 'unconscious memory' as a case of 'factual memory'; cf. sup. *nota cdxx* and inf.

Although I find Zemach's painstaking analysis winning in its brevity and perspicuity, I cannot bring myself to give up any meaningful use of 'unconscious memory as factual memory' in the sense of somebody remembering something but being unaware thereof. Think of the cases of traumas or of dispelled and suppressed experiences (and it is not only psycho-analysis which accepts this as a possibility not only for insane and mentally disturbed persons).

The fact narrated in example (X) from sup. *section III.III* could be the consequence of a traumatic distortion of a factual memory (M^X) referring to the looks of the lady mentioned in (X).

[cdxxv] Think of the example

(Y)   "*A* believes/knows that *q*";

(Y) expresses *A*'s attitude to the proposition *q*.

[cdxxvi] Think of the example

(Z)   "*B* believes/knows that *A* believes/knows *q*";

it expresses *B*'s attitude to (Y) and hence it states *B*'s attitude to *A*'s attitude to the proposition *q*.

[cdxxvii] "Iff" is an abbreviation of "if and only if" (today a quite often applied symbolic convention).

[cdxxviii] Cf. as well Malcolm 1977: 118.

[cdxxix] Plato's *anamnesis* is ruled out.

"the knowledge of p was acquired in the past",

and not necessarily a time-dependent knowledge itself, since p could be eternal or timeless, think of mathematical formulae.[cdxxx] Zemach's discussion of point *(4)* reveals that his epistemic definition of 'remembering a state of affairs' *contains a genuine constitution of the knowledge involved in remembering.-*[cdxxxi] Let's look at an example Zemach offers:

> <α>   "If I remember that my grandmother used to speak Russian[,] I must believe that, in the past, I came to know the fact" (Zemach 1968: 529).

Before I enter another reservation, I want to dwell upon the question whether this sort of talk about the

"concept of factual memory of q containing the belief in having learnt q"

is now about analytical entailment or not.[cdxxxii] I read this, enlightened by Zemach's own discussion, as *ruling out* Russell's fancy idea the hypothesis it is *logically* possible

> <β>   "that the world sprang into being five minutes ago [...] with a population that »remembered« a wholly unreal past" (Russell 1921: 159; cf. Malcolm 1977: 115 ff., Malcolm 1963a: 187 ff. or Schulte 1995b: 96 f.).

[cdxxx]   Cf. Hacker 1996: 483.- If the sentence p stands for "My past understanding of x", then my getting to know or recognition of my past understanding of x or my being confronted with it again (while I had already forgotten it) could still have taken place in some (later) past. The fact, yet, that it is not raining in Bergen, Norway, on the evening of Feb. 18th 2003, is certainly a state of affairs for particular time-space-coordinates and will tomorrow have been such a former state of affairs or 'past fact' (which as a term ought better be avoided), although it keeps being a true sentence corresponding to a fact to say that it surprisingly *wasn't* raining at this specific time at this place (it usually rains a lot in Bergen, at all seasons).

[cdxxxi]   But is the belief in knowledge-acquisition in *(4)* the only (propositional) attitude one could have in the case of 'factually remembering'?- I suggest replacing *(4)* with *(4)**, i.e.:
*(4)**   "*B* believes/knows that s/he knew that p in the past",
which opens up for the discussion whether my current knowledge about my former knowledge need not have been acquired itself? *How could I know now that I knew before?* By remembering, as a matter of fact – And we end up in a vicious circle!

[cdxxxii]   This is a different sort of analyticity than the one we dwelled upon in sup. *nota cccxxiii.*

Here, Russell's understanding of remembering does not imply any veridical propositional attitude towards a personal acquisition of knowledge of facts one later on can remember.[cdxxxiii] But why does he enter into this?

Russell's motive is to emphasize that there is no logical tie between our knowledge of the past and the past itself. That which distinguishes memories from other contents of consciousness for Russell are the feelings of pastness and feelings of familiarity (sec. Schulte 1995b loc. cit., Malcolm 1977 loc. cit.; cf. Russell 1921: 168 ff.). Against this, as we have seen above, Wittgenstein argues that these feelings might accompany memory-acts or memory-experiences, but that, conceptually assessed, remembering does not depend on these feelings as well as not on some memory-image or representation.

Russell's use of the word and concept 'remembering' is awkward, that is the immediate feeling one has when reading about it, because here it refers to something that could be addressed as 'faked fact', and it does so by means of a 'faked memory'. Why should this reference then not also be called just a 'faked reference'? What guarantee can an inhabitant of Russell's faked world have that his/her memory is not a dream or conflated with imagination and illusions, or that the memories of others are not? If these faked inhabitants share a common attitude to the pastness of remembered facts, they would share a belief in a fake − *without any chance to check if this agreement in a form of life[cdxxxiv] is a fake or not.* But if one in principle cannot check if one's idea of pastness of something remembered really refers to something past, one is free and as a philosopher vindicated to doubt any memory-expressions pretending the existence of such a reference.[cdxxxv]

Could there in Russell's faked world be any form of *documentation independent from (faked) memory-beliefs* apt to (falsely) convince these inhabitants of a faked world that they have 'factual memory' instead of their 'faked memory'? Perhaps memory-traces, some physiological change in these (faked)

[cdxxxiii] I entered "veridical" since in Russell's spirit one could argue that with this 'world' jumping into existence propositional attitudes are also implanted into persons and their minds. To maintain the logical possibility of *this* equals claiming that one's usage of language in doing so can, of course, not be affected by this very logical possibility.
But how, then, could we ever know that and be certain about it? How can we then decide that our whole discussion is not fancied as well? We touch here the theme of solipsism, cf. i.a. Bell 1992.

[cdxxxiv] Cf. loc. cit. sup. *nota ccclxxiii.*

[cdxxxv] A philosopher is also committed to doubt this.

people's (faked) brains?- No, these traces and engrammata[cdxxxvi] etc. would also be created, just in the way as these inhabitants are created!

Which commonly acceptable criterion could these faked inhabitants exhibit by which they come to an agreement about the factuality of such a documentation of the factuality of their memory? The definite answer is, almost too Wittgensteinian: *There would not be any difference between the judgement about the criteria for stating such an agreement and the criteria for the judgement about the existence of such an agreement*!

One can immediately conclude the (epistemic) necessity of a connection between factual memory and a factual belief in personally having acquired the knowledge of the fact recalled or being recallable, and such a necessary or even semantic link[cdxxxvii] might be seen as the actual and inevitable belief in personal acquisition of knowledge being analytically contained in the concept of 'factual memory' to be reconstructed here. The analyticity of the bond between a genuinely personal acquisition of knowledge of some fact and a 'factual memory' of it is a conceptually essential quality Russell overlooked.

But what, concerning the example <α> of my memory of my grandmother having spoken Russian, if I can remember that she talked strangely in a language unintelligible to me, about which I, at some time in my childhood, was told by my mother that this *was* Russian? To get to know that the language Granny was talking was Russian was then some *additional information*, thus my memory depicts a synthetical knowledge which depends on my taking for granted what my mother said – and later on I might discover that it was Bulgarian what my Granny spoke, and not Russian![cdxxxviii]

So *I have to learn now that I was misinformed then*, that I never acquired knowledge in this point and therefore *had only the right of naiveté to believe in it*, but nevertheless was remembering correctly the same fact of my Granny having spoken in a tongue alien to me which my mother (and I) mistook for Russian. So

---

[cdxxxvi] At least at the time of his "Analysis of Mind", Russell held a physiological-chemical theory of "mnemic phenomena", which he learned from the German Biologist Richard Semon's, whose book "Die Mneme als erhaltendes Prinzip im Wechsel des organischen Geschehens" he quotes (cf. Russell 1921: 77 ff. and Semon 1904).

[cdxxxvii] The semantic link consists in the possibility of the explication "Memory teaches us what is past" (cf. sup. *section III.1*).

[cdxxxviii] Let's say, after her death I discover an old tape in her belongings with her voice and let my friend, the Slavist Noam, find out which language it is one can make audible by listening to the recording.

my memory was justified, although I would need express it a bit differently to have the right to claim 'factual memory'. I believed that I had acquired knowledge about my Granny's linguistic abilities, but in fact I was misinformed, although my 'factual memory' still rings from her old vibrating voice, perhaps with such an accuracy that I hear her talking in this tongue still alien to me!

If the tight attachment of 'factual memory' to 'belief in acquisition of knowledge' *empirically* or through subsequent experiences with information value can be refuted, *we might not want to understand it as a necessary or a priori link any more*. So through this ramified train of thoughts we arrive at the insight that *the description of our belief in getting to know a fact might change, even though the fact we remember and our factual memory may epistemically still be the same.* Is this an indication that the connection between 'factual memory' and 'a belief in knowledge acquisition' is not a priori, although 'analytical', not necessary, but *contingent and conceptual?-*[cdxxxix] According to Glock, Malcolm holds that

> "the causal connection between experience and remembering is a contingent
> fact rather than part of the concept of remembering." (Glock 2000: 243)

I have just talked about the *conceptual* connection between an attitude towards knowledge acquisition and remembering being contingent and analytical; *I do not maintain the causality of this tie*, knowledge acquisition or the belief in it does not cause remembering or 'factual memory', and vice versa: *'factual memory' does not cause a belief in knowledge acquisition*. Otherwise Russell's fancy idea would be logically possible, i.e. by creating memory one would be able to cause that the persons having this construed 'factual memory' believe that they have acquired the knowledge about the things they remember.

But these persons do only believe that they remember, because by Russell's creation of a world they were made (in such a way as) to believe in having memory, they do not really have any 'factual memory', because they have not acquired any memory! Russell's thought-experiment fails because the link between causation of memory (through creation) and beliefs in knowledge-acquisition is not conceptual, and its contingency is empirical, whereas the tie between the concept of 'factual memory' and a belief in having acquired the knowledge of that what one remembers is analytical, although it can be called

---

[cdxxxix] This would be another form of "exotic necessary truth" as suggested by Donnellan 1983 in reflection on i.a. Kripke 1980 and Putnam 1979.

'contingent' in the sense that the same 'factual memory' can refer to some (expressible) knowledge about the fact in question whose ways of acquisition itself is then just contingent.

Couldn't the inhabitants of this creation of a world in Russell's thought-experiment come to this conclusion, reprimanding their creator for this logical fallacy (if they could only meet him?). No, in my point of view they can't (even if they could contact him in one way or other):

For the first-person-language-user the (claimed, imagined, indoctrinated, imposed, induced) 'factuality of memory' cannot be doubted on phenomenological grounds due to a *lack of criteria*: As Michel ter Hark diligently points out, the

> "descriptive interpretations of the first person [...] fail to do justice to what we call descriptions. And since these introspective 'descriptions' typically take the form of 'memories', they fail to do justice to the language-game of remembering as well" (ter Hark 1990: 104 f.),

and ter Hark calls it a "ground-floor fallacy" that all psychological concepts are reduced to the same introspective type.[cdxl] In his agreeable opinion, "Wittgenstein does not base his argument against private language on the fallibility of the memory" (loc. cit.).

Without denying inner sensations or the impression of an inner process in remembering,[cdxli] Wittgenstein rejects the idea that an image of an inner process gives us the right idea about applying the word 'to remember'; he remains

> "solely interested in the question of how we understand the language of the senses or the language of memories" (ter Hark 1990: 106).-

So the created memories' contents of the inhabitants of a five minute old world in Russell's scientific romance[cdxlii] *cannot* be taken as the inner referents of a private language, and because of that *Russell's speculation cannot be refuted on the grounds of a wrong idea about expressing psychological concepts* (which is, by the way, neither Wittgenstein's nor my attempt undertaken here). So what about the logical possibility of 'memory creation'? Wherein then lies the absurdity?

[cdxl]   M. ter Hark loc. cit. points to *MS 119* and *MS 120*, as well as to *MS 116* part I, to entries I date around autumn 1937 and winter 1937/38.

[cdxli]   Cf. i.a. "Philosophische Untersuchungen" I §§ 305 f., Wittgenstein 1984, Band 1: 377 and see Ayer 1985: 75 ff.

[cdxlii]   Cf. loc. cit. sup. <β>.

In departing a bit from Wittgenstein's argumentation I give the following reasons: The *genuine constitution of knowledge involved in 'factual remembering' is itself a fact*, sometimes worth remembering, and the logical possibility of it excludes the creation of memory ex nihilo, although the propositional attitudes towards one's genuine constitution of knowledge are under a description not necessarily, yet factually related to one's own factual memory (iff they are veridical). If one has not forgotten what one once got to know and hence still remembers it (as a fact), then one also knows that one has learnt it, even if one does not exactly recall how and when one learnt it. Therefore the possibility of Russell's 'creation of memory' becomes absurd.-

In his Cambridge lectures from the thirties, Wittgenstein called Russell's idea of the world being created five minutes ago "meaningless" (cf. Wittgenstein 1982a: 25 ff.). Let me quote a bit from this passage:

"Russell's hypothesis was so arranged that nothing could bear it out or refute it. Whatever our experience might be, it would be in agreement with it. The point of saying that something has happened derives from there being a criterion for its truth. To lay down the evidence for what happened five minutes ago is like laying down rules for making measurements. The question as to what evidence there can be is a grammatical one. It concerns the sorts of actions and propositions which would verify the statement. It is a simple matter to make up a statement which will agree with experience because it is such that no proposition can refute it [...]" (Ludwig Wittgenstein 1982a: 26).

Here, as an aside, Wittgenstein is closer than ever to Popper's conception of falsifiability.- A bit before this passage, still in the notes on the lecture "Philosophy" I § 22, we find: "Russell said that

remembering cannot prove that what is remembered actually occurred, because the world might have sprung into existence five minutes ago, with acts of remembering intact. We could go on to say that it might have been created one minute ago, and finally, that it might have been created in the present moment. Were this latter the situation we should have the equivalent of »All that is real is the present moment«. Now if it is possible to say the world was created five minutes ago, could it be said that the world perished five minutes ago? This would amount to saying that the only reality was five minutes ago. [...] There is a grammatical confusion here. A person who says the present experience alone is real is not stating an empirical fact [...]"(Wittgenstein 1982a: 25)

After this follows the passage quoted above.- Here, I think, Wittgenstein makes two closely intermingled points, or better: Wittgenstein makes his point be showing that there is a connection between two points, one *against a certain form of solipsism*, that only my present experience is real,[cdxliii] the other *against the possibility of a creation of memory along the lines of Russell.*

Wittgenstein's ingenious strategy to argue contra Russell and the imagined "creation of 'factual memory' together with a world" is *to shorten the age of such a creation until it coincides with the present moment*, thus letting the time of creation of reality and the time of creation of memory be the present experience; so the present experience *becomes* the creation of 'the world' and any 'memory' of it (in such a world, memory would then *not* tell us what is past, since the only past one could know of is the one of whose 'existence' we were created to have an impression at this very moment of experience). This is *a reduction of Russell's fancy idea to solipsism.* The refutation consists in hinting at the concept of (this form of) solipsism not being an empirical one.

So what Russell's fantasy creates is just as less real or as much real as a dream, and the inhabitants of this fancy world with their fancy memories are then like the inhabitants of a dream who are ascribed some memory about the dream *in the dream.* This amounts to Wittgenstein saying: The logical possibility of which Russell talks is nothing but a dream, and in dreams and in fantasy there is no logic. *Russell's suggestion does not prove anything about the logical possibility that the world was created five minutes ago with a population whose memory was created at the same instant*, in contrast to Russell's claim, it is just an evidence for Russell's creativity.-

Russell's idea, which was in favour of the logical possibility of such a combined memory-world-creation, is absurd since there cannot be a veridical description or ascription of propositional attitudes towards the genuine constitution of knowledge which is created together with this fake of a factual memory-creation.

Either the people in Russell's fancy world have these propositional attitudes to their knowledge-acquisition or they know that their memory is created and hence false (if the have a concept of 'factual memory' or at least of 'memory' at all) – unless one wants to go on *creating ad infinitum* foundations for memory-creations by assuming that:

[cdxliii]   That goes against William James 1890.

{1.}   the information about the world and the memory of the world is also created;

{2.}   that the propositional attitudes towards one's knowledge-acquisition, too, are created;

{3.}   the opinions these created inhabitants of a five minute old world have, that they are real, are created as well, thus excluding the possibility of inquiring into one's own solipsism;

{4.}   any criterion for checking whether something is a fact or not can accordingly be created on demand, what is the ultimate joker.[cdxliv]

All these creations 1. – 4. are set in action in order to found a supposition of created memory, and any doubt or possible objection can be done away with by further fancied creations, whereas the only way to create (cognitive, epistemic, factual) memory is the genuine constitution of memory in a personal history, and this creation has a recallable personal history itself which goes along with propositional attitudes towards it.-[cdxlv] Russell's talk about the simultaneous creation of (factually false) memory and the world is clever talk about something fancied which cannot have a correspondence in reality. The logical possibility of memory-creation in Russell's understanding is the logical possibility of fancying, nothing more.

Another point concerning propositional attitudes towards one's knowledge and the personal history of one's knowledge is that *one might remember things in which one does not (want to) believe or even cannot believe* (which one cannot accept to be true, due to other, e.g. moral, reasons). Whether this is now 'unconscious memory' or not (interesting for psycho-analysis), it might still be 'factual memory' by referring to a known or knowable fact *without leading to an*

[cdxliv]   It reminds me of the fairy tale where one encounters a fair lady which reveals herself as a fairy by offering to fulfil one three wishes. I would at least spare the last of these three wishes for wishing for at least two more of these free wishes (and then I would go on in the same way with every last wish of the still unused wishes). This would replenish me with an infinite list of free wishes on my demand.
This presupposes that the fair fairy sticks to her offer as promised. I do not know how I would react if the fairy turns out to be an evil ghost. (I just might think of Descartes and wish for an argument which could save the situation.)

[cdxlv]   This could serve us for defining 'historicity': The cultural concept of 'historicity' requires the personal memory-history of those people whose attitudes towards the reports on history act as a criterion for their assessments, whereby such a personal memory-history does not necessarily involve a personal acquaintance with the experiences and events historiographically described or taken account of.

explicit description of any such belief or acceptance of knowledge about this fact. An example of this could be a traumatic experience: one's conscious memory might detect some traces of what happened, either to oneself or to someone close, while at the same time not wanting to believe or to talk about it.

Yet I might have to admit here that the assertion of the factuality of such a form of memory might be met with a reluctance to ascribe it any credibility *by others*, even though it is 'factual memory' from the point of view of the knower who states "I remember *y*", meaning the factual memory of *y*.

This is connected to *the factual problem of witnessing*, of the rhetorical and pragmatic dependencies of the witness' report being regarded as reliable, supportive for a judgement, as effective, e.g. in a court. In the sense of the certainty of first-person statements about propositional attitudes[cdxlvi] the witness might truly be convinced that s/he knows this or that, just as certainly as I know it when I feel pain, but tragically enough, s/he could lack the very response to her/his testimony telling him/her that her/his reports *is met with belief*, s/he could even be regarded as an unreliable witness, a liar, as insane, etc.

The credibility of one's memory reports depends i.a. on the propositional attitudes of others towards one's claims of the acquisition of 'factual memory': Has s/he really experienced what s/he maintains to be able to recall? Is his/her story an account of the facts which make him/her produce these recollections? An important point in assessing the credibility of somebody else's memory report could be whether in telling what s/he insists is his/her memory s/he really believes in his/her own story! Even if giving an account of his/her own experience does not convince others, either because they attach little credibility to his/her claim to having an accurate 'factual memory' or because s/he does not clearly and consistently believe his/her own memory, she might nevertheless recall and give an account of facts!

This might be called "the tragedy of witnessing": one does not meet the attitude towards one's own 'factual memory' required for making publicly it accepted as 'factual memory'.[cdxlvii] Here I mean both, one's own attitude towards

---

[cdxlvi]   Cf. i.a. Malcolm 1986: 213; cf. inf. *section III.VI.*

[cdxlvii]   If Moore would have said, just to hint at the famous paradox (I don't want to enter further into this discussion, we shall take another turn at the very threshold), "I can't believe it" as an answer to "I remember that it rained", the problem would have been quite different.

one's own memory-report, as well as the attitudes of others towards one's own story about one's own 'factual memory'.-

All these complications just discussed show us that even in the case of 'factual memory' the *quest for a concept or norm of how to tackle the problem of definition does not lead to any ideal answer*. The logical-analytical spirit remains quite unsatisfied, especially if striving for a general concept of at least 'factual memory'; and on Wittgensteinian grounds (if I ever can stick to them) I get the impression that this lack of satisfaction is not unwelcome, since *this sort of 'factual remembering' is mistaken as a key feature of mind as such, independent from any other understanding of 'remembering' and 'memory'*, however well it may be analysed and defined. The term 'memory as such' as a hidden essentialism does not make sense, because the language-game of 'factual memory' is not the only language-game we play with memory-expressions, and not all of these language-games are semantic references to 'factual memory'.

So what Russell's fairy tale[cdxlviii] about a created world with created memories does, is to attempt (fruitlessly) to introduce a new game we can play with memory-expressions. In doing so, he walked along the borders of "logical possibility". But by going over the limits of language, the semantics changed, and he ended up with something equivalent to a phrase revealing

"somebody dreams having remembered something",

which is totally different from the (partial) phrase's meaning

"factually remembering something",

even if one recalls *this* particular memory-dream.- But there are other cases which additionally show us the manifold meaning of memory-phrases, some of which we have already touched upon. I shall now quickly discuss those with *a specific pragmatic aspect* we hitherto have not paid much attention to. Think of the appeal or recommendation, so frequently found among philosophers, who use this phrase, of course, to show off:

<γ>   "Remember to read this book!",

which is semantically equivalent to:

[cdxlviii]   Cf. loc. cit. sup. <β>.

<δ>   "Don't forget to read this book".

Yet in a pedagogical context it is advisable to use the first phrase, not the second, because the second contains a negation which pragmatically might be less inviting to follow, and since <δ> is less direct than <γ> it is less apt to serve overtly the purpose of boasting to being a well-read and helpful scholar. Or ponder the question (one could direct to Russell):

<ε>   "Do you remember how to use this word?"

More than <γ> or <δ>, the example <ε> refers to a *pragmatic dimension* and almost completely neglects the semantic sphere. The question <ε> is about (*the quality of) one's linguistic competence* and asks for a performance proving or re-establishing it (it can easily and with a similar effect be countered with a slight tone of it being question-begging). *The 'factual memory' of the usage of a word or term is not so much about semantic reference but about knowledge of language-games, i.e. about the capability of speech-acts.* Less intricate, at least at first glance, is

<ζ>   "Do you remember how to use this tool?",

since <ζ> does not ask for the performance of a speech-act but of a mere act; <ζ> could be answered by an act of ostension, i.e. by actually using the tool <ζ> is about (think of a hammer). Answering <ε> yet can also be regarded as an act of ostension, yet only *if the reply to <ε> is a speech-act applying the word and thus showing one's practical memory of the usage of this term.*
Performative speech-acts under (situational, contextual) conditions of that which could be called 'institutional or conventional remembering' like

<η>   "Let us recall our dear friend's long and successful life which recently
         found an unexpected end so many of us mourn over now",

held as a speech at a funeral or at Memorial Day,[cdxlix] are also examples of a pragmatic or rhetorical component in memory-phrases which are concealed by an

---

[cdxlix]   Other situations like these could be anniversaries, birthday parties, toasts, weddings, etc.; the formal traits of such performative speech-acts would resemble those of example <η>, the words and other circumstances chosen could vary.

all-embracing semantic concept called 'factual memory', because one need not factually remember the dead person to meet with the social conventions of a funeral, to listening to a speech there on behalf of the person to be buried. One is merely expected to display a certain respectful, mournful behaviour, might be supposed to wear a tie or dark clothes (and sun-glasses might be used to hide the joyful twinkles of one's eye).[cdl] I think, here the mere outward behaviour of pretending to mourn and remember suffices, there is no personal 'factual memory' required, and not even the speaker of <η> really is compelled to have any 'factual memory' of the deceased (yet s/he must have some capability in pretending to have some knowledge about the deceased).[cdli]

This list of examples of the pragmatic bearing of memory-phrases upon our communication could be enhanced indefinitely, and *not all of them need to be represented as appeals or invitations to remember*. Just think of:

<θ>　　"Capri is a memorable place",

which praises something one might not have the slightest personal acquaintance to, remarkably by appealing to memory, or look at

<ι>　　"Any evidence about the involvement of the US government in the assaults of Sept. 11th 2001 would be worth recollecting".

Both examples <θ> and <ι> are not about the things in question (i.e. Capri or the evidence about a certain crime) really recalled or actually kept in mind but *about an assessment of their quality in regard to our interests*, in other words: *recommendations to get to know and to treasure the things these statements are*

[cdl]　　Another, more trivial thing is that at funerals one need not know the deceased in order to attend it. Yet this is no pragmatic case of any language-game of remembering at all, it is not even such a case.

It might be, that what I describe above holds more for the priest or a funeral director or some other professional (journalists, professionally engaged mourners, etc.) than for the usual or casual attendant of a funeral.

The point of my example is that one can behave as if mourning a certain person's death at the occasion of a funeral, even at the occasion of somebody publicly bringing forth some recollections in calling for recalling the dead person, without actually remembering anything about this person, neither her/himself, nor any even or experience connected to her/him.

[cdli]　　I would say, academic anniversaries are good occasions to study all the ceremonies of 'conventional remembering' and the rhetoric and pragmatics they involve.

about. So Capri, indeed, might be memorable as such and of high interest to become acquainted with, and any evidence, if ever discovered and if extant, showing the involvement of the current US government in these terror-assaults would, indeed, be worth collecting and recollecting, for the records and for future memory, if not for other, say political or juridical purposes.

In this sense *memory-phrases function like a safe, one can put things into these phrases and thus make them most interesting*; but the things and expressions referred to in these phrases need not be facts or refer themselves to facts:

> <κ>   "It is important in studying for the examinations at the end of the semester to remind your pupils of the name of the King of France at the time of Charles de Gaulle's death, since the examiner likes this sort of questions"

is an example about recalling somebody, viz. the King of France in the year 1970, who does not and actually cannot exist;[cdlii] ergo <κ> cannot reveal anything about 'factual memory' about a French *roi*, and it as well cannot, if taken seriously, lead to the pupils acquiring 'factual memory' or knowledge about this king (whether he was bald or not …).

Yet <κ> *can perform something in the name of a certain authority*, which is not some monarch's magnamity to exist but the *authority of the speaker* of <κ>: imagine some strict headmaster in a school in Paris, for instance, mindlessly uttering <κ> at the occasion of ordering, preparing, and guarding a young history teacher in his first teaching experiences in class. Unfortunately, the situation of uttering <κ> is also *an example of a perfomative self-contradiction of the speaker's authority* thereby marshalled (and this is the real wit of <κ>), since the headmaster's authority is lessened by his factual mistake about the Republic of France being a monarchy.

<κ> is the interesting example of performing an authoritative appeal with intent to induce the retention of a certain name, and in this pragmatic function it seems to work without any references to facts at all. The point for us is here not so much the factual failure, on the headmaster's side, of an authority to perform

---

[cdlii]   The non-existence of a King of France during the Fourth *Republic* of France (for which Charles de Gaulle served as a soldier and general) or the Fifth *Republic* of France (whose first president de Gaulle was) is a conceptual point; even if there existed some infant of the last monarch of France who claimed the right of ancestry to the throne, s/he could not be the monarch of a republic!

accuracy, but that *this case carries a speech-act which involves a memory-phrase whose reference to facts is irrelevant*, even though <κ> distinctly points to an acquisition of knowledge and carries with it a certain belief in the correctness of knowledge thus acquired. *The attitude towards knowledge-acquisition is there*, at least in the intention of the speaker of <κ>, and the target of the authority imposed on the listener to <κ> seems to be *to firmly establish this attitude in the spirit of the context of teaching, learning, schooling, and training*. The person uttering <κ> exploits the notion of 'factual memory' even if the requirements for this concept being applied correctly are not fulfilled.-

Malcolm himself has later relativized his own definition of 'factual memory' when he writes that the

> "belief in the centrality of factual memory fits hand in glove with the picture of thinking" (Malcolm 1977: 142).

By saying this, Malcolm somehow has a tractarian kind of propositional conception in mind. Later on Malcolm resists to these tendencies,[cdliii] just as the later Wittgenstein did, by *denying* that

> "remembering is necessarily picturing or representing" (Malcolm loc. cit.).

'Remembering' behaves here just as 'thinking', for both 'representing' is not the essential feature. But if 'representing' is not central any more, then also 'factuality' of memory loses its core position, *especially if a representation or expression of memory shall refer to the representation or expression of facts in memory*.-[cdliv]

In a sort of crash-course through a pile of philosophical literature about and around the 'concept of 'memory', on 'remembering', 'recalling', etc., Norman Malcolm 1977 i.a. draws the conclusion that *for any attempt to define a general, all-embracing concept of memory there could be counter-examples* taken from our everyday language use. Empirically and conceptually these show that we apply the words 'to remember', 'to recall', or phrases containing 'memory' or 'recollection', etc., also in ways that do not go along with such a term restricted in its meaning to, e.g., a 'general concept of factual memory'.

[cdliii] This is one of the reasons why I like Malcolm 1986.

[cdliv] Cf. sup. *section III.IV.*

III.VI. **Memory as a Socially Construed Attribute of Mind**

"The question, »In what does remembering consist?«, should be answered in this way: It doesn't consist in anything." (N. Malcolm 1977: 53)

It is, for a well versed scholar at least, *no* surprise that *one quite quickly infers the family-resemblance*[cdlv] *of words like 'memory' or 'remembering' in our human language.*[cdlvi] The uses of these words live their linguistic lives quite undisturbed by any philosophical analysis in the stream of intertwining language-games where speech is accompanied by acts, talk by deed[cdlvii] – and no unique or complete, unambiguous, fundamental meaning of these words can be singled out.[cdlviii]

"The moral to be drawn from [...] countless other passages in *The Brown Book* is one that we shall encounter again in the *Investigations* [i.e. "Philosophische Untersuchungen"; G.G.]: that the application of a word to a number of instances does not depend on their having a character, or a set of characters, in

---

[cdlv] Cf. *MS 111*: 139 from Aug. 1931, *TS 211*: 72 from Sept. 1931, *TS 211*: 745 from Jan. 1932, finally *MS 115*: 56 from Dec. 1933, edited in "Eine Philosophische Betrachtung" ad exempla 21 *et* 70, Wittgenstein 1984, Band 5: 129 *et* 170; see also "Philosophische Untersuchungen" I §§ 65-71, Wittgenstein 1984, Band 1: 276 ff.; "Vermischte Bemerkungen", Wittgenstein 1984, Band 8: 469; etc.
The oldest entry of "Familienähnlichkeit(en)" is *MS 111*: 119 from Aug. 1931, the last is from Jan. 1948 in *TS 232*: 740 and from March 1948 in *MS 137*: 37.

[cdlvi] Malcolm 1977: 211 comes to talk about Wittgenstein's concept of 'family-resemblance', yet he *fails to make explicit its application to similar words* like 'memory', 'retention', 'recollection'.-
I agree with Wittgenstein, and take the term 'family-resemblance' as a central and algebraic term, applicable in a wide sense.

[cdlvii] Cf. i.a. Seekircher 1995; Malcolm 1977: 221 observes:
"[...] that what determines whether an expression of a language is understood or misunderstood[,] is the common practice of a community of users of that language, i.e., of a community of people. Such a practice is a pattern of responses and actions. *Language is embedded in actions – in deeds.*" (comma and italics mine; G.G.).
This is a most concise explanation of the term 'language-game' whose usage itself cannot be kept from obtaining the character of family-resemblance to concepts like 'speech-act' (cf. Biletzki 1997 and my comment in footnote 16 ad Gelbmann 2002e) or 'performatives' (in Gelbmann 2002c I somehow come near to this). Cf. for substantial support of the thesis that acting is at the bottom of our language e.g. Stroll 2002: 451 ff. and "Über Gewißheit" § 204, i.e. Wittgenstein 1984, Band 8: 160 f.

[cdlviii] In contrast to us is Benjamin 1956, who refuses to regard the word 'remember' as equivocal.

common, but rather in their possession of a variety of features which constitute what Wittgenstein calls »a family resemblance«" (Ayer 1985: 59; italics original; G.G.),

as Alfred Jules Ayer concisely summarizes in his book "Wittgenstcin", saving us any further elaborations of this well-known term, central in Wittgenstein's post-tractarian period(es).[cdlix]

We can apply this description to the *family-resemblance of memory-phrases* in discovering that *not only different semantic usages, but also pragmatic aspects* are employed in the way we talk about memory, apply memory-phrases, play the language-games of remembering, and communicate in speech by using expressions containing words like 'memory', 'to remember', 'recollection', etc.- This leads to the final inquiry, namely *when and how do we attribute to somebody having memory or to remember something*, now taken more narrowly in the sense of 'factual memory'? When are we justified in our attitude towards somebody else's memory-claims? Partly *this can be answered by looking at the detectable propositional attitudes towards one's memory-claims and the truth-conditions for a description of these.*[cdlx]

On the other hand one has to talk about the socio-epistemic side of this coin: above in *section III.II* we have already touched the terms 'semantic memory' and 'semem' embedded in the *social language-gaming* and in *section III.I* the term 'situation' was introduced.[cdlxi] Interestingly enough it seems to complete our relativism that the term 'factual memory' is contained in the 'semantic universe' of which my 'semantic memory' becomes a part in my social language-gaming. At the same time my personal 'factual memory' contains the term 'semantic memory', although I hardly ever play a language-game in everyday life employing this term.

But the riddle is dissolved when one realizes that the occurrence of a word or *lexem* does not automatically entail that it is a generally definable concept and a cultural unit or *semem* with a unequivocal usage; the concept of 'semantic memory',[cdlxii] as a model of (linguistic and semantic) reference was not designed

---

[cdlix] The term 'Familienähnlihchkeit' is chiefly from Wittgenstein's middle-period, i.e. from the thirties (cf. sup. *nota cdlv*), not so much from the time after having finished and abandoned what is today called "Philosophical Investigations" part I.

[cdlx] Cf. sup. *section III.V*.

[cdlxi] Cf. sup. *nota cccxxx*.

[cdlxii] As explicated in Gelbmann 1998.

to serve as a definition of 'factual memory', and the occurrence of the term or *lexem* 'factual memory' in a semantic memory and its transformation into a cultural unit or *semem* thereby does not enlighten its conception or definition. We all use terms without being able to define them logically and analytically; but *what I try to show in this essay is even a bit stronger, namely that not only do the language-games of remembering go further than the term 'factual memory' does, the term 'factual memory' itself seems not to be semantically definable* if one looks at the variance and pragmatic aspects of its application.

Eco 1976 explicitly introduced the 'Model Q' to try to represent the pragmatic features of semantic reference with the idea of a 'semantic memory' sec. M. Ross Quillian 1968. But the 'Model Q' uses the 'semantic memory' of Quillian only *via analogia*, as *a picture for the language-gaming in a semantic universe*. For every *semem* occurring in this 'semantic memory', represented as a node in the huge multi-dimensional network called 'Model Q' of a *culturally organized semantic mind*, it holds that it belongs to family-resemblances.The crucial question then is,[cdlxiii] in what sense the terms 'Model Q' and 'family-resemblance' themselves have a clear reference to an unequivocal meaning. My answer today is that this is only so relative to a certain, personal 'semantic memory'. *The language-games of Wittgensteinian terminology cannot be played with everybody.*

Here I only want to *draw a difference between two memory-situations* occurring within this language-gaming of 'remembering', and this shall throw a spotlight on to what extent the *attribution of (semantic) memory is a social and semiotic act of qualifying subjectivity*.[cdlxiv] In my terminology, as subsequently shall be developed and enhanced, the case

> *(€)* to *remember a state of affairs involving persons*, to have a memory with at least a tinge of a *communication-situation*,[cdlxv] and thus implying the recalling of a constellation of persons to states of affairs in a situation involving attitudes these persons take to the states of affairs they refer to,

---

[cdlxiii] As I already addressed in Gelbmann 1998.

[cdlxiv] I pondered titling this section or the whole essay with "Semiotic Subjectivity IV", in continuation of a series of lectures I gave in Bergen, cf. Gelbmann 2002c, Gelbmann 2002d, Gelbmann 2002e.

[cdlxv] For the term 'communication-situation' cf. Gelbmann 2000b and Gelbmann 2002b.

shall be distinguished from a case

> *($)*   of *recalling a mere constellation of things* or of events or a *memory of a state of affairs*, i.e. a case where the attitude of the persons in the case remembered does not play any role;

yet I do not venture to speculate on a '(temporally distributed) constellation of states of affairs' as recallable.[cdlxvi]

In case *($)* there is *no thought of the phenomena themselves being remembered as having minds and retention.*[cdlxvii] So as a memory-act *($)* is a phenomenon free of any hindsight to socio-semiotic subjectivity as an object of memory, whereas in the case *(€)* there is not only the touch of other minds present, but in fact *a form of recollection depicted which could practically be counter-checked with the expression of the memories of the communicants* (or a sufficient documentation of it).

Therefore *(€)* reveals something about socio-semiotic subjectivity of memory in the sense that one attributes to other minds the same ability in retention and in language-gaming. So *the case (€) will involve actual language-games in social situations*, it depicts even cases of attitudes towards memory-reports, whereas the case *($)* could occur in solitude or at least without any hindsight to the attitudes being taken to its report! The difference depends on what is recalled, whether the recalled phenomena itself was situational sec. *(€)* or constellational sec. *($)*, to venture these adjectives.

This does *not* mean that *($)* is not performed by language-games, but in case *($)* there are *no social, communicative criteria for the correctness of a memory.* Look for example at remembering a dream; there is no contrast between 'correctly remembering' and 'seeming to oneself to remember' (cf. Malcolm 1956: 32). In contrast to this, in case *(€) one has to reckon with some way of being corrected*, either through direct intervention by persons involved and present in one's own expression of memory, or by some documentation rendering evidence about others who could confirm our refute them.

[cdlxvi]   This would lead to an ontological problem of its own complexness, viz. the question of temporally distributed sortals like persons who are identical with themselves and recallable as such during their life-times, although their circumstances, the states of affairs in which they are found, their situations, language-games, even their memories are under change.

[cdlxvii]   For the term 'phenomena' cf. sup. *nota cccv.*

In remembering along the lines of *($)*, *one does not need to see memory as a social attribute of mind*, i.e. as something potentially involving other persons for the correct ascription of 'factual memory', one simply ascribes the ability to recall and the correctness of one's recollection to oneself. Yet if memory is enacted and displayed according to aspect *(€)*, the *social attribute of mind called 'memory' is a part of the rules of the game*, and the judgment or trust in the 'factuality of memory' becomes a socio-semiotic task requiring not only the settlement of the question whether the propositional attitudes towards the facts remembered and the memory expressed are justified and reliable, but also whether one is convinced or can convince others.

This is the reason why someone might feel forced to make public a recollection in sense *($)* in order to give it the validity and reliability of sense *(€)*; it is not only the publication of e.g. *memoirs* that have this purpose of turning *($)* into *(€)*, the situation in court called "witnessing" is of exactly the same strain.-[cdlxviii] There seem to me to be two interesting points connected to this distinction between the aspects *($)* and *(€)*:

<χ>   The distinction between *($)* and *(€)* is *not a priori*, since one cannot without any empirical hindsight be certain in the assumption that the expression of a memory-act recalls a mere state of affairs without involving any situational aspect, although one's intention might go in this direction.

<ψ>   The conviction itself, that a certain memory-expression is of type *($)* or *(€)*, *depends on a social situation* or on a communication situation.

The first-person-statement,

(J)   "I remember (that) X",

intended as a case of knowledge of 'factual memory',[cdlxix] could be both, a case of *($)* or of *(€)*, uttered to oneself in isolation about something only I can know and

---

[cdlxviii] Cf. *section III.V.*

[cdlxix] It could also be understood in other ways, e.g. in phrases where X stands for dreams, cf. Malcolm 1956: 32. This is another reason (for which an exception can be found sup. in *nota cccxxiii*) to think that this sign 'X' can just deputize for any sentence or speech-act or any type of meaningful expression. Exactly this logical fact makes it impossible to construe an "algebra of memory".

relate to, or brought up in a conversation or in such a form that it is *about a situation*, either by affecting the situation in which (J) occurs, or by being about a situation of social dimension.

In case *($)*, if I use the words properly, one simply cannot doubt that (J) is true, i.e. that I really remember that *X, X will be some inner state, feeling, sensation*, or an expression reporting on the occurrence of such an inner state, feeling, sensation, something which I and only I can see, feel, experience. So the usage of

(Ä)   "I remember that I had a toothache exactly on the same day a year ago"

is comparable to the often discussed Wittgensteinian interpretation of the expressivist account of first-person psychological statements as:

"I am in pain";[cdlxx]

it expresses an *incorrigible personal experience* by directly expressing memory itself, just as "I feel pain" can be read as an expression of pain, or as demeanour caused by pain.[cdlxxi] In Wittgenstein's mode we could clothe it in the words:

(Ö)   "Only I can know if I really remember ...".

Yet *this form of first-person-factual-memory-of-experiences is no form of knowledge*, since if my memory deceives me (because an operation of my brain, to imagine a science fictional situation,[cdlxxii] causes me to have this memory), I would still believe that I have it and hence I would qualify a description of my remembrance as true or correct, even though it factually does not deserve that.

But to use (J) in the sense of *(€)* means to witness or report on something (which might be related to the current situation in directly affecting it or not),

---

[cdlxx]   Cf. i.a. "Philosophische Untersuchungen" I §§ 404 ff., Wittgenstein 1984, Band 1: 407 f.; Edoardo Zamuner is to be credited with drawing my attention to these passages.

[cdlxxi]   Cf. N. Malcolm 1954: 542; cf. i.a. "Philosophische Untersuchungen" I § 246, Wittgenstein 1984, Band 1: 357.

[cdlxxii]   Russell's invention of a 'created memory' would also cause one to have a subjectively indubitable memory; yet to turn (Ö) into a statement about 'factual memory', involves the aspects *(€)* and <ψ>: The communication-situations with others sec. <ψ> might licence one to use (Ö) without making explicit that one keeps in mind that others conventionally granted one this special status.

which can be checked and confirmed or refuted, at least on grounds of the possibility of some documentation; so even if (J) is only an expression and not a statement, it asserts something in the context of its occurrence, viz. having a knowledge about X combined with an epistemic attitude towards the genesis of one's acquaintance with X. If I say

(Ü)   "I remember having been at the dentist lately",

it expresses a fact which due to some investigation could prove to be falsely asserted, by simply showing that I was lying or that my memory failed or that I was made to believe in having been there, since *it does not fit with the reports of others or the documentation and evidences others can produce*. In this sense to say "I remember ..." means "I assert/believe/assume to have factual memory of ...", and it comes up to a *claim of knowledge combined with the claim of an attitude towards the personal history of this knowledge.*

The point seems to be that expressions of first-person-factual-memory of situations or states of affairs claim knowledge in interpersonal situations, whereas first-person-factual-memory of subjective experiences simply expresses a personal attitude towards one's experiences beyond knowledge, even though it might rethorically be accompanied by an explanation of

(#)   "I know that I remember ...".[cdlxxiii]

In the latter sense memory, indeed, resembles pain ..., viz. insofar the expression of a sensation or experience is the personal attitude itself, with the difference between the case of pain and the case of memory that the first could be substituted by natural expressions like moaning (pain-behaviour), whereas in the latter case the natural expression of remembering for the first person is just *not able to* take the attitude of hesistating, doubting, qualifying one's confidence in it.

If "I am in pain" is (like) pain-behaviour, "I remember ..." is *the* memory-behaviour, it is the only form of how we can take and express a propositional attitude to a past knowledge we entertain again, to a re-gained knowledge; in the first case one might think of substituting the linguistic phrase with something else, in the second case the linguistic phrase *is* the memory-behaviour. Consider especially the *seemingly* obvious truth of:

[cdlxxiii]   Cf. Malcolm 1951: 335.

(§)   "I cannot have your memory".

According to sup. $\langle\psi\rangle$ a social situation could be brought about which excludes any reply of (§) on the grounds of a memory-report of a witness under aspect *(€)* without violating $\langle\chi\rangle$. And this seems to be *the institutional achievement of witnessing about one's memory-contents*, where memory-expressions are taken as speech-acts under aspect *(€)* in order to lead to *a commensurabilisation of the propositional attitudes towards the facts memorized and reported as factually recalled.*

Such a consensus is neither a priori constituted nor empirically discovered but ideally socio-semiotically construed through the logical force conviction enacts upon the semiotic subjects taking part in the communication situation; memory as an attribute of mind is then socialized and shared if it as such an attribute of mind depends on the social presuppositions of language-gaming. The agreement on the factuality of a memory-report will then depend on the documentation of evidence for the facts remembered and reported, and the fact that somebody remembered correctly will further the judgements about the memory-claims consistent or inconsistent with this one displayed here.

'Good memory' then is *both*, 'factual memory' displayed in personal as well as public records, and grounded in the control of the language-games that constitute our form of life as a participation in the semantic memory of our culture, the heritage of our semiotic being.—

Essay IV. Hintikka's Blind Spot:
Social Conceptualisation of Pragmatics[cdlxxiv]

IV.I. Pragmatics as a Non-Empirical Science

My criticism of an outstanding analytic philosopher's view on pragmatics starts with a quotation I take from a known paper "Language-Games", delivered by Jaakko Hintikka in honour of Georg Henrik von Wright in 1976.[cdlxxv] Although this paper is worth reading for a variety of reasons,[cdlxxvi] I shall, almost in a

---

[cdlxxiv] This essay has two main sources of which it was re-composed in the present form: In spring 2002 I gave the first of a series of three lectures at the University of Bergen, Norway (i.e. Gelbmann 2002c), whose (a bit more elaborated) text was concomitantly rendered as a web-site. This is the background for the first half of this essay. This essay's second half has its source in two slightly different e-mails, presenting a draft of *section IV.VIII* to *section IV.X*, which I wrote in reaction to the paper Jaakko Hintikka gave at the 2001 Wittgenstein Conference in Kirchberg am Wechsel, Austria (the very paper which was published as Hintikka & Hintikka 2002).

In late summer 2002 I had already discussed with colleagues (chiefly with Anat Biletzki from the University of Tel Aviv and Ludovic Soutif from the Sorbonne University, Paris, both research colleagues at the Wittgenstein Archives at the University of Bergen) the thesis of Wittgenstein's dyslexia that was advocated by Hintikka & Hintikka 2002. Nevertheless it was only until early 2003 that I could get hold of the article itself, to which I reacted with sending out these e-mails.

The feed-back was that Edoardo Zamuner from the University of Bologna, Italy, at that time my research colleague at the Wittgenstein Archives at the University of Bergen, and Allen Janik from the Brenner Archives in Innsbruck, Austria were supportive. Ludovic Soutif in Paris and Alois Pichler from the Wittgenstein Archives at the University of Bergen promised to write back, a promise they so far (mid May 2003) have not achieved to make true. I also have to add that Kevin M. Cahill meant that such a project is always worth while.

The reaction of Anat Biletzki in personal communication in April 2003 is worth retelling: she said that Hintikka sometimes is provocative and ironical. To my retort that I could not sense any irony in those of Hintikka's writings I refer to, since nothing in his style marks any irony, she replied that this is just the essence of irony that it is *not* marked. Well, she knows Hintikka personnally, could be that he means things ironical which I take serious. But if this is so, then my critique can just be ironical as well.

[cdlxxv] Cf. Hintikka 1976, re-edited as Hintikka 1996l.

[cdlxxvi] For an anticipation of the later game-theoretical approach to the semantics of language-games, cf. Hintikka & Sandu 1997.

Wittgensteinian manner, pick out only one passage. I do not want to criticize Jaakko Hintikka's philosophy in its impressive entirety but only on some crucial points *his concept of 'pragmatics'*, that he himself relates to Wittgenstein, as I shall soon demonstrate.

I have not digested Wittgenstein,[cdlxxvii] and probably have nothing at all to say about him, but let me comment on others who comment on him, and then let's see if it is possible to get anything out of Wittgenstein's various writing for my current purpose: *to take a stand against a certain idea about pragmatics and the social aspect*; about the connection or relation between these two notions. Hintikka seems to see it as a contingent and empirical relation, whereas *I sense a conceptual necessity to see pragmatics under a social aspect*, particularly with regard to communication.

Let me begin by rather naively questioning *whether pragmatics really can be conceived of as not being an empirical science.*[cdlxxviii] I was bewildered when I came across some lines by Hintikka written in 1976 – and I take the liberty to quote at length:

"Since the basic representative relationships between language and reality were left unanalyzed [...] also in logical semantics, Wittgenstein's idea of language-games as establishing those relationships marks an at least potential advance over the customary logical semantics and not only over the picture theory. Unfortunately this relevance of Wittgenstein's later philosophy to contemporary logical and linguistic theorizing has been overlooked virtually completely until recently. One reason has been the unsystematic character of most of Wittgenstein's thought and of the thought of most of his followers. Another reason has been a misunderstanding concerning the kind of use of language exemplified by Wittgenstein's language-games. This misunderstanding is often embodied in definitions of the familiar trichotomy syntax-semantics-pragmatics [...] [[cdlxxix]; G.G.]. Syntax is the study of language (and its logic) without

---

[cdlxxvii] I wonder if one could ever reach such a state of accomplishment.

[cdlxxviii] My surprise's background lies in my own personal biography, i.a. in my doctoral dissertation about the Pragmatic Theory of (Interpersonal) Communication (*PTC*) by Gregory Bateson, Don D. Jackson, Janet H. Beavin, Paul Watzlawick and others, cf. Gelbmann 2000b and Gelbmann 2002b.

[cdlxxix] Here Hintikka quotes (among others) Colin Cherry's still valuable compendium "On Human Communication", which is an important source for Watzlawick & Beavin & Jackson 1967. Cherry 1965 takes a much wider and full-blown semiotic account of Communication and pragmatics than Hintikka seems to have realized. Yet *the famous definition of pragmatics* as *the study of use of language* is a myth, it is not what Cherry says, as we shall see. Cf. inf. *nota **cdlxxxii**.*

reference to its representative function, while this function is studied in semantics. Pragmatics is defined as the study of the use of language. The misunderstanding I am speaking of consists in taking pragmatics, so defined, to be an empirical science, part of the psychology and sociology of the language-users. The fallaciousness of this idea is less surprising than its prevalence. For of course we can study certain aspects of the rules governing the use of a language in abstraction from the idiosyncrasies of the people using it. This feat is no more remarkable, I am tempted to say, than studying syntax in isolation from the idiosyncrasies of handwriting and typeface. If pragmatics is a part of psychology and sociology of language, syntax ought to be by the same token a part of graphology.

Yet the *idea of pragmatics as an empirical science* was for a long time surprisingly prevalent. Applied to Wittgenstein's language-games, it of course had the effect of sweeping them right away into the 'pragmatical wastebasket'. [...] Even though in the last few years serious attempts have been made to develop explicit logical and philosophical pragmatics, little notice has been taken by most of the logicians working in this area of Wittgenstein's ideas." (Jaakko Hintikka 1976: 119 f., i.e. Hintikka 1996l: 290; emphasis by G.G.)

Why is it so startling that somebody, who might be far more important in the academic business of philosophy than I am, *declaredly addresses pragmatics as a non-empirical science*? And what sort of science would it then be?-

First of all, let's look at *how Hintikka himself defines 'pragmatics'*: He sees pragmatics merely as the study of the use of language;[cdlxxx] *not* as the study of the

---

[cdlxxx]   In Hintikka & Halonen 1995, one can still find narrow and one-sided understanding of pragmatics as language-use. Yet in this paper, there is at least more consideration of the empirical side and the role it plays in explanation. They suggest a re-evaluation of Hempel's famous explanation-scheme (cf. Hempel 1965), which, in its "covering-law model", is

"not a purely deductive task, namely, the logical derivation of the explanandum from the covering law plus the initial condition [...] an explanation [...] consists of an interrogative derivation of the initial condition and of the specific covering law starting from some background assumptions *T*. [...] the task of explanation means a search for a derivation of the explanandum from *T* interrogatively. This normally involves putting questions to nature and is therefore an empirical rather then a purely logical task." (Hintikka & Halonen 1995: 657)

To describe the process of questioning nature as a pragmatic one is fine enough, yet as a process it is inevitably social. *The pragmatic side of this interrogation is idealized if its social complexity is neglected.* Since Hintikka et al. here are chiefly interested in the structural and formal components of the interaction of such an interrogation with regard to explanation, their focus is not on the practical implementation of this process in socio-epistemic sign-processes; rather, they concentrate only on certain aspects and features of pragmatics.

triangular relation between signs, meanings, and sign-users, which is the semiotic definition stemming from Ch. W. Morris[cdlxxxi] and applied by C. Cherry, whose book "On Human Communication" Hintikka himself quotes![cdlxxxii] Many authors adopted the definition of pragmatics as the study of semiotic phenomena in the fully developed semiotic dimension

> (1)   of the sign-character(s) themselves,
> (2)   of the semiotic character(s) of reference/denotation/meaning/sense, and
> (3)   of the semiotic character(s) of interpretants/sign-users/semiotic subjects.

It is not too far fetched to roughly identify aspect[cdlxxxiii] (1) with 'syntactics',[cdlxxxiv] aspect (2) with 'semantics', and aspect (3) with 'pragmatics' (actually, writers as early as Cherry 1965 and also Watzlawick & Beavin & Jackson 1967 do exactly this).

If pragmatics studies the use of language, as Hintikka loc. cit. sup. says, then I ask: *Who is it that is using language? What sorts of interaction does their*

[cdlxxxi] Cf. Morris 1938.

[cdlxxxii] Cf. how Cherry sees pragmatics as the full dimension in which syntactics and semantics are contained:
"It is at this level that the true process of human communication can be considered – the use of signs by people in specific circumstances and environments, the whole »effectiveness« problem of Warren Weaver. To the pragmatic level we must relegate all questions of value or usefulness of messages, all questions of sign recognition and interpretation, and all other aspects which we would regard as psychological in character. Again, the concepts of meaning *to* specific people reaches this level; associations of signs and designata in the mind of someone, in some specific situation, are semantic-pragmatic questions." (Cherry 1965: 244)
W. Weaver formulated the "effectiveness problem" in his preface to the famous study by Shannon: "The Mathematical Theory of Communication" (i.e. Shannon & Weaver 1949), which gave a physico-syntactical theory of the transfer and transformation of signals in communication without any further hind-sight to pragmatics.
I agree with Cherry's view that the effectiveness problem belongs to pragmatics and has *also* to do with the psychology (and the sociology) of the transformation and reception of messages. The reader should also acknowledge that Cherry defines pragmatics as "the use of signs", and has a wider notion of it as Hintikka with the definition "use of language".

[cdlxxxiii] As a matter of fact, Morris 1938 talks about "dimensions" and not about "aspects".

[cdlxxxiv] Or 'syntax', but this term I would reserve for purely logical purposes, whereas the more general word 'syntactics' is Morris' semiotic term.

communication via language bring about? What sort of being or expert must a sign-user be, if not merely a single empirical subject, a person who can easily fall prey to some empirical, social or psychological investigation, subjected, e.g., to an opinion poll about the expected results of the coming elections? *Is there anything conceptually specific about the sign-user that could turn pragmatics from being a pure empirical matter into some other sort of problem?* Can a pragmatic study of language-use exhaust the concept of pragmatics if from the very start one excludes the social aspect in its empirical embodiment?

Even if language were *only* a tool, there should be some *communicants*, applying it – not to mention that language, indeed, is not only a tool but a *social institution.*[cdlxxxv] Therefore, the use of language is, to some degree, unavoidably "collectivistic", to use an ill-fitting phrase I borrowed from Michael Luntley (who might have objected, as I presume).[cdlxxxvi] When I disagreed with Luntley on the occasion of his previous lecturing, by saying that *'use'* (*and 'practice'*) *itself already presupposes some social sphere*, some societal settings, if this term occurs in combination with terms like 'symbol', 'language', or 'communication', then *the use of language cannot be a private conceptual affair*; it always requires a multitude of users, and *'practice' used as a frame of reference for Wittgensteinian 'language-games' is tightly knitted to the social sphere.*[cdlxxxvii]

One cannot have a form of life all to oneself, and if I refer to a practice as the basis of my language-gaming, then I refer to the practical application of a form of life by making use of the public and social institution of language, *by being a social subject.* From my point of view, and I do not intend to exploit this subject further, *a solipsist would neither have a language nor the concept of language,* since s/he would never communicate.

The usage of communicational means is social per se, and communication, for example in the form of (verbal or written) actual natural language, can only be understood as enacted by practices of a social character, involving other social subjects. What I am going to approach here is *a demonstration of the under-*

[cdlxxxv] Cf. "Bemerkungen über die Grundlagen der Mathematik" VI § 32, Wittgenstein 1984, Band 6: 334. Cf. i.a. also G. E. M. Anscombe 1976, Searle 1995: 76 ff., David Bloor 1996.

[cdlxxxvi] Prof. Michael Luntley (from the University of Warwick, United Kingdom), was a guest researcher at the Wittgenstein Archives at the University of Bergen in spring 2002. Unfortunately he had already left when I gave my lecture, cf. sup. *nota cdlxxiv*, which partly also criticized him.

[cdlxxxvii] Cf. e.g. "Philosophische Untersuchungen" I § 197, Wittgenstein 1984, Band 1: 343.

standing of 'pragmatics' as a social and even communicational concept, a demonstration of the social character of sign-use and of *the practical being of sign-users as the conceptual point about their essence and not only as an empirical and contingent attribute*. At the same time, our lives as sign-users *must be empirical* since sign-use itself could not take place if it were not for our experience and sensations. Sign-use is based on the phenomena of interaction and our semiotic being with *materia*.

Therefore, contrary to Hintikka, my view is that *pragmatics is not only a conceptual, but also an empirical undertaking*, and this holds *in virtue of its social implications*. To say, as Hintikka does, that pragmatics is not an empirical science is just as wrong as to say that mathematics has nothing to do with logic (what does not entail that mathematics can be reduced to logic[cdlxxxviii]); just as logic and mathematics are formal, pragmatics has an empirical aspect, which *consists in the only possible realization of pragmatics in a social sphere, in communication and sign-use*. This does not entail that there are formal and abstract traits about pragmatics, which can only be reduced to a socio-empirical level; in the same sense there are formal and abstract traits about physics, which cannot be reduced to mathematics, although they can be described by mathematical means.

IV.II. **Internal Relations Socio-Semiotically Scrutinized**

Let us enter a more Wittgensteinian subject (which was only at the margin of Luntley's talks, although he mentioned it in his eloquence), and let me attempt to apply a semiotic reading which, to my knowledge, hasn't been yet done. Michel ter Hark, in his excellent study of Wittgenstein's philosophy of psychology, titled "Beyond the Inner and the Outer",[cdlxxxix] deals with the crucial term of 'internal relation', which we find throughout Wittgenstein's writings.[cdxc] If what he says

---

[cdlxxxviii] I am not favouring some form of foundationalism; pragmatics, in my understanding, is a subject neither for (syntactical-semantical) logicians nor for sociologists or psychologists, but for semiotics. Yet *semiotics involves a social conceptualisation of its subject*!

[cdlxxxix] Cf. ter Hark 1990.

[cdxc] The theme of "interne Beziehung" and "interne Relation" can be traced through Wittgenstein's whole Nachlass and life, although the meaning of these terms seems to vary. The earliest occurrence stems from the notebooks of his time in the Austrian-Hungarian Army: an entry from Oct. 24th 1914, cf. *MS 101*: 61r, edited in Wittgenstein 1979b: 18. The last occurrence seems to be from April 1st 1951 in *MS 176*: 1r, published in

holds, then *we must rebuff Michael Luntley's reading, which excluded a conceptual role for social life*, who, despite everything, referred[cdxci] to this term of 'internal relation' but did not give its definitional reconstruction.

In contrast to Luntley, Michel ter Hark made a painstakingly accurate study a decade before the Bergen Electronic Edition of Wittgenstein's *opera omnia* was published,[cdxcii] where he extracted the following *definition of 'internal relation'*:[cdxciii]

> "(i) It is impossible that both relata do not have this relation to each other. (ii) The relation is not mediated by a third term. (iii) The internal relation exists in a practice, in a language." (ter Hark 1990: 47)

With this in mind, I'd say that *the relations between signs, their meaning(s), and the sign-users have to be carried by internal relations* Wittgenstein[cdxciv] sees prevailing and conceptually constituting the relationship between 'aspect' and 'object', 'emotion' and 'object', 'image' and 'object', between 'inner' and 'outer', between 'pain' and 'expression', 'sensations' and 'descriptions'[cdxcv] (and perhaps also between 'fact' and 'memory').[cdxcvi] Let me first rephrase ter Hark's definition for clarity sake, before I go into detail. For the *concept of 'internal relation'* it necessarily holds that:

ad (i)   the relata of an internal relation *necessarily* have this relation to each other;

ad (ii)   there is *no indirect, representational, or interventional mediation*, no means by which this relation is brought about; there is nothing in between or supporting this relation;

"Bemerkungen über die Farben" I § 1, Wittgenstein 1984, Band 8: 13.

[cdxci] I refer to Luntley's lectures at the University of Bergen from spring 2002.

[cdxcii] A critical masterpiece on the several edition projects dealing with Wittgenstein's literary heritage and being explicitly critical against Michael Nedo has my full consent: cf. Hintikka 1996b. It firstly came out 1990 and again in 1991 and describes not only the failures of the Tübinger Wittgenstein Archive and the project(s) of Nedo, but supportively refers to the Norwegian edition project, that in the meantime has resulted in the Bergen Electronic Edition.

[cdxciii] This is one of my favourite citations, cf. i.a. Gelbmann 2002b: 32.

[cdxciv] Sec. ter Hark's reconstruction.

[cdxcv] It may be hardly noticeable, but *this* is the gist of my lecture.

[cdxcvi] I implicitly head in this direction in *Essay III*.

> ad (iii) the actualization of this internal relation takes place *in practice*, in language, i.e.: *the internal relation is realized within a social dimension.*

In other words, the relations between certain entities or concepts as occurring in Wittgenstein's philosophy of psychology: are firstly, *not semantic or representational.*[cdxcvii] Secondly, the are *empirical insofar as they are socially performed*, embodied, and enacted. And thirdly, they are *indispensable and factual insofar as they are constitutive for the "internality" of these concepts.* The internal relation between these relata are constituted by their experienced social performance, and by the indispensable factuality of their existence. If one can rely on anything at all, then one should rely on this.

The internal relations depict the framing structure for our (social) reality, and for being able to refer to anything real about others or oneself. Therein lies the reason for pragmatics depicting the full dimension of our social life in sign and signification. As an example let us think about 'aspect': We see a change of meaning or interpretation when we see an aspect-change;[cdxcviii] and when we see something as something else, we have already an interpretation or a meaning of this new aspect of the image or thing. The meaning is based on an institutional framework of concepts that are ready to arrange our accurate ability in intending and expressing meaning.[cdxcix] This implies, in applying the aforementioned definition, that the relation image-aspect is realized in a social dimension, it is unmediated and impossibly inexistent.

But what does it mean other than this, that the pragmatic dimension of a conceptualisation of sign-use is constitutive for such internal relations? For it is internal relations which allow us perceive a sign as a sign! *That we see an object under the aspect of it being a sign, is due to the persistence of internal relations*! The habits of sign-use, the conventions and the institutional framework are the manifestation of such internal relations in our socio-semiotic life!-

Already as a young man Wittgenstein came upon some thoughts about 'internal relations', which I see as close to the semiotic concept of pragmatics I

[cdxcvii] This trait kept me from conceptualising 'factual memory' via internal relations, cf. sup. *nota cdxcvi.*

[cdxcviii] Cf. inf. See also M. B. Hintikka & J. Hintikka 1985a.

[cdxcix] Cf. the exclamation: "But how is it possible to *see* an object according to an *interpretation?*" in "Philosophical Investigations" II xi, Wittgenstein 1991: 200.

employed above.[d] Let me quote from his "Notebooks" from Oct. 26th 1914:[di] "[I]t looks", he writes,

> "as if the logical *identity* between sign and things signified were not necessary, but only *an* internal, *logical*, relation between the two. (The holding of such a relation incorporates in a certain sense the holding of a kind of fundamental – internal – identity.)
> The point is only that the logical part of what is signified should be completely determined just by the logical part of the sign and the method of symbolizing: sign and method of symbolizing *together* must be logically identical with what is signified." (Wittgenstein 1979b: 19; cf. *TS 101*: 63*r* f.)

How shall we read this? I venture a reading in favour of the conceptual approach I try to advocate in this essay.

Therefore I would say that, within a natural language, things can work as signs because then the relation between things and sings is socially realized, unmediated and necessary.[dii] Here, the necessity Wittgenstein denies, is that of (logical) identity. I read the whole passage as a clumsy way to talk about the *pragmatic constitution of reference*, yet without having a full conception of it, but yet in being aware of the need for a semiotic dimension which enables one of signification. That's why he talks about the tie between the method of symbolizing and the sign as an identity.[diii]

Can this quotation from the early Wittgenstein be *taken as a definition of pragmatics by the use of the term 'internal relationship'*? I fear the answer to this is that such an internal relation in its realization depends on

---

[d]   I am aware of the fact that there are other concepts of 'pragmatics' I have not touched or employed here, e.g. linguistic concepts. But it deserves being mentioned that I agree on several points with the Polish linguistic Roman Kopytko from the University of Poznan in Polen, especially on the "non-Cartesian" conception of pragmatics, on a distinct distance to a formal-analytical and non-social understanding of 'pragmatics', on the many-factored aspects of pragmatics in communication; cf. Kopytko 2001 (this, at least, was my impression of our conversations in early autumn 2003 in Bergen, Norway).

[di]   Cf. sup. *nota cdxc*.

[dii]   "Logical", as Wittgenstein loc. cit. calls it, probably in clear contrast to any ontological reading.

[diii]   This rests upon *pragmatics forming our signification and sign-use in a way which enables it to force itself upon us* (the later Peirce wrestled with exactly this problem, but I do not want to be distracted here).- Furthermore, it entails that *a notation cannot be arbitrarily chosen*, something the early and more nominalistic Wittgenstein might not have noticed.

<ξ>   signification and codification,
<τ>   communication via sign-use, and
<υ>   communication of and about sign-use.

Hence it is a matter for pragmatics, if not even *the* matter of pragmatics as the full semiotic dimension. The points <τ> and <υ> imply a social dimension. This is why I think that the themes of 'aspect-change', 'seeing as' (especially in the case of sign-perception) and of *seeing some object or entity as a sign*, asks for a pragmatic inquiry,[div] because it involves *an investigation of the functioning of internal relations*. Let me dwell a bit on this point:

If I see e.g. the drawing of a rabbit as a duck, *I must already share some sign-practice and language with others* in order to be told that there is another aspect which mutually excludes seeing the drawing under the first aspect, or in order to actually see this thing signifying something else. We see some things as signs because of a pragmatically installed internal relation; *under other cultural and semiotic circumstances a sign-post might not signify at all or could signify in a different way*, and what, for a German reader, could be a handwritten "e" in one of Wittgenstein's manuscripts, might for an illiterate child be a picture or, for a Chinese, be a slip of the pen. Within a common language, the presuppositions <ξ>-<υ> are fulfilled; but *we actually only share a language if there are internal relations manifest in our practice of communication*!

Therefore, that there is a code-system according to <ξ> and communication according to <τ> are just basic conditions, but even condition <υ> is surely met, because we can communicate our sign-use to others and can clarify our sign-use by talking it. We can even talk about our communication, if we have a language in common.[dv] If we can read Wittgenstein's handwriting and know German well enough, we can discuss whether this or that letter was an "e" or an "r" or not, and we can determine our interpretation on the grounds of our language-use.

[div]   Hintikka 1976 loc. cit. does not even ask for the reasons why something can function as a sign!

[dv]   For a discussion of 'metacommunication' cf. i.a. Gelbmann 2002b.

IV.III. A Brief Interlude about a Transcription-Problem

Since this essay was written at the Wittgenstein Archives at the University of Bergen,[dvi] and since the transcription of Wittgenstein's Nachlass into the Bergen Electronic Edition provides us with an astonishing example of the *dependency of philological transcription on interpretation*, grounded in the knowledge of a language, I would like to briefly discuss how a handwritten word can be read either as the German "vor" (in English "before") or the German "von" (in English "from").

The case I have in mind is a passage in the Bergen Electronic Edition, where the transcriber(s) transcribe a hardly readable German letter in handwriting as a "v" whereas the editors of "Last Writings" II (G. H. von Wright and H. Nyman) read it as an "r". The detail of interest is that, founded on the internal relation between 'reading' and 'context', 'sign' and 'meaning',[dvii] and between 'interpretation' and 'context', I think there is a method of coming to a final decision about what the correct transcription and hence the intended reading should be.

I shall now quote both problematic passages, accompanied by an English translation. The first transcription, which I regard as *wrong*, renders:

German: "[...] Die Einstellung kommt *von* der Meinung" (*MS 169*: 60v from Jan. 1949 in the Bergen Electronic Edition; original emphasis in underlining, here rendered in italics; G.G.)
English Translation: "[...] the attitude comes *from* the opinion." (my translation; emphasis in italics; G.G.)

The second transcription has:

German: "[...] Die Einstellung kommt *vor* der Meinung" ("Letzte Schriften über die Philosophie der Psychologie. Das Innere und das Äußere. 1949–1951" II, I *MS 169*, Wittgenstein 1992b: 38; emphasis in italics original in the edition; G.G.)
English Translation: "[...] the attitude comes *before* the opinion." ("Last Writings on the Philosophy of Psychology. The Inner and the Outer. 1949–1951" II, I *MS 169*, Wittgenstein 1992b: 38e, translated into English by C.

[dvi] The original lecture (cf. inf. *nota cdlxxiv*) did not contain the following philological-philosophical critical interlude.

[dvii] Or between 'sign-appearance' and 'reading'.

Grant Luckhardt and Maximilian A. E. Aue; emphasis in italics original in the edition; G.G.)

Before I give my reasons why I think that the *second transcription*, and hence the reading of the problematic letter as "r" is *right*, I have to express my gratitude towards Simo Säätelä from the University of Bergen (currently at the University of Uppsala) for this example of a strange deviation of two editions of the same manuscript.[dviii] As far as I can remember, Simo did not give any reasons for why one should prefer one and not the other reading, but in a paper, Säätelä 2001, he clearly takes the same position I am taking now (that is: he reads and quotes the passage with "before"; the same does, by the way, a real expert on Wittgenstein's Nachlass, viz. Michel ter Hark 1994).

I think Wright and Nyman are more trustworthy in their knowledge of Wittgenstein's handwriting than any of the transcribers working at the Wittgenstein Archives at the University of Bergen for the Bergen Electronic Edition, who were among the best experts in this field one could recruit, and for this alone I have the good reason (also from other sources and cases) that Wright as a pupil of Wittgenstein and long-time editor, trustee and personal friend of Wittgenstein is more liable to be credited with a better acquaintance of Wittgenstein's handwriting than any other reader or transcriber.

But even if one had no knowledge of who the editors of the second reading are, what might bias one, or if one does not think that highly of their ability in reading this particular case of Wittgenstein's handwriting, one has enough reason to agree with me in my assessment, since *my reading can be inferred from the context of the problematic passage.* After having pondered that one always could say of a human being that he is an automaton, Wittgenstein asks and comments:[dix]

[dviii] He pointed it out to me in a private conversation in spring 2002; I think Simo knew it already in 2001, since his conference-paper Säätelä 2001: 258 quotes the passage from "Last Writings" II loc. cit. sup.

[dix] Cf. "Philosophische Untersuchungen" II iv, Wittgenstein 1984, Band 1: 495; edited again in "Letzte Schriften über die Philosophie der Psychologie. Das Innere und das Äußere. 1949–1951" II, I *MS 169*, Wittgenstein 1992b: 38.
The Cartesian *opinion* that all bodies of living entities (like animals, plants, or other human beings) are automota as *res extensae*, has not influenced Descartes' *attitude* towards other human beings as having a soul, since he eventually attributes others having a mind/soul (*res cogitans*)! Ergo, it is *wrong* to read this famous citation as an anti-cartesian account of Wittgenstein's concept of 'person'.

German: "Was aber ist der Unterschied zwischen einer Einstellung und einer Meinung?

Ich möchte sagen: Die Einstellung kommt *vor* der Meinung.

(Ist aber nicht der Glaube an Gott eben eine Einstellung?)

Wie wäre dies: Nur der *glaubt* es, der es als Mitteilung aussprechen kann.

Eine Meinung kann sich irren. Aber wie sähe hier ein Irrtum aus?" ("Letzte Schriften" loc. cit.; emphasis in italics original in the edition; G.G.)

English Translation: "But what is the difference between an attitude and an opinion?

I would like to say: the attitude comes *before* the opinion.

(*Isn't* belief in God an attitude?) [[dx]; G.G.]

How would this be: only one who can utter it as information *believes* it.

An opinion can be wrong. But what would an error look like here?" ("Last Writings" loc. cit., translated into English by C. Grant Luckhardt and Maximilian A. E. Aue; emphasis in italics original in the edition; G.G.)

I think the difference between 'attitude' and 'opinion' *cannot* be sought in a dependency of 'attitude' on 'opinion'. There are four reasons for this.

Firstly, one cannot utter an attitude as information. Yet if one could, one would automatically believe it. Therefore, if belief in God were (only) an opinion and not an attitude, those who utter it and avow to it would not have to believe it, against all evidence.

Then, opinions can be right or wrong, i.e. correct/true and erroneous, whereas it makes no sense to say that an attitude as belief in God would be an error, since we have no criteria for deciding whether it is an error or not. Furthermore, due to our lack of criteria, the ascription of a possible error to an attitude in belief is meaningless.

Thirdly, the whole page of this passage suggests that the case of 'attitude' in connection to 'belief in God' is just a paradigmatic case-study, brought

---

[dx] The italics *here* are only in the English addition and do not correspond to an original emphasis or underlining.

In the terminology of *GMT* (cf. i.a. Stachowiak 1973, Gelbmann 2000c, Gelbmann 2002d), I would say that these italics of "isn't" are *an abundant attribute of the normalized transcription* Wright and Nyman offer us. This does not say that these italics do not express anything or are superfluous, because in the representation Wright and Nyman have chosen these italics render an *emphasis* stressing a rhetorical tone of the question, which *therefore clearly has to be answered in the affirmative*. Rendering their translation with this part in italics, corresponds to the same prosodic or rhetorical attribute of the German original, which is expressed in the word-order of " Ist aber nicht ...". This clearly suggests that only an affirmative answer can be given to the inquiry.

up in order to give an example, viz. religious belief, where it is quite clear that the opinion *about* a (or better: the) belief in God presupposes an attitude *as* this very belief, of which the opinion then is only an expression. Therefore, belief in God *is* an attitude about which one can express opinions. The attitude comes before the opinion, and to inform others that one believes in God is *an opinion about one's own attitude as belief, in which one cannot be wrong.*

Finally, *We cannot be wrong in our own attitudes.* Thus our attitudes towards others will always come before our opinions about others. Even if the latter are wrong, *our attitudes towards others determine the frame for our opining;* and the opinion that somebody is a human being or has a soul depends on our attitude towards the other I encounter as a person, i.e. as somebody having a soul. Therefore, *the ascription of having a soul or mind towards others is not a question of opinion but of attitude.*

I have to admit that it is a tricky problem, but the other option, that the attitude comes from the opinion, would mean *that our opinion about the other as being a person can be wrong, in spite of our attitude towards him/her as having a soul.* This is unreasonable and practically irrational.

Moreover, belief in God would be an attitude that depends on an opinion. Now I could imagine that this opinion would be about a central question of belief and religion (if not of theology), i.e. about the existence of God. Belief in God would therefore depend on an opinion concerning the question of whether God exists or not. Hence in the event that one believes in God, one might think that God exists. *Yet this sort of belief is not an attitude but an opinion!* If belief is taken as an attitude, rather than as an opinion, it cannot depend on an opinion, *for that is the point of Wittgenstein's rhetorical question put in paranthesis* (cf. loc. cit. sup.).

It seems to me that the Bergen Electronic Edition's transcription committed the philological mistake of disregarding the *option of inferring from the meaning of the context the correct reading of the passage in question.* This option is objectively given by virtue of the *internal relation between the reading of a text and the understanding of the meaning within a context, on the background of a practice and common language.*[dxi] How this mistake came about? My suspicion is that the staff of the Wittgenstein Archives at the University of Bergen transcribed

---

[dxi]   By "objectively given", I mean a form of social objectivity or *institutionality.* Cf. sup. *nota cdlxxxv.*

as they did[dxii] by *concentrating too much on the pure syntactical or even physical appearance of graphemes*, and by focusing too exclusively on whether a certain word can be read as the German "vor" or the German "von". They seem to have decided by simply throwing a coin, *instead of starting with the best fitting and consistent semantic meaning of the passage, placed in its context*, in order to then decide which possible aspect was suggested by reading the skript-string[dxiii] in question.

This philological mistake is connected to *a philosophical unawareness* of what Wittgenstein himself expresses in "Zettel" § 216,[dxiv] namely that *one does not see or read a change of aspect but a change of interpretation*. I interpret this as the methodological and hermeneutical principle that *the reading of a meaning is prior to the recognition of a word or letter*, and *determining the meaning should always be made dependent on the meaning revealed in the appropriate context*.

We do not see something under the aspect of being a sign and apart from it a possible meaning of the sign. But in seeing something as a textual sign and hence under the aspect of it being a readable sign, we have already realized the sign's meaning and hence know what the sign does mean, how it has to be read, and therefore how it ought to be transcribed. The meaning is something we learn from the context of the thing that is to be regarded as a sign or grapheme. Hence in a situation where a whole reading of meaning(s) has happened,[dxv] any new occurrence of something obviously belonging to the text (of which this situation has already provided a context in its meaning) has to fit with all of what one has grasped in meaning(s).

Otherwise we would insulate the thing in question in its significance as a grapheme while reading it, and *we would not consider it as text or grapheme at all*, but as something covering the text, as a stain on the paper, etc.! This happens to spots or dirt on the pages to be transcribed or read, *even if they resemble a letter*. One might then guess what letter or grapheme was intended or was covered or destroyed by this stain. This would put one back on the same track of *evaluating the meaning of the reconstructed or conjectured string in question, on*

[dxii]   Probably after a long discussion without reaching complete agreement.

[dxiii]   By "skript-string" I mean the handwritten composition of letters "vor/n", if I may render it here in this sort of alternative transcription. Cf. also sup. section *II.V.* at (D11).

[dxiv]   Loc. cit. inf. *section IV.IV.*

[dxv]   One could hermeneutically speak of a "history of reading".

the grounds of what meaning one has read in the foregoing passage and in the whole context. Any part of an allegedly missing text or chain or token of graphemes has to be reconstructed on the basis of such a methodologically ruled assessment, and exactly in taking this principle into consideration our poor transcribers have failed.

Actually, a transcription would find my consent, if it (on the level of a so-called 'diplomatic edition') rendered the text-string "vor/n" in question as, e.g.

"vo¤",

where the sign '¤' stands for "not readable", if and only if, at the level of a 'normalized edition' of *MS 169*: 60v,[dxvi] this transcription would come to the same conclusion, i.e. the reading and printing of:

"vor".

The (current release of the) Bergen Electronic Edition[dxvii] does not come to this conclusion, which is unfortunate; its normalized edition renders the passage as shown above, and its diplomatic edition does *not* differ from the normalized edition[dxviii] in this respect.- But let's go back to the issue:

IV.IV. Internal Relations and Aspect

Where in Wittgenstein can one locate a connection between the concept of 'internal relation' and the theme of 'aspect' for our semiotic interests in pragmatics? Wittgenstein writes:

"Does »seeing an aspect« mean that one perceives the internal relation? What is there in me which speaks against this?" ("Last Writings on the Philosophy of Psychology. Preliminary Studies for Part II of Philosophical Investigations" I § 506, Wittgenstein 1990b: 66; cf. *MS 137*: 127 from Dec. 16th 1948)

[dxvi]   There is no question what the original for the modelling called "transcription" would be. The source is indubitable and could be checked by having a look at the physical original, kept in a safe in Oxford by the trustees.

[dxvii]   At least at the time when this excurse was written, viz. beginning of March 2003.

[dxviii]   The text-string in question is underlined in the diplomatic edition as well as in the original.

Well, the expression "perception of the internal relation" is problematic, but that there is an internal relation enacted in seeing something as some definite other thing, is undeniable, since *we have to interpret what we perceive as that other thing we see*, and this interpretation involves meaning and language. *If one sees an aspect, one notices that an internal relation takes place*; one might even feel homely, because now the usual sign-use or the sign-use of other persons can be attended to. The actualization of internal relations is a semiotic matter, bringing about sign-use in a social field. Look at the following piece:

> "Seeing aspects is built on other language-games." (sec. "Remarks on the Philosophy of Psychology" II § 541, Wittgenstein 1998b: 96e; the quotation is the translation by Michel ter Hark 1990: 184; G.G.)[dxix]

So realizing an aspect based upon an internal relation, presupposes that this internal relation is founded on some other sign-uses. In other words: *we are always already involved in a socio-semiotic use of signs.*[dxx] To see something under the aspect of it being significant as a sign, rests upon an already existing sign-use. Therefore, to realize internal relations, which introduces us to a sign-use, is conditioned by internal relations incorporated in language-games.

If I see the rabbit-aspect of a certain drawing,[dxxi] until having looked at it as a duck, I have engaged myself in some other game, the game that makes the semiotic manifestation of an internal relation more explicit; *now* one is talking about attributes of a drawing as being aspective, and not only of the drawing representing either a duck or a rabbit. I deeply believe that *the possibility of aspectivity is the back-bone of our ability to use signs, and hence of the human culture*. That is why we can use things as signs in communication!

[dxix]   The German original of "Bemerkungen über die Philosophie der Psychologie" II § 541, Wittgenstein 1998b: 96 reads:
"Das Sehen der Aspekte ist auf anderen Spielen aufgebaut." (*TS 232*: 736 § 540 from Jan. 1948 and *MS 137*: 34 from March 10th 1948)
C. Grant Luckhardt and Maximilian A. E. Aue translate it into English as
"Seeing aspects is built up on the basis of other games" ("Remarks on the Philosophy of Psychology" II § 541, Wittgenstein 1998b: 96e)
That ter Hark has "language-games", is a *contextually motivated* expansion of the original text. For his citation in indirect speech it is appropriate and permissible.

[dxx]   This avoidance of a socio-semiotic emptiness has a transcendental-pragmatic freature.

[dxxi]   I mean Joseph Jastrow's famous duck-rabbit from "Philosophische Untersuchungen" II xi, Wittgenstein 1984, Band 1: 519 f.

But this possibility is *rooted in the existence of internal relations, which always already presuppose a social environment or even culture.*[dxxii] Is this not a vicious circle, a fallacious mutual conditioning? I think, this circularity, since it is pragmatic, is *not* vicious; it is not causal in a physical sense and not inconsistent in a logical sense, but it is based on the *interaction of the Conceptual with the Empirical.* We might never be able to explain how this complexity genetically developed, but we can, with the means of this complexity, conceptualize and understand how it works. The philosophical task is not to show how it evolved, but to point out *that* the concepts of 'internal relation', 'sign', and 'aspect' are interwoven, and how.

What do we really perceive when seeing something as something, when seeing a thing X under the very aspect that immediately leads to an interpretation of X? When an aspect change takes place, the internal relation between the 'percept' and that which we see in it – between the image and *that* as *what* it is seen – is already performed! *The empirical application of an instance of the concept goes hand in hand with the realization of the concept in its token.*[dxxiii] The lack of time-delay, one might feel tempted to say, is a sign or better: a signal that this situation, although experienced, is conceptually constituted.

Take another striking passage in Wittgenstein's works, which dwells on the philosophy of psychology. It is obviously one of the central themes of his whole philosophy, and let me remind you that, as early as in "Tractatus Logico-Philosophicus", the theme of 'aspect-change' can be found in Wittgenstein's writings.[dxxiv] Wittgenstein explicitly states:

> "By noticing the aspect one perceives an internal relation, and yet noticing the aspect is related to *forming an image.*" ("Last Writings on the Philosophy of Psychology. Preliminary Studies for Part II of Philosophical Investigations" I § 733, Wittgenstein 1990b: 93e; translated by C. Grant Luckhardt and Maximilian A. E. Aue from *MS 138*: 5 from Jan. 20th 1949; original emphasis in underlining, here rendered in italics; G.G.)

[dxxii]   This is a Peircean thought; recall Eco's word about semiosis, which never develops ex novo or ex nihilo (cf. Eco 1991: 338).

[dxxiii]   Here I definitely use the word "realization" as a translation for the German "Erkennen"; it has a cognitive function, to constitute the instance of a concept.

[dxxiv]   Cf. e.g. "Tractatus Logico-Philosophicus" § 5.5423, Wittgenstein 1984, Band 1: 64 f.

This citation is worth a thorough discussion before we continue with our general theme, viz. the pragmatics of internal relation and aspectivity. The German original as well as the German edition of *MS 138*: 5 has:

"Man nimmt durch das Bemerken des Aspekts eine interne Relation wahr[,] und dennoch ist es dem *Vorstellen* verwandt." ("Letzte Schriften über die Philosophie der Psychologie" I § 733, Wittgenstein 1990b: 93; emphasis in italics original in the edition; the German original, *MS 138*: 5, has a grammatical mistake in punctuation which was corrected in brackets; G.G.)

I am *not at all* satisfied with the English translation, since it renders the verb[dxxv] "vorstellen" with "forming an image", thus *invoking an idea of pictorial or representative imagination and of an activity*! Without reiterating a detailed discussion by repeating some points about the translation of the German term "vorstellen" (which I have already laid down somewhere else),[dxxvi] let me suggest my own version:

"By noticing the aspect one perceives an internal relation, and yet it is related to *imagining*."

Another, probably even more agreeable alternative is:

"By noticing the aspect one perceives an internal relation, and yet it is related to *forming an idea*."

The element of imagination is not one of forming an image or even a (mental) picture, but of an *idea about presentation*,[dxxvii] invoked by the perception of

---

[dxxv]   This verb loc. cit. is *used as a noun*, that's why it is written with a capital letter in German and best translated into English with a Gerund. My criticism of the translation done by Aue and Luckhardt is not directed against the Gerund they introduce but *against the implication of an active construing of an image*, cf. inf.

[dxxvi]   Cf. i.a. my report on a former project at the Wittgenstein Archives at the University of Bergen, accessible at *http://h2hobel.phl.univie.ac.at/~yellow/projects/TPTME.htm#17* (last access in March 2003).

[dxxvii]   One cannot have an idea about 'presentation' as a 'pictorial image', if this idea about presentation should represent "vorstellen", in the sense of a deliberation about a method of a representative presentation. One can paint a picture of a picture, but the second picture then is not a "Vorstellung" about the first, although it might reveal such an idea.
The attributes or properties of a representation reveal something about an idea, and will essentially be different from the attributes or properties of an image or picture. With "essentially different", I mean that the means of representation of these attributes will be different; an idea about presentation will not be represented in the same way as some physical object is represented in a picture or in a mental image.

something objectively real or institutional, namely the *internal relation of the significance and sign-function of the aspect noticed*. This imagination is related to noticing an aspect since *one can only notice an aspect if one notices the significance of the novelty of this idea of presentation, which goes along with the representation of something under a new aspect*.-

Back to our issue: In noticing an aspect or a new aspect, *there is a constructive element involved*, but it is not totally free in its execution; the "forming of an idea" as related to noticing the aspect-change is *sustained by already existing conditions, manifest in internal relations*. The conclusive remark in the light of what I have said, is this:

> "We see, not change of aspect, but change of interpretation." ("Zettel" § 216, Wittgenstein 1998c: 38)[dxxviii]

The change of interpretation is only possible on pragmatic grounds, i.e. on the *thirdness* of signification.[dxxix] We can see things as something different because they are like pure objects of mind, or objects for the senses. Because we have the ability to see something as something else, we can refer to our sign-use and can form our sign-use. Thus *our socially implemented semiotic subjectivity has an active part to play within the life of signs*; the multiplicity that lies within sign-use makes perception of aspects and their dynamics possible.

That we immediately understand the expression of pain, depends on a *shared convention*, deeply rooted in the institution of our sign-use; there is an *internal relation between expression and pain*. Language-use would not be an institution if

---

[dxxviii] In German it originally reads:
"Nicht den Aspektwechsel sieht man, sondern den Deutungswechsel." ("Zettel" § 216, Wittgenstein 1984, Band 8: 319; cf. *TS 233a*: 45 § 520 from Jan. 1946, *TS 232*: 733 § 520 from Jan. 1948, *MS 137*: 32 from Aug. 3rd 1946)
So Wittgenstein's insight (that the realization of the pragmatic-semantic significance of an interpretation is prior to the perception of an aspect) is *older* than his insight into the connection between 'aspectivity' and 'internal relation'. His thoughts seem to have developed from what we present as the consequence to its premises.
This is an observation about the history and development of his thinking, not about the conclusiveness of his thoughts (the context of discovery is not a mirror or justification for the context of validity). Yet, if Wittgenstein noticed the truth of our consequence, it might have made him look for what could support it, and hence it guided his research.

[dxxix] In a Peircean sense, of course, cf. Peirce 2000a-c.

it were not social in the every-day sense.[dxxx] The constitution of a social sphere is the prerequisite for the conceptualisation of language *de dicto*, but also for the constitution of language itself *de re*. So the thing called "language" is constituted by communication organizing a social sphere, and we (can)[dxxxi] grasp language as an institution by making use of the organisational power of communication, by applying language; but in applying language, we automatically perform speech-acts and *enforce* the institutional sphere of language, which deepens the social sphere in return.[dxxxii]

A social sphere is constituted by sign-use, in communication between different subjects who are mutually "others" for each other, who are subjected to a semiotic sphere and who are subjects of a semiotic sphere. I like to picture this[dxxxiii] as *a net, where knots are the concepts and signs in our social and linguistic practice*; a net that is *used by many* persons, and is made for being used by many, in order to get the meanings right.[dxxxiv] What we cannot catch with this conceptual net simply cannot be said or expressed. (Hence the 'meanings', in a certain, constructivistic sense, are fit for being caught by this net.)- This analogy can even help to imagine dynamic conception of 'language':

By forming, distorting, and changing this net we sometimes even constitute the social facts of our common conceptualisations; it is as if a fisherman's net catches the fisherman. There are facts brought about within the social sphere of our conceptualisations, and these facts are not less brute than death and taxes.

[dxxx]   Even essence would not be expressible by grammar; cf. "Philosophische Untersuchungen" I § 371, Wittgenstein 1984, Band 1: 398. See also "Philosophische Untersuchungen" I § 116, Wittgenstein 1984, Band 1: 300.

[dxxxi]   Indeed, I think that we cannot avoid conceptualising language and at the same time creating the institutional dimension of language; it is *a pragmatic fact*, comparable to the fact that by pondering the physical Laws of Nature, one is bound and subjected to these laws of Laws of Nature (although a difference is that one does not create the Laws of Nature by trying to formulate them).

[dxxxii]   *By conceptualising language, we enforce its institutional power* (and with a pun a la James Joyce, I therefore dare say that these are "infective facts")!

[dxxxiii]   Here I am sticking to Luntley's fine metaphor near the end of the last of his aforementioned lectures.

[dxxxiv]   This actually draws on Eco's 'Model Q', cf. Gelbmann 1998.

IV.V. The Constitutive Function of Pragmatics

What is wrong with a sentence like the following?

"If pragmatics is a part of psychology and sociology of language, syntax ought to be by the same token a part of graphology." (J. Hintikka 1976: 119 f.; i.e. J. Hintikka 1996l: 290)

Hintikka sees pragmatic*s as the study of the formal, abstract features of the use of language*, features which abstract from empirical, psychological, social attributes and properties. Since syntax (according to Hintikka) is the study of the *use of graphic tokens* as objects studied by graphology, it seems as if syntax (or syntactics) were a part of graphology. This is clearly wrong, for *syntax does not study sign-tokens but sign-types, and the rules of formative and transformative character*, which concern the construction of well-formed formulas or sentences, of correct conclusions and derivations, and of proofs and deductions.[dxxxv]

So Hintikka *compares pragmatics with syntactics*, and infers from a certain syntactical fact (namely that *syntactics is not an empirical science like graphology*[dxxxvi]) the statement about pragmatics, viz. that pragmatics is not an empirical science. Why then, if this parallel really holds, *differ at all* between pragmatics and syntactics? Why not go back to the simple system of two semiotic notions, viz. syntactics and semantics, and nothing else?

I personally think that this is Hintikka's consequence, if he only would go that far!-[dxxxvii] Let me list up some points against Hintikka in this respect:

<*1.*> Cherry 1965, op. cit., (whom Hintikka quotes) and the classic Morris 1938, op. cit.,[dxxxviii] do not speak of "syntax" in the rather restricted sense of formal logic, but use the semiotic term "syntactics" covering the semiotic dimension which deals with the interrelations of signs. This is a terminological point.

[dxxxv] If one counts the notion of 'validity' among syntactical concepts, the study of arguments would become a matter of syntactics. Then one starts with semantics.

[dxxxvi] Granted that graphology is one; I am not that sure of myself on this point, as Hintikka seems to be, so we let him go through with this.

[dxxxvii] There is an author in the field of semiotics who really wants to base pragmatics on semantics, it is the Italian semiotician and philosopher Umberto Eco from the University of Bologna; cf. Eco 1976.

[dxxxviii] Cf. inf. *section IV.1.*

<2.>   Even if pragmatics (wrongly, and in contrast to Cherry's approach) is defined as "the study of the use of language", why must it then not be taken as a part of (linguistic) psychology and (linguistic) sociology? If such a study is sufficiently abstract and formal, it could at least be a part of any general psychology or sociology in its linguistic branch. In other words, *if (linguistic) psychology and (linguistic) sociology study the use of language in an abstract and formal approach, which is not only an empirical sampling of data, then they are integrated parts of semiotics.* Moreover, *pragmatics has become an essential conceptual part of these sciences* (think of the Group of Palo Alto around Bateson, Watzlawick et al., op. cit.).

<3.>   I have to stress that Hintikka seems to think of (linguistic) psychology and (linguistic) sociology as being *nothing but* empirical sciences. In his understanding of (linguistic) pragmatics, these sciences represent no satisfactory frame for the study of the use of language. Yet are (linguistic) psychology and (linguistic) sociology necessarily restricted to empirical scienticity? And would Hintikka be satisfied if, in his understanding, 'pragmatics' were the *only* theme for linguistics or for logic? This is hardly imaginable, *unless one reduces scientific enterprise to formal studies alone.*

<4.>   In my point of view, *pragmatics is not a part of any single science,*[dxxxix] *but an approach to studying the effects and manipulations of signs.* Hintikka's understanding of pragmatics is as a "pure conceptual science" in contrast to an "empirical conception" (and the pragmatic wastebasket, as mentioned by Hintikka,[dxl] would then only contain the "empirical dirt", wouldn't it). I fear this is a bit shallow and does not really get the "grammatical point" about pragmatics. When I say that pragmatics is the study of the effects and manipulation of signs, it, *a fortiori and obviously, is a socio-semiotic study, since sign-users are manipulated signs*, and society and communication depend on sign-use. Furthermore, *the observation and perception of other persons has always already a semiotic character.*[dxli] Therefore, being in the presence of others involves observable behaviour as communication.

<5.>   I would even go further, and as a semiotician I feel free to say that the semiotic dimensions, sec. Morris, Cherry, Carnap and others signified

---

[dxxxix]   Except semiotics, in so far as this is a science and not much more an *interdisciplinary undertaking.*

[dxl]   Hintikka takes this expression about the "pragmatic wastebasket" from Yehoshua Bar-Hillel, cf. Hintikka & Halonen 1995: 636.

[dxli]   Cf. i.a. Gelbmann 2002b and Gelbmann 2002e.

as syntactics, semantics, and pragmatics, are *aspects of the study of the semiotic universe*, and of the various ways of dealing with signs. Why should a psychological, sociological, empirical or logical approach be denied access to this aspect of one's own sign-use and of one's own approach to semiotics? *Seeing things under a semiotic aspect is not necessarily a non-empirical or a non-conceptual undertaking!*[dxlii]

<6.>   I wonder if this artificial contrast between "the Empirical" and "the Conceptual" is, firstly, really something Ludwig Wittgenstein would have approved of,[dxliii] and secondly, if it is the right frame for dealing with pragmatics, since the pragmatic dimension is, in my point of view, *the link between the empirical aspect in sciences like psychology and sociology*, and the conceptual aspect of such sciences. There is nothing bad in seeing certain philosophical traits in conceptual and theoretical branches of these sciences. *As it is not true that physics is only an empirical science, neither is it true that psychology or sociology are merely empirical.* If pragmatics is to be conceptual and formal, it would be so as a basis for the entire social field by asking for the semiotic experience's intelligibility to be enacted and conceptualized, just as the concept of speech-act asks for social institutions.

The question is not by what token pragmatics could be either an empirical or a conceptual science, but what type of pragmatics is involved in empirical and conceptual aspects of the various sciences. Asking whether pragmatics is not better understood as a non-empirical, i.e. a conceptual science, leads to false assumptions about the objects of psychology and sociology, viz. that language, the human soul, social problems are exclusively empirical matters. It is a philosophical point to see that this is not the case. In this sense I believe that I am applying something like "a method of Wittgensteinian philosophy".[dxliv]

For me, pragmatics has a constitutive function for the social sphere as a whole, just because of its empirical effects and realization; the conceptualisation of the social field in terms of pragmatics can be very elucidating about our human

---

[dxlii]   I am now afraid to notice that Hintikka has no notion of semiotics; his notion of "pragmatics" betrays this short-coming. He throws the phemic sheet into the pragmatic wastepaper basket.

[dxliii]   I think the difference is relative to a conventionalistic "Aggregatzustand des Wissens", so a knowledge comparable to states of matter, sometimes fluid and sometimes solid, cf. Pollok 2001.

[dxliv]   I venture to state this even though Wittgenstein might probably have disapproved of it, as well as of the term "pragmatics".

reality. The concept 'social' requires a concept of pragmatics that is empirically and practically realized, via intersubjectivity, conventions, co-operation, and communication. A conceptual study of pragmatics has to take account of its possible and actual embodiment. I would study the content of a wastebasket if I suspect some valuables or commodities there!

IV.VI. **Is the Social Only Empirical?**

I think, it is time to shift the focus of our attention to somebody else: In his four lectures on "Wittgenstein: the conditions for the possibility of judgement",[dxlv] Michael Luntley gave me the impression that, for him, the social sphere is exclusively a case for empirical studies. This seems to be a common and rather old position, and in Jaakko Hintikka we find yet another example of it.[dxlvi] Perhaps this sort of subtle division is a temptation for philosophical professional thinking, and I might myself be encumbered by it.

Curiously enough, both, Hintikka and Luntley seem to expect a solution for certain problems from Wittgenstein, regarding the concepts of "judgement" and "pragmatics". I see this as a very *instrumentalist reading of Wittgenstein*, a reading based on a deep mistake which I could, in Wittgensteinian terms, almost call *a grammatical confusion about the terms 'social' and 'empirical'*.

If we return to some themes put forth by Luntley, we arrive at the Wittgensteinian notions of 'aspect' and 'attitude'. One of my critical remarks in the discussion of Luntley's lectures was that *attitudes are performatives of a non-linguistic sort*, viz. under the condition that they are displayed in the presence of others.[dxlvii] Performatives refer to a social framing by virtue of their realization;

[dxlv]   Cf. sup. *notae cdlxxiv, cdlxxxvi, cdxci*.

[dxlvi]   If I ascribe to Luntley and Hintikka positions they have not held at the times I refer to (in Luntley's case 2002, in Hintikka's case at least until 1976), I apologize herewith.

[dxlvii]   Cf. for some entries on 'attitude' in the sense of performatives:
"Meine Einstellung zu ihm ist eine Einstellung zur Seele. Ich habe nicht die *Meinung*, daß er eine Seele hat" ("Philosophische Untersuchungen" II iv, Wittgenstein 1984, Band 1: 495, i.e. *MS 137*: 110b from Nov. 27th 1948, *MS 144*: 10 from Jan. 1949)
This passage is quoted by Säätelä 2001: 258 in English.- See also:
"»If exception and rule change place then it just is not the same thing any more!«– But what does that mean? Maybe that our attitude toward the game will then change abruptly [...]" ("Remarks on the Philosophy of Psychology" § 146, Wittgenstein 1998b: 28e, cf. *MS 136*: 27 on Dec. 24th 1947, *TS 232*: 638 from Jan. 1948).

this lies in their concept. And performatives bring about a "situation" or a "state of affairs" through their enactment or application. For example, a man who is having an affair with a woman presents her with withered flowers – this might change the state of their affair, mightn't it?

It is important to see that the situation or state of affairs affected by performative actions is of a social character essentially, involving interacting persons as semiotic subjects.[dxlviii] A performative speech-act makes use of conventions and conditions of application, which are socially embodied by the institution of a so-called "ordinary language" that is intersubjectively shared with others, at least as *a standard for actual language use.* If I say

"I herewith declare my lecture as finished!" or

"Thanks for your attention!"

as an effective declaration of my lecture *being* finished, and if I do so *appropriately* at the end of my lecture and in front of an auditorium,[dxlix] my lecture *is* finished (please, remain seated …).

If I take the attitude towards this very situation of lecturing as if this matter were closed, I would change the situation and bring the conversation to an abrupt end, probably by simply refusing to enter or to prolong a dialogue. *My attitude would be performed together with accompanying gestures and body-behaviour,* which you, as an auditorium sharing a more or less European culture with me, could easily read as my emotional status and opinion of having brought this to an end.- I do not take this position. My attitude actually is a different one: *I really think there are performatives that are not linguistically expressed,* although their execution has communicational effects via non-verbal signals and other forms of behaviour that are institutionally encoded.[dl] *If I take a certain attitude to a certain subject, those observing me might infer my opinions and could guess some of my*

That on Christmas Eve 1947 Wittgenstein thought about exception and rule and their connection to 'attitude' should not bother us too much.

[dxlviii] And not only "things that can say 'I'", as Luntley seems to conceptualize persons. (I hope that the reader is laughing.)

[dxlix] The setting and appropriateness of such a performative declaration is, indeed, indispensable.

[dl] It is just the essence of performatives that they have communicational effects.

further behaviour before I express anything explicitly, just from my personality and the appearance of my behaviour. Attitudes as performatives form a certain *gestalt* of the current social context and *raise anticipation*; they constitute a social context that effects the subject's point of view.

For Luntley the social level was scaffolding whereas the conceptual level was constitutive,[dli] and, I dare say that the constitutive was for him conceptual. Yet the *network of concepts used by a speaker, can also be used by others*, and the possibility that others use the concepts' network conforms to the certainty and reliability we have in expressing ourselves by using language or other means of communication. In this sense, pragmatics as the study of the use of signs by sing-users, used in order to express meanings (and emotions), is *socially constitutive for the conceptual field.* Concepts are neither private nor scaffolding, and the empirical side is not only a fact, but necessary.- Here I would like to interrupt my train of thoughts with a remark of the young Wittgenstein:

> "Since language stands in *internal* relations to the world, *it* and these relations determine the logical possibility of facts." ("Notebooks 1914 – 1916" from April 25th 1914, Wittgenstein 1979b: 42, cf. *TS 102*: 75r)

Again, if we take the term 'internal relation' as unmediated, persisting in a social dimension, and necessary,[dlii] then *the relation between world and language is, already in the pre-tractarian Wittgenstein, one which necessitates the social field.* Facts depend on these internal relations, because without language there would not be any facts, nor would there be the concept of 'fact'.

For sign-use and for socio-semiotic practice, *a formal access to empiricity is constitutive*; if signs were only mental and private, there would be no communication between empirical subjects like human beings, who factually have perception, and who are *turned into semiotic subjects for each other just because of the communicational use of signs.* That we can share a concept of 'the empirical' is already the result of us con-forming our forms of life. Even though it has empirical effects, pragmatics is *constitutive* for conceptions like 'language', 'psychology', because *it regulates the grammar of our language-games*[dliii] (*the possible participation in which embodies our agreement in form of life*).

[dli] He alluded to "Philosophische Untersuchungen" I § 240, Wittgenstein 1984, Band 1: 355.

[dlii] Cf. sup. *section IV.II.*

[dliii] "Philosophische Untersuchungen" I § 241, Wittgenstein 1984, Band 1: 356.

The study of the empirical features of pragmatics can be performed after a certain form of abstraction has already been processed, viz. the abstraction from the very pragmatic features of this certain study and its social implementation, and also the abstraction from any empirical embodiment of sign-use. What Hintikka loc. cit. sup. tries to do, is to make pragmatics a formal idealisation. This is justified, but could then not serve to explain the phenomenality of pragmatics.

An observer normally does not observe himself being observed, but *others* as being observable; so *otherness corresponds to observability*. A sociologist questioning "the plain man in the street" does not question himself in his questioning the plain man in the street, since such a sociologist is not "plain" any more.[dliv] Hintikka's use of the rather complex sign 'pragmatics' does obviously not take account of his own pragmatics in doing so, and *his preoccupation with an understanding of pragmatics as essentially non-empirical drives him into overlooking the constitutive function of pragmatics for the social field.*

It *is* clear that *Hintikka neither wants to understand the social*, as a conceptual notion, nor as empirically constituted by pragmatics and communication. He sees pragmatics only as linguistic pragmatics as well, some formal traits of it, which fit into his syntactic-semantic approach of a pure statement-view, are of philosophical interest. *While this is legitimate, his attacks on psychology and sociology are not*, since they can also contribute to a conceptual understanding of formal (linguistic) pragmatics.-

Luntley (and perhaps also Hintikka) overlook the pragmatics of making differences. *A difference, that makes a difference, is informative.*[dlv] If pragmatics is seen as strictly non-empirical, then I ask myself what else the effect and use of performatives *in praxi* would be; *obviously pragmatics has to do with the form of social experience via communication.*[dlvi] *The inter-linking of the empirical and the conceptual aspect is essentially constitutive for the social sphere*, and this interaction is always of a semiotic (namely pragmatic) character, *since sign-*

[dliv]   Obviously, it is *a definitional requirement* for being such a plain man in the street *not* to question oneself in a sociologist's manner; well, philosophers remain largely unaffected by this.

[dlv]   To rephrase a well-known saying by Gregory Bateson (cf. e.g. Bateson 1990: 272); differs from William James known phrase by using it as *a pragmatic definition for information*!

[dlvi]   If speech-acts cannot even be seen as belonging to pragmatics, we better live the lives of computers, what would be rather boring!

tokens can be taken as realizations of sign-types, and thus contribute to an institutional level of common reference.[dlvii]

Our empirical *social* life is much deeper and much more infiltrated by conceptuality than any of us are usually aware of. However, *the conception of sign-use relies on it being able to become empirical*. Even the notion of privacy is a product of the socially implemented grammar of conceptuality. In other words, the sign 'private' has a certain pragmatic sense that is socially shared.[dlviii] *A non-empirical understanding of pragmatics and an only-empirical understanding of the Social are a bit too far apart from each other*. That's why I tend to read Wittgenstein's term 'grammar' from a perspective that dismantles the so-called unbridgeable difference between 'conceptuality' and 'empiricity'. This is because *grammar is itself social, for conceptually constitutive pragmatic reasons*.[dlix]

IV.VII. The Pragmatic Constitution of Empiricity

I do not like Jaakko Hintikka's approach to pragmatics, since he construes an understanding of empiricity that fails to see it constituted in socio-semiotic (communicational and not only linguistic) pragmatics. What Hintikka probably wants to study are the formal-semantic characteristics of general pragmatics, a kind of model-theoretical pragmatics.[dlx] The task – to figure out how pragmatics is fundamental for social life and how the possibility of (communicable) experience is based upon this conception of pragmatics – is not even addressed by Hintikka, but I sense its solution in Wittgenstein's term of 'grammar'.[dlxi]

[dlvii] Cf. inf. *section IV.V.*

[dlviii] Cf. Gelbmann 2002a.

[dlix] Private property is only possible if the public allows it.

[dlx] But not in the sense of Heinrich R. Hertz' or Herbert Stachowiak's understanding of "picture" or "model" (cf. i.a. Gelbmann 2000c or Gelbmann 2002d), and in my point of view, also not in the sense of the earlier Wittgenstein, who talks about "pictures" under the influence of Hertz (cf. e.g. "Tractatus Logico-Philosophicus" § 4.04, Wittgenstein 1984, Band 1: 29).

[dlxi] I think that in this sense a *conception of pragmatics as grammar* goes beyond the Kantian gap between the empirical and the transcendental, 'intuition' and 'mind'.
I do not want to hide some sympathy for Karl-Otto Apel's program of a transcendental-philosophical foundation of Philosophy of Language (*cf.* Apel 1993).

Luntley, probably without intending, *arrives at a change of aspects,*[dlxii] which shows him (and us) that what *once was thought of as scaffolding, namely the Social, turns suddenly out to be constitutive.* It does so via its semiotic function, its pragmatics. The social and the conceptual seem to have changed their role, if one realizes that *the network of concepts and performatives necessarily involves other persons as their users.* There would be no communication of meaning and no attitude about something, displayed on others, if the medium of the expression and manifestation of any such semiotic act were not social.

The fact that the social sphere is fundamental is, in itself, *not empirical,* although the fact that there are others and that there is something like "the social" can be and is experienced. *The possibility of this experience involves the empirical subject as a semiotic subject,* whose subjectivity is constituted by his/her sign-use, within a context of others' sign-use. If sign-use did not essentially involve others participating in this semiotic practice, it would be an empty concept.

I do not know what Wittgenstein would have said, if confronted with such strong opinions about "pragmatics" and "the social sphere". He might have brought (empirical or possibly fancied) examples that make one doubt these positions' tenability.- Hintikka lacks a certain recognition of the empirical subject that is independent from his/her ability to perform socio-semiotic representations of valuable thoughts, which have implications for the conceptualisation of the social field and its semiotics. This lack can be sensed in his attitude towards Wittgenstein's style; *I accuse him of inferring from an contingent property of Wittgenstein as a writer,*[dlxiii] *an interpretation of Wittgenstein's therapeutic concept of philosophy that is crudely misapplied and totally wrong.* It is indicative of his *lacking exegesis,* which, at least within the text, is contextually oriented, even if it is not detached from a pure immanent reading.

The pragmatic considerations guiding Hintikka (and his co-authoring wife[dlxiv]), which let them to go too far with what I shall present below, were most likely *oriented towards putting on a performance at one of the most theatrical conferences I have ever heard of.* Such considerations exceed any serious concept of 'pragmatics'. In this case, I am not at all happy about Hintikka's success.

[dlxii]   As I have predicted during the discussions in his lectures.

[dlxiii]   I do not deny the possibility of Wittgenstein having had this property.

[dlxiv]   I.e. Hintikka & Hintikka 2002; I sometimes talk about this text in phrases like "the Hintikkas".

IV.VIII. The Example of an Argumentum Ad Hominem

In the paper by Jaakko and Anna-Maija Hintikka, "Wittgenstein the Bewitched Writer" an *argumentum ad hominem* was raised against Wittgenstein. The Hintikkas addressed the mode and composition of Wittgenstein's skripts[dlxv] by maintaining that Wittgenstein suffered from dyslexia. This was done instead of addressing the structure of those skripts that actually were put together in book-form in their various editions from "Philosophical Investigations" onwards, as *formations of the texts essentially adapted to their subject*. This is at least the gate I see open for entering into an interpretation, when I read once again the "Vorwort" to "Philosophische Untersuchungen", a preface which essentially belongs to the whole text edited under this title[dlxvi] (here we might focus on "Philosophische Untersuchungen" part I[dlxvii]). On this I agree with David Stern or Alois Pichler.[dlxviii]

Although prefaces have a "paratextual position", as Stern 2002 points out,[dlxix] they (in most cases) are added to the text by the author and *are designed in such a way as to refer to the text* in question. In Wittgenstein's case, the Preface to "Philosophical Investigations" reveals that *the author's intention in applying a certain style and in giving his writings a certain gestalt, were accomplished* to a degree that allows us to conclude that the formation of the text matches Wittgenstein's theme(s) and hence *is authorized as intended*.

If Wittgenstein now is ascribed dyslexia due to the form of his texts, i.e. because of his style,[dlxx] I sense the danger of an argumentum ad hominem, which expresses *a weakness in the presentation of his philosophy caused by a personal disadvantage*. This *overlooks the possibility that the weak form of presentation of Wittgenstein's philosophy probably was inevitable*, not due to an inability of Wittgenstein himself, but *due to the nature of what should be presented*; the

---

[dlxv]   I use the term 'skript' as an over-all significator for 'manuscript', 'typescript', and 'dictate'.

[dlxvi]   Besides the motto, of course.

[dlxvii]   I shall henceforth use this well-known abbreviation.

[dlxviii]   Cf. Stern 2002, Pichler 1997a, Pichler 2001a, Pichler 2001b, Pichler 2002.

[dlxix]   Because of this seemingly marginal position, these sorts of texts are easily and preferably neglected, as happened to Wittgenstein's Preface to "Philosophische Untersuchungen" in the exegesis of text-immanentists like Eike von Savigny.

[dlxx]   Yet Hintikka 1996b: 8 reasons with Wittgenstein's impatience having inflicted his writings with spelling mistakes and the like.

Wittgensteinian style was thus not characteristic for his dyslectic mode of writing but for his philosophy.[dlxxi]

Before I go into detail in developing my partly polemical criticism of the Hintikkas, let me define what I mean with "argumentum ad hominem". One has come across an argumentum ad homimem *if the validity of the argument in question depends on a property or quality of the person confronted or criticized with such an argument*, or *if it depends on the person bringing forth this argument*.[dlxxii] Let us take this as a definition for the latin expression 'argumentum ad hominem'.

It is unfortunate that the scholar Hintikka has attributed the style of "Philosophische Untersuchungen" to dyslexia. By doing so, he commits a logical, or better, rhetorical fallacy against Wittgenstein. I appreciate Jaakko Hintikka as a scholar, a philosopher, and as a man, independently from any fame he might enjoy. He diagnoses Wittgenstein's dyslexia *as if this psycho-linguistic weakness were the reason why* "Philosophische Untersuchungen" *have their album-character, and lack a wished-for structure of step-by-step argumentation*.[dlxxiii] Instead, as we all know, "Philosophische Untersuchungen" are the *result of a project* with *a criss-cross of intertwining trains of thought*, and *the question is now whether this feature of the text contributes to its philosophical import or not*: Hintikka seems to desperately long for an 'ordinary book' and concludes with:

> "there is no serious evidence that Wittgenstein's expositional and argumentative methods are necessitated by the nature of his subject matter" (Hintikka & Hintikka 2002: 139 f.).

Well, at least he attributes him some methods!- *I do not deny that Wittgenstein might have suffered from dyslexia*; as a philosopher and not specially trained pedagogue I am not capable in judging this, but I argue against the conclusions and approach to interpreting Wittgenstein's writings encountered in Hintikka & Hintikka 2002. I do not want to disrespect them, but *I am afraid that they are disrespecting Wittgenstein as a philosopher and also as a person*; therein lies the draw-back of an 'argumentum ad hominem': it's a logical fallacy to attack

---

[dlxxi]   A reservation might be found along the lines of the notion of 'seduction by language' in Friedrich Kainz 1976 and the discussion of aphasia, apraxia, etc. to be found therein.

[dlxxii]   Cf. also Gelbmann 2002b: 92.

[dlxxiii]   Cf. Hintikka & Hintikka 2002: 137.

the person instead of his/her argument.[dlxxiv] This form of arguing is irrational because it does not take seriously what the person is bringing forth (whereas I take the Hintikkas deadly seriously). The barbs of this critique are directed against the human being "Wittgenstein", instead of against the views he held.[dlxxv]

At Hintikka & Hintikka 2002: 143, they even go so far as to lay down how "a normal, non-dyslexic person" would handle the task of dictating a book (something Wittgenstein did several times: think of the dictations of the "Blue Book"[dlxxvi] and the "Brown Book"[dlxxvii] to his students in the Cambridge sessions of 1933-1935). The Hintikkas give their prescription of how this should be done, and they end with saying that in "Philosophische Untersuchungen" part I, Wittgenstein did not manage to give a book the desired and acceptable form.

Do they want to imply that Wittgenstein came up to their standards, at least once? Does it not occur to them that Wittgenstein might have had different standards, probably standards that are inconceivable to the Hintikkas?

> "One can hence apply the notion of style [...] to Wittgenstein only if one realizes that Wittgensteinian style was not a freely chosen literal convention or genre" (Hintikka & Hintikka 2002: 140),

they announce, as if this were the *only* understanding of how a certain style came to be applied! Could there be no other reason for "Wittgensteinian style" except his dyslexia, *independent from his dyslexia, in spite of his dyslexia*? Could the "Wittgensteinian style" not be just the form Wittgenstein *finally arrived at* in dealing with his subject(s), *satisfied with the outcome of the project, at least in the sense that he thought it could not be improved in principle and hence not by himself, because the nature of these investigations force one to travel through a wide area of thoughts in all directions*[dlxxviii] (whereas the Hintikkas might soon start re-writing "Philosophische Untersuchungen")?

It is true that, firstly, Wittgenstein does *not* say that his book cannot be improved upon in principle, he only writes that *he* cannot improve it; but *this does*

[dlxxiv] Cf. the electronic documents of Stephen Downes' "Guide to the Logical Fallacies", mirrored at *http://www.intrepidsoftware.com/fallacy/* (last access in March 2003).

[dlxxv] An argumentum ad hominem has to do with rhetoric and hence with pragmatics.

[dlxxvi] I.e. *D 309*.

[dlxxvii] I.e. *D 310*.

[dlxxviii] Cf. the "Vorwort" to "Philosophische Untersuchungen", Wittgenstein 1984, Band 1: 231; my free translation.

not mean that the project of philosophical investigations can be improved in principle; I think that Wittgenstein did not believe in a reasonable notion of improvability of this project. Secondly, we have to keep in mind that the influence of dyslexia or other personal property upon Wittgenstein's manner of writing cannot really be quantified. The Hintikkas certainly do *not* want to say that Wittgenstein did not succeed in representing anything of his philosophical doctrines through his writings, they still ascribe him with a philosophy. They only deplore the way this philosophy was put into a more or less readable text.

As we all know, Wittgenstein shows some signs of resignation towards the end of the Preface in finishing with a sad gesture, what could be seen in support of the Hintikkas. He says that he would have liked to produce a good book, but

> "[i]t did not work out; the time yet is over within which it could be improved by me" (sec. Wittgenstein 1984, Band 1: 233),

if I might translate it myself. Yet it depends how one reads these signs of resignation, viz.

(ı)   as being sad about the unsatisfactory presentation of his thinking he arrived at through his journey of re-writing and altering, or
(ıı) as a resignation in face of the realization that any attempt in improving the current result would spoil it.

I cannot read these lines *as if Wittgenstein was awaiting somebody else to do a better job than he was able to do,* but I am afraid that the Hintikkas' reading might open up for this suspicion. What Wittgenstein writes a few lines above is reason for me to suspect that the form and style of Wittgensteinian writing should produce an effect in the reader:

> "I do not want my writing to spare others the troubles of thinking. Instead, I want to stimulate someone to thoughts of his/her own, if possible." (my translation sec. Wittgenstein 1984, Band 1: 233)

Hence the aim of the presentation of Wittgenstein's thinking in the form of "Philosophische Untersuchungen" is to *make others participate in the project of philosophically investigating the mind and language,* or to make them start such a project for themselves. Does not Wittgensteinian style serve this purpose, just because of its "brokenness"? Avrum Stroll 2002, e.g., clearly sees the use of "broken text" as *purposive*!

In the context of the Hintikkas' criticism, another crucial question about the intentions of Wittgenstein's philosophical project, and his intention to write a book, is: *Could one calculate the influence of dyslexia on writing, in the event that Wittgenstein was aware of his mishap?*[dlxxix] This appears to be an absurd perspective!

Although the Hintikkas loc. cit. correctly quote from the Preface to "Philosophical Investigations" that *Wittgenstein originally intended a book in the so-called ordinary form*, they fail to notice that *Wittgenstein himself regarded the deplored lack of the required textual traits as unavoidable per se, due to* "the nature of these investigations".[dlxxx] *The nature of these investigations is philosophical, not psycho-linguistic!* Therefore the outcome of the text, the appearance and style of the argumentation in "Philosophische Untersuchungen", do not mirror some psycho-linguistic characterisation of the writer, but the philosophical characterisation of the writer's *sujet!* Was then, in the Hintikkas' point of view, Wittgenstein

either	unaware of his own dyslexia? If he suffered from it, did he deceive us readers, even himself?
Or	was he, despite a likely awareness of this probable handicap, nevertheless convinced (or even because of that conscious thereof) that *his philosophical undertaking could never lead to a documentation in the form he himself once wished for* and the Hintikkas still dream of?

To clarify: I vote for the latter. I think that the project he was devoted to made Wittgenstein realize that *an ordinary form of representation would pragmatically fail in carrying out the project.*

Kristóf Nyíri gives a more moderate assessment of Wittgenstein's dyslexia as "beyond any possible doubt". This is in order to see his "striving to overcome the pitfalls of written language" (Nyíri 2002: 335 f.) as a basis for Nyíri's own interesting theory of Wittgenstein elaborating a theory of spoken language by working towards a philosophy of pictures. This is a psycho-genetic outlook on a

---

[dlxxix]   I do not doubt that Wittgenstein might have been aware of his "Legasthenie", to use a German term, at least I do not doubt the possibility of this.

[dlxxx]   Cf. his Preface to "Philosophische Untersuchungen" in Wittgenstein 1984, Band 1: 231; my own, free translation.

characterisation of the person and writer Wittgenstein,[dlxxxi] it does not diminish the accomplishment of "Philosophische Untersuchungen" and Wittgenstein's later writings (i.e. his Nachlass) but characterizes them as a philosophical project.

At any rate, *I do not want to say that Wittgenstein's philosophising was caused by dyslexia*, but I am not sure whether the Hintikkas do not end up in actually maintaining this.

IV.IX. On the Wickedness of Attributing Bewitchment

The Hintikkas grossly misinterpret "Philosophische Untersuchungen" part I § 109[dlxxxii] at the very beginning of their article[dlxxxiii] in such a way that if the "bewitchment of our understanding by the means of language" becomes *a bewitchment of Wittgenstein's abilities to express himself, caused by dyslexia*! The Hintikkas give the impression that

> "a thinker as personally engaged as Wittgenstein [... were ...] impossible not to assume that he [here] is speaking of his own experience" (Hintikka & Hintikka 2002: 131).

Was poor Wittgenstein *bewitched by dyslexia*, and did he talk about *that* in the famous § 109. Was he so unable to express himself any better? (This is a rhetorical question, the answer obviously has to be *NO*!)

To reword Wittgenstein § 109 loc. cit. (or am *I* now in danger of being seen as suffering under dyslexia?): through gaining philosophical insights into how our language works we get rid of the bewitchment of the mind by the means of language![dlxxxiv] The philosophical spell is not to be located in Wittgenstein's dyslexia, but in ignorance or philosophical unawareness about the subtlety of

---

[dlxxxi] Cf. also Pichler 1997b.

[dlxxxii] Cf. "Philosophische Untersuchungen" I § 109, Wittgenstein 1984, Band 1: 298 f.; originally this remark occurs the first time in *MS 142*: 102 § 110 in Nov. 1936, was taken over into *TS 220*: 76 f. § 96 in Jan. 1937, then into *TS 239*: 76 f. § 114 in Jan. 1942, until it eventually appears in *TS 227*: 84 as § 109 with Jan. 1945.

[dlxxxiii] I am still referring to Hintikka & Hintikka 2002. But in Hintikka 1996d: 79 (this paper originally was a conference-contribution from 1988, another Kirchberg-occasion I am happy to have missed) he has already hinted at this interpretation of this § 109, and again in Hintikka 1996g: 145.

[dlxxxiv] I seem to hold a standard-interpretation, at least here.

natural language. It is not a psycho-linguistic obstacle Wittgenstein loc. cit. is talking about; it is about philosophical problems arising because we misunderstand how language functions.

This paragraph could then also be read as *a (meta-textual) remark on the project of philosophical investigations of language and mind as such*, the project[dlxxxv] Wittgenstein was labouring with. Under this reading, the very beginning of this observation ("Philosophische Untersuchungen" I § 109) already gives *enough evidence for rejecting any explanation of the style and structure of* "Philosophische Untersuchungen" *by particular shortcomings of the person Wittgenstein.* As Wittgenstein loc. cit. alludes, *he wants to describe the way language works by depicting this through his project of philosophical investigations.* This is the reason for all this criss-cross, which obviously confuses. Solving philosophical problems then becomes *a question of reassembling and rearranging the already known.*[dlxxxvi] There is *a performative background of the therapeutical intention* expressed in "Philosophische Untersuchungen" I § 109! And besides: even if Wittgenstein had dyslexia, would not this mishap, if he were aware of it, rather have made him think on how language works?-[dlxxxvii]

The Hintikkas just have not got the point, or they say something which is philosophically pointless. "Philosophical Investigations" are not the sorry product of someone with troubles in expressing himself; they are *written in the best possible way* for their purpose(s), written by someone who spent a great deal of time and energy on improvements and successive versions of his intended text, and *the pragmatic element contained in the text, and its structure, is informative exactly about the philosophical challenge one undertakes in addressing the subjects Wittgenstein devoted himself to.*

There is no deficiancy in the apparent text of "Philosophische Untersuchungen" that could have been overcome, had Wittgenstein not had this personal deficiancy the Hintikkas diagnose; "Philosophische Untersuchungen"

[dlxxxv] About the project and not about text! "Philosophische Untersuchungen" I § 109 is about the project of (his) philosophy, not about Wittgenstein's own writing. As a "meta-textual remark" it is not about the apparent and final text of "Philosophische Untersuchungen" but *a comment on the project* (and this understanding of my term "meta-textual" is not well-chosen)!

[dlxxxvi] Which is, by the way, a hidden reference to H. R. Hertz and his plea for a perspicuous overview. Cf. Allan Janik 1994/95, Janik 1999, Janik 2003.

[dlxxxvii] Nyíri 2002 goes in this direction.

could not have had any other textual appearance than they have in order to be what they are. That Wittgenstein himself calls his work an "album"[dlxxxviii] rather than a book should be evidence enough that *Wittgenstein himself was aware of the interconnection between textual structure and the matters his writings dealt with,* much more than the Hintikkas will ever be able to pay tribute to. I reproach them for reading not Wittgenstein, but some ideal text they think Wittgenstein ought to have composed. I think "Philosophische Untersuchungen" I § 109 can be read in the light of this as well.

In my wrath, and wicked as I sometimes am, I feel now liable to diagnose the Hintikkas with "hypolexia", namely with *the professional disease of reading texts for stylistic defects,* and seeing these textual defects as caused by some personal misfortune of the author. I think that *Wittgenstein ex post came to intend the album-structure* of "Philosophische Untersuchungen", that's why he was satisfied with it. For his project, he attained what he stated in op. cit. I § 109: *he did not advance a theory about his own philosophical project*!

The style of "Philosophische Untersuchungen" presents us with a readable everyday language, an avoidance of intricate and adorning terminology, and a striving for clarity in expression. This should not embarrass any analytic philosophers today, if they are only able to recognize the simple truth that *the way certain things are said cannot arbitrarily be chosen, due to reasons inherent in the particular interaction. Subjects represent their thinking through language,* and this shows itself unavoidably in style. *Style is a necessary and memorable attribute of the arrangement of the already gained.* In this sense, Wittgenstein gracefully noticed how to get rid of the bewitchment of one's thinking by the linguistic surface, in undergoing the cure of his philosophical project.

IV.X. A Graceful Comparison

That the German composer Ludwig van Beethoven was deaf did not affect his compositions, at least his music has kept its specific quality. One can listen to his grand music without even paying the slightest attention to his waning hearing. Yet I am afraid *the Hintikkas would rather tell Beethoven how he should have produced better symphonies, than think of the fact* (and wonder!) *that the aging*

[dlxxxviii] Cf. the Preface in "Philosophische Untersuchungen", Wittgenstein 1984, Band 1: 232.

Beethoven's ability to compose was unaffected, or at least not destroyed or disqualified, by the deafness he suffered in his late years!

The same holds for Wittgenstein; even if he might have suffered under dyslexia, the expression of his thinking is not only the more admirable, but it is, in its form, style, and gestalt *to be taken serious* and not as a defective and hence an improvable product. *If Wittgenstein had dyslexia, it might only have enticed him all the more to express himself clearly, and to clarify thinking.*

It might have led him to the philosophical depth the organic composition his writings offer us. I purposefully have written "organic composition" because, *to me, the criss-cross of roots in a wood have an order*, if I may introduce a metaphor,[dlxxxix] and *these roots depict an order in itself, although it is hard or even impossible to follow one of them from their beginnings to their very end.* If one wants to investigate a wood, its structure, one should not cut it down and re-build a model-wood of well-analysed toothpicks instead. Wittgensteinian style is *not* a mere symptom of a psycho-linguistic defect he deplorably might have had,[dxc] but a pragmatic reflection of the performance of thinking in writing, an effect of his philosophical endeavour, *a strikingly necessary feature of the project of the philosophical investigations*, as Wittgenstein himself had to discover. The way in which this project is enacted cannot be arbitrarily or freely chosen.

The ability to discover this might have a source in this mishap – in his dyslexia – but whether he had this misfortune or not, does not make any significant difference with regard to the philosophical import of his writings, be it "Philosophische Untersuchungen" part I, or some other material.—

[dlxxxix] To make it perspicuous: this metaphor compares philosophically perceived natural language to a natural wild wood.

[dxc] For me there remains the steadfast hope and confidence that the Hintikkas did not want to treat Wittgenstein's philosophy in terms of medicine, viz. on the lines of a citation to be found in "Culture and Value", Wittgenstein 1998c: 33 f., cf. sec. Bergen Electronic Edition *MS 118*: 113r from Sept. 24th 1937.

Acknowledgements

Among the many people to whom I am indebted for various reasons, some have a professional connection to the Wittgenstein Archives at the University of Bergen, Norway, be it that they were guest researchers there like I was, or that they worked at the University of Bergen or were otherwise connected to these institutions.

It is not possible to give a complete list of all these people, I just want to mention a few to whom I feel particularly grateful for the animated and constructive discussions I enjoyed with them:

Daniel Apollon (*HIT*-Centre and University of Bergen, Norway), Michael Biggs (University of Hertfordshire, United Kingdom), Anat Biletzki (University of Tel Aviv, Israel), Jeff Bernard (Institute for Socio-Semiotic Studies, Vienna; International Association for Semiotic Studies; Austrian Association for Semiotics), Kevin M. Cahill (University of Bergen, Norway), Herbert Hrachovec (University of Vienna, Austria), Allan S. Janik (Brenner Archives, Innsbruck, Austria), Ralph Jewell (University of Bergen, Norway), Harald Johannessen (University of Bergen, Norway), Michael Luntley (University of Warwick, United Kingdom), Aleksander Motturi (Åbo Akademi, Finland), Alois Pichler (University of Bergen, Norway), Simo Säätelä (University of Bergen, Norway; University of Uppsala, Sweden), Richard Sørli (University of Bergen, Norway), Ludovic Soutif (Sorbonne University, Paris, France), Edward Vanhoutte (Centre for Scholarly Editing and Document Studies, Gent, Belgium), Edoardo Zamuner (University of Bologna, Norway).

For their marvellous job in proofreading I am deeply oblidged to Deirdre C. P. Smith (University of Bergen), who carefully examined *Essay III.*, and to Arlyne Moi (University of Bergen), for her excellent correction of *Essay IV.*, whereas Henrike Banauch (Vienna) largely improved *Essays I.* and *II.* and did the final overall proofreading in a reliable and such an outstanding way that this book would never have been finished without her cooperation. All of these proofreaders gave me valuable hints, criticism, and feedback. I also relied several times on the linguistic abilities of my office neighbour Martha Thunes (*HIT*-Centre, now called *AKSIS*, Bergen), who readily interrupted her own work whenever I came knocking to ask for advice. My proofreaders took their arduous job very seriously; I can only marvel at their patience with such an impatient Austrian as I am. Any remaining linguistic mistakes and lack of idiomatic expressions in a language still alien to me are all to blame on the author.

I would also like to express my special gratitude towards Tom Ballhausen (Vienna), Eugen and Ike Banauch (Vienna), Jeff Bernard (Vienna), Anat Biletzki (Tel Aviv), Anna Hartmann Cavalcanti (Rio de Janeiro), Zhihong Gong (University of Bergen, now back in Taiyuan City, China), Eldbjørg Gunnarson (Wittgenstein Archives at the University of Bergen and *HIT*-Centre, Bergen), Niki and Shannon Rotheneder (Albuquerque, New Mexico), Ludovic Soutif (Paris), and Edoardo Zamuner (Bologna) for their friendship and personal support.

I am extremely sorry if I have left out anybody, it was not done on purpose but can only be the fault of my weak memory.

A small grant from the European Union at the beginning of the year 2003 and a parttime teaching job at the University of Bergen (thanks chiefly to Knut Ågotnes and Vigdis Songe-Møller), combined with the permission of the *HIT*-Centre (now AKSIS) to use the infrastructure at the Wittgenstein Archives at the University of Bergen, made it possible for me to compose this book. For its publication my publisher, capable Norbert Willenpart, was able to attract a subsidy from the Austrian Federal Ministry for Education, Science and Culture, that was to cover the printing costs.—

References[dxci]

Aldrich, Virgil Charles (1958): "Pictorial Meaning, Picture-Thinking, and Wittgenstein's Theory of Aspects", *Mind 67*: 70-79

Ambrose, Alice; Lazerowitz, Morris (1972): *Ludwig Wittgenstein. Philosophy and Language*. London: Allen & Unwin

Ambrose, Alice (1972): "Ludwig Wittgenstein: A Portrait". In: Ambrose & Lazerowitz 1972: 13-25

Amundson, Ron (1981): "Memory and Mind. Review", *Noûs 15, 1*: 101-106

Anscombe, Gertrude Elizabeth Margaret (1976): "The Question of Linguistic Idealism", *Acta Philosophica Fennica XXVIII, 1-3, Essays on Wittgenstein in Honour of G. H. von Wright*. Amsterdam: North-Holland: 188-215

Apel, Karl-Otto (1993): "Pragmatische Sprachphilosophie in transzendentalsemiotischer Begründung". In: Stachowiak 1993: 38-61

Austin, John Langshaw (1962a): *How to do things with Words*. Oxford: Clarendon

Austin, John Langshaw (1962b): *Sense and Sensibilia*. Reconstructed from the manuscript notes by G. J. Warnock. Oxford: Clarendon

Averill, Edward Wilson (1978): "Memory and Mind. Review", *Philosophy and Phenomenological Research 39, 1*: 140-141

Ayer, Alfred Jules (1985): *Wittgenstein*. Chicago: UCP

Baecker, Dirk (Ed.) (1993): *Kalkül der Form*. Frankfurt am Main: Suhrkamp

Baker, Gordon (2002): "Wittgenstein on Metaphysical / Everday Use", *The Philosophical Quarterly 52, 208*: 289-302

Bartley, William Warren (1974): *Wittgenstein*. London: Quarted Books

Bateson, Gregory (1934): "Personal Names Among the Iatmul Tribe (Sepik River)", *Man 34, Royal Anthropological Institute: Proceedings 130*: 109-110

Bateson, Gregory (1936, 1958): Naven: A Survey of the Problems Suggested by a Composite Picture of the Culture of a New Guinea Tribe Drawn from Three Points of View. Cambridge: CUP; Stanford, Calif.: SUP

Bateson, Gregory (1942, 1972c, 1994c): "Comment on »The comparative study of culture and the purposive cultivation of democratic values« by Margaret Mead". In: Bryson & Finkelstein 1942: 81-97 *et* reprinted widely *qua*: "Social Planning and the Concept of Deutero-Learning". In: Bateson 1972a: 159-176. Translation into German by Günter Holl as: "Sozialplanung und der Begriff des Deutero-Lernens". In: Bateson 1994a: 219-240

Bateson, Gregory (1954, 1955a, 1972g, 1994g): "A Theory of Play and Fantasy; a report on theoretical aspects of the project for study of the role of paradoxes of abstraction in communication". *Paper read by Jay Haley to the Symposium of the American Psychiatric Association on Cultural, Anthropological, and Communications Approaches, March 1954, Mexico D. F. et Approaches to the Study of Human Personality. American Psychiatric Association. Psychiatric Reports II, 2*: 39-51. In: Bateson 1972a: 177-193. Translation into German by Günter Holl as: "Eine Theorie des Spiels und der Phantasie". In: Bateson 1994a: 241-261

[dxci] This list of references follows the *rules of citation* given in Gelbmann 2002b: 127 f.; also in this book I tried to keep to it.- For a great article on the philosophical implications of quoting cf. Harald Johannessen 1976.

Bateson, Gregory (1955b, 1972f, 1994f): "How the deviant sees his society", Mimeographed in: *The Epidemiology of Mental Health, Brighton, Utah, May 1955*: 25-31. Reprinted *qua* "The Epidemiology of a Schizophrenia". In: Bateson 1972a: 194-200. Translation into German by Hans Günter Holl as: "Epidemiologie einer Schizophrenie". In: Bateson 1994a: 262-269

Bateson, Gregory; Jackson, Don D.; Haley, Jay; Weakland, John H. (1956, 1972, 1992, 1994): "Toward a Theory of Schizophrenia", *Behavioral Science I, 4*: 251-264. In: Bateson 1972a: 201-227. Translation into German by Hans Werner Saß as: "Auf dem Weg zu einer Schizophrenie-Theorie". In: Bateson *et al.* 1992: 11-43 *et* translation into German by Hans Günter Holl as: "Vorstudien zu einer Theorie der Schizophrenie". In: Bateson 1994a: 270-301

Bateson, Gregory (1959, 1960, 1972e, 1994e): "Minimal Requirements for a Theory of Schizophrenia", Second annual Albert D. Lasker Memorial Lecture at the Institute for Psychosomatic and Psychiatric Research and Training of the Michael Reese Hospital, Chicago, April 1959 et Archives of General Psychiatry 2: 447-491. In: Bateson 1972a: 244-270. Translation by Hans Günter Holl as: "Minimalforderungen für eine Theorie der Schizophrenie". In: Bateson 1994a: 321-352

Bateson, Gregory (1964 & 1971, 1968, 1972d, 1994d): "The Logical Categories of Learning and Communication, and the Acquisition of World-Views", *Paper given at the Wenner-Gren Symposium on World Views: Their Nature and Their Role in Culture, August 1968, Burg Wartenstein, Austria*. In: Bateson 1972a: 279-308. Translation by Hans Günter Holl as: "Die logischen Kategorien von Lernen und Kommunikation". In: Bateson 1994a: 362-399

Bateson, Gregory (1967, 1972b, 1994b): "Cybernetic Explanation", *American Behavioral Scientist 10, 6*: 29-32. In: Bateson 1972a: 399-410. Translation by Hans Günter Holl as: "Kybernetische Erklärung". In: Bateson 1994a: 515-529

Bateson, Gregory et al. (1969, 1992): Schizophrenie und Familie. Beiträge zu einer neuen Theorie von Gregory Bateson, Don D. Jackson, Jay Haley, John H. Weakland, Lyman C. Wynne, Irving M. Ryckoff, Juliana Day, Stanley J. Hirsch, Theodore Lidz, Alice Cornelison, Stephen Fleck, Dorothy Terry, Harold F. Searles, Murray Bowen, Ezra F. Vogel, Norman W. Bell, Ronald D. Laing und J. Foudrain. Frankfurt am Main: Suhrkamp

Bateson, Gregory (1972a, 1977, 1981, 1990, 1994a): *Steps to an Ecology of Mind. Collected Essays in Anthropology, Psychiatry, Evolution and Epistemology*. San Francisco: Chandler *et* New York: Ballantine. Translation into German by Hans Günter Holl as: *Ökologie des Geistes. Anthropologische, psychologische, biologische und epistemologische Perspektiven*. Frankfurt am Main: Suhrkamp

Bateson, Gregory (1979, 1980, 1982, 1995): *Mind and Nature. A Necessary Unity*. London: Wildwood House *et* New York: Dutton *et* New York: Bantam. Translation into German by Hans Günter Holl as: *Geist und Natur. Eine notwendige Einheit*. Frankfurt am Main: Suhrkamp

Beavin, Janet Helmick; Watzlawick, Paul (1966/1967, 1980): "Some Formal Aspects of Communication", *American Behavioral Scientist 10*. Translation into German by Eva Foppa and Paul Watzlawick as: "Einige formale Aspekte der Kommunikation". In: Watzlawick & Weakland 1997: 95-110

Becker, Oskar (1930): "Zur Logik der Modalitäten", *Jahrbuch für Philosophie und Phänomenologische Forschung XII*: 6-15 *et* 502-511. In: Berka & Kreiser 1984: 165-172 (gekürzter Nachdruck von Becker 1930)

Bell, David (1992): "Solipsismus, Subjektivität und öffentliche Welt". In: Vossenkuhl 1992: 29-52

Benjamin, B. S. (1956): "Remembering", *Mind 65, 259*: 312-331

Benthem, Johan van; Meulen, Alice G. B. ter (Eds.) (1997): *Handbook of Logic and Language*. Amsterdam: Elsevier

Berka, Karel; Kreiser, Lothar (Eds.) (1984, 1986): *Logik-Texte. Kommentierte Auswahl zur Geschichte der modernen Logik*. Berlin: Akademie

Bertalanffy, Ludwig von (1968, 1995): General System Theory. Foundations, Development, Applications. New York: Braziller

Bigelow, Julian; Rosenblueth, Arturo; Wiener, Norbert (1943): "Behavior, Purpose and Teleology", *Philosophy of Science, 10*: 18-24

Biletzki, Anat (1997): "Are Speech Acts Language Games (and Vice Versa)?". In: Weingartner & Schurz & Dorn 1997a: 60-65

Biletzki, Anat (2002): "Overinterpreting vs. Misinterpreting Wittgenstein". In: Haller & Puhl 2002: 13-20

Blau, Ulrich (1978): *Die dreiwertige Logik der Sprache*. Berlin: de Gruyter

Blau, Ulrich (1993): "Zur natürlichen Logik der Unbestimmtheiten und Paradoxien". In: Stachowiak 1993: 353-380

Bloor, David (1996): "What did Wittgenstein Mean by »Institution«?". In: Johannessen & Nordenstam 1996: 60-74

Boltzmann, Ludwig (1974a): *Theoretical Physics and Philosophical Problems. Selected Writings* (edited by Brian McGuinness, translated from German into English by Paul Foulkes). Reidel: Dordrecht

Boltzmann, Ludwig (1902 *et* 1910-1911, 1974b): "Model", *Article in the Encyclopaedia Britannica* (edition 1902, reprint 1910-1911). In: Boltzmann 1974a: 213-220

Braithwaite, Richard Bevan (1946, 1968): Scientific Explanation. A Study of the Function of Theory, Probability and Law in Science. Cambridge: CUP

Brandt, Richard (1979): "Memory and Mind. Review", *The Philosophical Review 88, 1*: 105-109

Bryson, Lyman; Finkelstein, Louis (Eds.) (1942): Conference on Science, Philosophy and Religion in Their Relation to the Democratic Way of Life. Second Symposium, New York, September 1941. New York: Columbia University

Bühler, Karl (1934, 1982): Sprachtheorie. Die Darstellungsfunktion der Sprache. Jena: Gustav Fischer

Candlish, Stewart (2002): "Russell and Wittgenstein". In: Haller & Puhl 2002: 21-29

Cassirer, Ernst (1938, 1944): "The Concept of Group and the Theory of Perception", *Journal de Psychologie*: 368-414; *Philosophy and Phenomenological Research 5, 1*: 1-36

Cherry, Colin (1957, 1965): On Human Communication. A Review, a Survey, and a Criticism. Cambridge, Mass.: M. I. T.

Church, Alonzo (1936a): "A Note on the Entscheidungsproblem", *Journal of Symbolic Logic 1, 1*: 40-41 *et* 101-102

Costa, Claudio F. (2000): "Das Paradox der privaten Erfahrung". In: Gehlhaar 2000: 29-56

Descartes, René (1637, 1961): *Discours de la méthode pour bien conduire sa raison et chercher la vérité dans les sciences*. Translation into German by Kuno Fischer as: *Abhandlung über die Methode des richtigen Vernunftgebrauchs*. Stuttgart: Reclam

Descartes, René (1641, 1986): *Meditationes de Prima Philosophia. Meditationen über die Erste Philosophie* (Latein / Deutsch, translation into German by Gerhart Schmidt). Stuttgart: Reclam

Drury, Maurice O'Connor (1973, 1996): *The Danger of Words and writings on Wittgenstein*. London: Routledge & Kegan; Bristol: Thoemmes

Donnellan, Keith S. (1983): "Kripke and Putnam on Natural Kind Terms". In: Ginet & Shoemaker 1983: 84-104

Eco, Umberto (1968, 1972, 1994a): *La struttura assente*. Milano: Bompiani. Translation into German by Jürgen Trabant as: *Einführung in die Semiotik*. München: Fink

Eco, Umberto (1973, 1977): *Segno*. Milano: Istituto Editoriale Internazionale. Translation into German by Günter Memmert as: *Zeichen. Einführung in einen Begriff und seine Geschichte*. Frankfurt am Main: Suhrkamp

Eco, Umberto (1976, 1987, 1991): *A Theory of Semiotics*. Bloomington, Ind.: IUP. Translation into German by Günter Memmert as: *Semiotik. Entwurf einer Theorie der Zeichen*. München: Fink

Eco, Umberto (1993, 1994b, 1995): *La ricerca della lingua perfetta nella cultura europea.* Roma: Laterza. Translation into German by Burkhart Kroeber as: *Die Suche nach der vollkommenen Sprache.* München: Beck

Edmonds, David; Eidinow, John (2001): Wittgenstein's Poker. The Story of a Ten-Minute Argument Between Two Great Philosophers. London: Faber and Faber

Elster, Jon (1980, 1981, 1984): "Négation active et négation passive: Essai de sociologie Ivanniene", *Archives Européennes de Sociologie 21, 2*: 329-349. Translation into German as: "Aktive und passive Negation". In: Watzlawick 1994: 163-191. Translation into English as: "Active and Passive Negation: An Essay in Ibanskian Sociology". In: Watzlawick 1984a: 175-205

Evans, Gareth (1982, 1995a): *The Varieties of Reference* (edited by John McDowell). Oxford: Clarendon

Evans, Gareth (1995b): "Memory". In: Evans 1995a: 235-248

Fann, K. T. (1969): *Wittgenstein's Conception of Philosophy.* Oxford: Blackwell

Fjelland, Ragnar (1999): *Vitenskap mellom sikkerhet og usikkerhet.* Oslo: Gyldendal

Foerster, Heinz von (Ed.) (1949-1953): *Cybernetics* (Five volumes). *Transactions of the 6th, 7th, 8th, and 9th Conferences.* New York: Josiah Macy Jr. Foundation

Foerster, Heinz von (1963, 1965, 1999c): "Memory without Record". In: Kimble 1965: 388-433. Translation by Wolfram Karl Köck as: "Gedächtnis ohne Aufzeichnung". In: Foerster 1999a: 133-171

Foerster, Heinz von (1973a, 1981, 1984): "On Constructing a Reality". In: Preiser 1973/74: 35-46. In: Watzlawick 1984a: 41-61. Translation into German by Wolfram Karl Köck as: "Das Konstruieren einer Wirklichkeit". In: Watzlawick 1994: 39-60

Foerster, Heinz von (1979, 1993c): "Kybernetik der Kybernetik". In: Foerster 1993a: 84-91

Foerster, Heinz von (1991, 1993b, 1995, 2001): "Ethics and Second-order Cybernetics", *International Conference on Systems and Family Therapy: Ethics, Epistemology, New Methods in Paris, France, October 4th 1990.* In: Rey & Prieur 1991 (o. w. A.). Translation into German by Birger Ollrogge as: "Ethik und Kybernetik zweiter Ordnung" in: Foerster 1993a: 60-83, and by Michael von Killisch-Horn in: Watzlawick & Nardone 2001: 71-89. Re-edited in *Cybernetics & Human Knowing. A Journal of Second Order Cybernetics & Cyber-Semiotics (C&HK) 1, 1: http://www.imprint.co.uk/C&HK/vol1/v1-1hvf.htm.* Reprinted in: Franchi & Güzeldere 1995: *http://www.stanford.edu/group/SHR/4-2/text/foerster.html* (electronic documents, last access July 2001)

Foerster, Heinz von (1993a): *KybernEthik.* Berlin: Merve

Foerster, Heinz von (1999a): *Sicht und Einsicht. Versuche zu einer operativen Erkenntnistheorie.* Konstruktivismus und systemisches Denken. Heidelberg: Carl-Auer-Systeme

Foerster, Heinz von (1999b): "Über das Konstruieren von Wirklichkeiten". In: Foerster 1999a: 25-41

Foerster, Heinz von; Glasersfeld, Ernst von (1999): *Wie wir uns erfinden. Eine Autobiographie des radikalen Konstruktivismus.* Heidelberg: Carl-Auer-Systeme

Franchi, Stefano; Güzeldere, Güven (Eds.) (1995): *Constructions of the Mind: Artificial Intelligence and the Humanities. Special issue of Stanford Electronic Humanities Review (SEHR) 4, 2: http://www.stanford.edu/group/SHR/4-2/text/toc.html* (electronic documents, last access Sept. 2000)

Frankl, Viktor Emil (1959, 1973): *Der Mensch auf der Suche nach Sinn. Zur Rehumanisierung der Psychotherapie (Originaltitel: Das Menschenbild in der Seelenheilkunde).* Stuttgart: Hippokrates; Freiburg im Breisgau: Herder

Frege, Gottlob (1879a, 1964, 1993): *Begriffsschrift und andere Aufsätze.* Hildesheim: Georg Olms

Frege, Gottlob (1879b): "Anwendungen der Begriffsschrift", *Sitzungsberichte der Jenaischen Gesellschaft für Medizin und Naturwissenschaft, Sitzung vom 10. 1. 1879*: 1-5. In: Berka & Kreiser 1984: 107-112

Frege, Gottlob (1893/1903, 1966): *Grundgesetze der Arithmetik, begriffsschriftlich abgeleitet.* 2 Bd. Jena: Pohle; Hildesheim: Georg Olms

Gadamer, Hans-Georg; Vogler, Paul (Eds.) (1975): *Neue Anthropologie. Band 7. Philosophische Anthropologie. Zweiter Teil*. Stuttgart: Thieme; München: dtv

Garrett, Brian (2001): "Wittgenstein's Private Language Arguments". In: Haller & Puhl 2001a: 245-250

Gehlhaar, Sabine S. (Ed.) (2000): *Ludwig Wittgenstein*. Dartford: Junghans

Gelbmann, Gerhard (1997a): "Abgeschiedenheit und Transzendenz", *Wiener Jahrbuch für Philosophie XXIX*: 7-33

Gelbmann, Gerhard (1997b): "Grundlagen der Automatentheorie. Dialogsequenzen". *S - European Journal for Semiotic Studies (S - EJSS) 9 (3, 4)*: 557-603

Gelbmann, Gerhard (1998): "Zum Problem der Referenz: Frege versus Eco. Zwei Pole im Universum semiotischer Gestaltung", *S - European Journal for Semiotic Studies 10 (1, 2)*: 73-158

Gelbmann, Gerhard (1999): "Was ist das, »Text«? Eine Anmerkung zum Unverständlichen einiger Selbstverständlichkeiten", *http://h2hobel.phl.univie.ac.at/~yellow/textual/textual.htm* (electronic document, last access: April 2003)

Gelbmann, Gerhard (2000a): "Traumzeit und die Nachzeit der Vorzukunft. Eine philosophische Reaktion auf Herbert Hrachovecens Text »Vorzukunft«", *http://h2hobel.phl.univie.ac.at/~yellow/kant/tempDB.htm* (electronic document, last access: Jan. 2003)

Gelbmann, Gerhard (2000b): *Die pragmatische Kommunikationstheorie. Rekonstruktion, wissenschaftsphilosophischer Hintergrund, Kritik*. Dissertation, Universität Wien; Frankfurt am Main: DHS

Gelbmann, Gerhard (2000c): "The Neopragmatistic Conception of Model", *Proceedings of the 10th International Symposium of the Austrian Association for Semiotics »Myths, Rites, Simulacra. Semiotic Viewpoints«, University of Applied Arts Vienna, Dec. 2000, Angewandte Semiotik 18/19, Vol.I, 2001*: 595-614

Gelbmann, Gerhard (2001a): "Gibt es Prinzipien zwischenmenschlicher Kommunikation? Der Clou des Konstruktivismus". In: Schallhart *et al.* 2001: 25-32 *et Sammelpunkt. Elektronisch archivierte Theorie, http://sammelpunkt.philo.at/* (electronic documents, last access March 2003)

Gelbmann, Gerhard (2001b): "Watzlawick (et al.) und Wittgenstein: Anregungen, Bezugnahmen, Parallelen", *Jahrbuch der Deutschen Ludwig Wittgenstein Gesellschaft 2001/2002*: 9-44 *et Sammelpunkt. Elektronisch archivierte Theorie: http://sammelpunkt.philo.at/* (electronic document, last access: March 2003)

Gelbmann, Gerhard (2002a): "Skript, Text, Werk, Album. Zu Alois Pichlers Umgang mit Wittgensteins Schreiben", *Sammelpunkt. Elektronisch archivierte Theorie, http://sammelpunkt.philo.at/ et http://h2hobel.phl.univie.ac.at/~yellow/Wittgenstein/Pichler.html* (electronic document, last access: Jan. 2003)

Gelbmann, Gerhard (2002b): *Observations on Transaction. A Discussion of Watzlawick's Second Axiom*. European University Studies: Ser.20, Philosophy, Vol.645. Frankfurt am Main: Peter Lang

Gelbmann, Gerhard (2002c): "Pragmatics and the Conceptual Constitutivity of the Social (contra Hintikka and Luntley). Semiotic Subjectivity I", *Lecture at the Department of Philosophy, University of Bergen, Norway, May 2002. Sammelpunkt. Elektronisch archivierte Theorie, http://sammelpunkt.philo.at/ et http://h2hobel.phl.univie.ac.at ~yellow/projects/lecture1.htm* (electronic document, last access: Aug. 2002)

Gelbmann, Gerhard (2002d): "An Outline of Pragmatologic Model-Theory (sec. Stachowiak). Semiotic Subjectivity II", *Lecture at the HIT Centre, Bergen, Norway, June 2002. Sammelpunkt. Elektronisch archivierte Theorie: http://sammelpunkt.philo.at/ et http://h2hobel.phl.univie.ac.at/~yellow/projects/lecture2.htm* (electronic document, last access: Feb. 2003)

Gelbmann, Gerhard (2002e): "Persons as Socio-Semiotic Subjects. Semiotic Subjectivity III. Presentation of Observations on Transaction", *Lecture at the HIT Centre, Bergen, Norway, August 2002. Sammelpunkt. Elektronisch archivierte Theorie: http://sammelpunkt.philo.at/ et http://h2hobel.phl.univie.ac.at/~yellow/projects/lecture3.htm* (electronic document, last access: Sept. 2002)

Gelbmann, Gerhard (2002f): "Sind Zahlen Attribute?", *Sammelpunkt. Elektronisch archivierte Theorie*: *http://sammelpunkt.philo.at/* et *http://h2hobel.phl.univie.ac.at/~yellow/Stachowiak/attribut.html* (elec-tronic document, last access: May 2003)

Ginet, Carl; Shoemaker, Sidney (1983): *Knowledge and Mind. Philosophical Essays* (in honour of Norman Malcolm). Oxford: OUP

Gleick, James (1987): *Making A New Science*. New York: Viking

Glock, Hans-Johann (1996, 2000): *A Wittgenstein Dictionary*. The Blackwell Philosopher Dictionaries. Oxford: Blackwell

Gödel, Kurt (1931): "Über formal unentscheidbare Sätze der Principia Mathematica und verwandter Systeme I", *Monatshefte für Mathematik und Physik 38*: 173-198. In: Berka & Kreiser 1984: 347-370

Gombrich, Ernst Hans (1960): *Art and Illusion. A Study in the Psychology of Pictorial Representation*. Bollingen Series XXXV, The A. W. Mellon Lectures in the Fine Arts 5. New York: Pantheon

Grice, Herbert Paul (1957): "Meaning", *The Philosophical Review 66, 3*: 377-388

Grice, Herbert Paul (1969): "Utterer's Meaning and Intention", *The Philosophical Review 78, 2*: 147-177

Gumin, Heinz; Meier, Heinrich (Eds.) (1985): *Einführung in den Konstruktivismus. Mit Beiträgen von Heinz von Foerster, Ernst von Glasersfeld, Peter M. Hejl, Siegfried J. Schmidt und Paul Watzlawick*. München: Piper

Hacker, Peter Michael Stephan (1996): *Wittgenstein. Mind and Will. An Analytical Commentary on the Philosophical Investigations*. Vol.4. Cambridge, Mass.: Blackwell

Haller, Rudolf; Puhl, Klaus (Eds.) (2001a): *Wittgenstein and the Future of Philosophy. A Reassessment after 50 Years. Papers of the 24th International Wittgenstein-Symposium, Kirchberg am Wechsel 2001*. Vol.1. Österreichische Ludwig Wittgenstein Gesellschaft, Kirchberg am Wechsel

Haller, Rudolf; Puhl, Klaus (Eds.) (2001b): *Wittgenstein and the Future of Philosophy. A Reassessment after 50 Years. Papers of the 24th International Wittgenstein-Symposium, Kirchberg am Wechsel 2001*. Vol.2. Österreichische Ludwig Wittgenstein Gesellschaft, Kirchberg am Wechsel

Haller, Rudolf; Puhl, Klaus (Eds.) (2002): *Wittgenstein and the Future of Philosophy. A Reassessment after 50 Years. Proceedings of the 24th International Wittgenstein-Symposium, Kirchberg am Wechsel 2001*. Vienna: ÖBV&HPT

Hark, Michel ter (1990): *Beyond the Inner and the Outer. Wittgenstein's Philosophy of Psychology*. Dordrecht: Kluwer

Hark, Michel ter (1994): "Wittgenstein and Russell on psychology and other minds", *Wittgenstein Studies 2*: *07-2-94.txt et http://sammelpunkt.philo.at/* (electronic document, last access: April 2003)

Hark, Michel ter (1995a): "Wittgenstein und Russell über Psychologie und Fremdpsychisches". In: Savigny & Scholz 1995: 84-106

Hark, Michel ter (1995b): "Electric Brain Fields and Memory Traces: Wittgenstein and Gestalt Psychology", *Philosophical Investigations 18, 1*: 113-138

Heisenberg, Werner (1969, 1985): *Der Teil und das Ganze. Gespräche im Umkreis der Atomphysik*. München: dtv

Hejl, Peter M. (1985): "Konstruktion der sozialen Konstruktion. Grundlinien einer konstruktivistischen Sozialtheorie". In: Gumin & Meier 1985: 109-146

Hempel, Carl Gustav (1965): *Aspects of Scientific Explanation and Other Essays in the Philosophy of Science*. New York: Free Press

Hertz, Heinrich Rudolf (1894, 1910, 1956): *Gesammelte Werke* Band III. *Die Prinzipien der Mechanik in neuem Zusammenhange dargestellt*. Leipzig: Barth. English translation by Jones & Walley: *The Principles of Mechanics, presented in a new form*. New York: Dover

Hintikka, Jaakko (1958): "On Wittgenstein's »Solipsism«", *Mind 67, 265*: 88-91

Hintikka, Jaakko (1962): "Cogito, Ergo Sum: Inference or Performance", *The Philosophical Review 71, 1*: 3-32

Hintikka, Jaakko (1976, 1996l): "Language-Games", *Acta Philosophica Fennica XXVIII, 1-3, Essays on Wittgenstein in Honour of G. H. von Wright*. Amsterdam: North-Holland: 105-125. In: Hintikka 1996a: 275-295

Hintikka, Jaakko; Hintikka, Merrill B. (1985a, 1996h): "Ludwig Looks at the Necker Cube: The Problem of 'Seeing As' as a Clue to Wittgenstein's Philosophy", *Acta Philosophica Fennica XXXVIII*: 36-48. In: Hintikka 1996a: 179-189

Hintikka, Jaakko; Halonen, Ilpo (1995): "Semantics and Pragmatics for Why-Questions", *The Journal of Philosophy 92, 12*: 636-657

Hintikka, Jaakko (1996a): *Ludwig Wittgenstein: Half-Truths and One-and-a-Half-Truths*. Dordrecht: Kluwer

Hintikka, Jaakko (1991, 1996b): "An Impatient Man and His Papers", *Synthese 87*: 183-201. In: Hintikka 1996a: 1-19

Hintikka, Jaakko (1996c): "An Anatomy of Wittgenstein's Picture Theory". In: Hintikka 1996a: 21-54

Hintikka, Jaakko (1996d): "Die Wende der Philosophie: Wittgenstein's New Logic of 1928". In: Hintikka 1996a: 79-105

Hintikka, Jaakko; Hintikka, Merrill B. (1985b, 1996e): "Wittgenstein's *Annus Mirabilis*: 1929". In: Hintikka 1996a: 107-124

Hintikka, Jaakko (1996f): "Ludwig's Apple Tree: On the Philosophical Relations between Wittgenstein and the Vienna Circle". In: Hintikka 1996a: 125-144

Hintikka, Jaakko (1996g): "The Original *Sinn* of Wittgenstein's Philosophy of Mathematics". In: Hintikka 1996a: 145-177

Hintikka, Jaakko (1996i): "Wittgenstein as a Philosopher of Immediate Experience". In: Hintikka 1996a: 191-208

Hintikka, Jaakko (1996j): "Wittgenstein and the Problem of Phenomenology". In: Hintikka 1996a: 209-240

Hintikka, Jaakko (1996k): "Wittgenstein on Being and Time". In: Hintikka 1996a: 241-274

Hintikka, Jaakko (1996m): "Rules, Games and Experiences: Wittgenstein's Discussion of Rule-Following in the Light of His Development". In: Hintikka 1996a: 315-333

Hintikka, Jaakko; Sandu, Gabriel (1997): "Game-theoretical semantics". In: van Benthem & ter Meulen 1997: 361-410

Hintikka, Jaakko; Hintikka, Anna-Maija (2002): "Wittgenstein the Bewitched Writer". In: Haller & Puhl 2002: 131-150

Hofstadter, Douglas R. (1995): "on seeing A's and seeing As". In: Franchi & Güzeldere 1995: *http://www.stanford.edu/group/SHR/4-2/text/hofstadter.html* (electronic document, last access Sept. 2000)

Houser, Nathan; Roberts, Don D.; Evra, James Van (Eds.) (1997): *Studies in the Logic of Charles Sanders Peirce*. Bloomington, Ind.: IUP

Hoyningen-Huene, Paul (1989): *Die Wissenschaftsphilosophie von Thomas S. Kuhn. Rekonstruktion und Grundlagenprobleme*. Braunschweig: Vieweg

Hrachovec, Herbert (1994): "Vorzukunft", *Wittgenstein Studien 1*: *11-1-94.txt* et *http://hhobel.phl.univie.ac.at/~herbert/vorzukunft/vorzukunft.html* et *http://sammelpunkt.philo.at/* (electronic document, last access: Jan. 2003)

Jackson, Don D. (1967, 1977, 1980): "The Myth of Normality", *Medical Opinion and Review 5*: 28-33. Translation into German by Eva Foppa and Paul Watzlawick as: "Der Mythos der Normalität". In: Watzlawick & Weakland 1997: 225-233

James, William (1890, 1990): *The Principles of Psychology*. New York: Holt; Chicago: Encyclopædia Britannica

Janik, Allan; Toulmin, Stephen (1973): *Wittgenstein's Vienna*. New York: Simon & Schuster

Janik, Allan (1994/95): "How Did Hertz Influence Wittgenstein's Philosophical Development?", *Grazer Philosophische Studien 49*: 19-47

Janik, Allan (1999): "Wittgenstein, Hertz and Hermeneutics", *Paper at the Wittgenstein Symposium at the Royal Irish Academy, Dublin, Nov. 22nd 1999* (electronic document): *http://www.ria.ie/committees/abstract%201999.PDF* (last access: August 2002)

Janik, Allan (2002): "On the Limits of Language and Other Nonsense". In: Haller & Puhl 2002: 171-175

Janik, Allan (2003): "Art, Craftsmanship and Philosophical Method According to Wittgenstein", *Rue Descartes. Revue Collège International de Philosophie 39*: 18-27 et Sammelpunkt. Elektronisch archivierte Theorie: *http://sammelpunkt.philo.at/* (electronic document, last access: Feb. 2003)

Jastrow, Joseph (1900): *Fact and Fable in Psychology*. Boston: Houghton & Mifflin

Jastrow, Joseph (1916): "Charles S. Peirce as a Teacher", *The Journal of Philosophy, Psychology and Scientific Methods 13, 26*: 723-726

Johannessen, Harald (1976): "On Quoting. An Essay on the Ontology of Words", *Det Kongelige Norske Videnskabers Selskab Skrifter 6*: 1-54

Johannessen, Kjell S.; Nordenstam, Tore (Eds.) (1995): *Culture and Value. Philosophy and the Cultural Sciences. Papers of the 18th International Wittgenstein-Symposium, Kirchberg am Wechsel 1995. Contributions of the Austrian Ludwig Wittgenstein Society* Vol.III. Vienna

Johannessen, Kjell S.; Nordenstam, Tore (Eds.) (1996): *Wittgenstein and the Philosophy of Culture. Proceedings of the 18th International Wittgenstein-Symposium, Kirchberg am Wechsel 1995.* Vienna: HPT

Kainz, Friedrich (1972): *Über die Sprachverführung des Denkens*. Erfahrung und Denken, Schriften zur Förderung der Beziehungen zwischen Philosophie und Einzelwissenschaften, Band 38. Berlin: Duncker & Humblot

Kant, Immanuel (1781, 1787, 1966): *Kritik der reinen Vernunft*. Stuttgart: Reclam

Kant, Immanuel (1783, 1989): *Prolegomena zu einer jeden künftigen Metaphysik, die als Wissenschaft wird auftreten können*. Stuttgart: Reclam

Kant, Immanuel (1788, 1961): *Kritik der praktischen Vernunft*. Stuttgart: Reclam

Kapitan, Tomis (1997): "Peirce and the Structure of Abductive Inference". In: Houser & Roberts & Evra 1997: 477-496

Keicher, Peter (2003): "Aspekte malerischer Gestaltung bei Ludwig Wittgenstein". Appears in: Neumer, Katalin (Ed.) (2003): *Traditionen Wittgensteins* [working title]. Wittgenstein Studies. Frankfurt am Main: Peter Lang

Kenny, Anthony (1976): "From the Big Typescript to the Philosophical Grammar", *Acta Philosophica Fennica XXVIII, 1-3, Essays on Wittgenstein in Honour of G. H. von Wright*. Amsterdam: North-Holland: 41-53

Kienzle, Bertram; Pape, Helmut (Eds.) (1991): *Dimensionen des Selbst. Selbstbewusstsein, Reflexivität und die Bedingungen von Kommunikation*. Frankfurt am Main: Suhrkamp

Kimble, Daniel Porter (1965): *The Anatomy of Memory. Proceedings of the First Conference on Learning, Remembering, and Forgetting, Princeton, New Jersey, 1963*. Palo Alto: Science and Behavior Books

Kleene, Stephen C. (1943): "Recursive Predicates and Quantifiers", *Transactions of the American Mathematical Society, 53*: 41-73

Kopytko, Roman (2001): "From Cartesian towards non-Cartesian pragmatics", *Journal of Pragmatics 33*: 783-804

Kraft, Victor (1950, 1997): *Der Wiener Kreis. Der Ursprung des Neopositivismus*. Wien: Springer

Kreuzer, Franz (Interview) (1982): *Die Welt als Labyrinth. Die Unsicherheit unserer Wirklichkeit. Franz Kreuzer im Gespräch mit Friedrich Dürrenmatt, Paul Watzlawick*. Wien: Deuticke

Kripke, Saul A. (1963a): "Semantical analysis of modal logic I. Normal modal propositional calculi", *Zeitschrift für mathematische Logik und Grundlagen der Mathematik 9*: 67-96. In: Berka & Kreiser 1984: 177-181 (abbreviated translation into German of Kripke 1963a: 67-70)

Kripke, Saul A. (1963b): "Semantical Considerations on Modal Logic". *Acta Philosophica Fennica XVI*: 83-94

Kripke, Saul A. (1980): *Naming and Necessity*. Oxford: Blackwell

Kripke, Saul A. (1982, 1987): *Wittgenstein on Rules and Private Language. An Elementary Exposition*. Oxford: Blackwell. Translation into German by Helmut Pape as: *Wittgenstein über Regeln und Privatsprache. Eine elementare Darstellung*. Frankfurt am Main: Suhrkamp

Krüger, Heinz Wilhelm (1993): "Die Entstehung des *Big Typescript*". In: Puhl 1993: 303-312

Kuhn, Thomas Samuel (1962, 1967, 1969, 1970c, 1991): *The Structure of Scientific Revolutions*. Chicago: UCP. In: Neurath & Carnap & Morris 1970: 53-272. Translation into German by Kurt Simon, revised by Hermann Vetter as: *Die Struktur wissenschaftlicher Revolutionen*. Frankfurt am Main: Suhrkamp

Kuhn, Thomas Samuel (1965a, 1970a): "Logic of Discovery or Psychology of Research?". In: Lakatos & Musgrave 1970: 1-20

Kuhn, Thomas Samuel (1965b, 1970b): "Reflections on my Critics". In: Lakatos & Musgrave 1970: 231-278

Kuhn, Thomas Samuel (1977, 1992): *The Essential Tension. Selected Studies in Scientific Tradition and Change*. Chicago: UCP. Translation into German by Hermann Vetter as: *Die Entstehung des Neuen. Studien zur Struktur der Wissenschaftsgeschichte*. Frankfurt am Main: Suhrkamp

Laing, Ronald David (1967, 1969): *The Politics of Experience*. Harmondsworth: Penguin. Translation into German by Klaus Figge and Waltraud Stein as: *Phänomenologie der Erfahrung*. Frankfurt am Main: Suhrkamp

Laing, Ronald D. (1970): *Knots*. London: Tavistock

Lakatos, Imre (1965, 1970): "Falsification and the Methodology of Scientific Research Programmes". In: Lakatos & Musgrave 1970: 91-195

Lakatos, Imre; Musgrave, Alan (Eds.) (1970): *Criticism and the Growth of Knowledge*. Cambridge: CUP

Leinfellner, Elisabeth; Haller, Rudolf; Leinfellner, Werner; Weingartner, Paul (Eds.) (1993): *Philosophy and the Cognitive Sciences. Papers of the 16th International Wittgenstein-Symposium, Kirchberg am Wechsel 1993*. Vol.1. Österreichische Ludwig Wittgenstein Gesellschaft, Kirchberg am Wechsel

Lenk, Hans; Maring, Matthias (1987): "Pragmatische Elemente im Kritischen Rationalismus". In: Stachowiak 1987a: 257-278

Locke, Don (1978): "Memory and Mind. Review", *Mind 87, 348*: 631-633

Luckhardt, C. G. (Ed.) (1979, 1996): *Wittgenstein. Sources and Perspectives*. Cornell University; Bristol: Thoemmes

Lukasiewicz, Jan (1930): "Philosophische Bemerkungen zu mehrwertigen Systemen des Aussagenkalküls", *Comptes Rendus des Séance de la Société des Sciences et des Lettres de Varsovie Cl. III, XXIII*: 51-74. In: Berka & Kreiser 1984: 135-150 (gekürzter Nachdruck von Lukasiewicz 1930)

Malcolm, Norman (1942): "Certainty and Empirical Statements", *Mind 51, 201*: 18-46

Malcolm, Norman (1951): "Philosophy for Philosophers (Philosophy and Ordinary Language)", *The Philosophical Review 60, 3*: 329-340

Malcolm, Norman (1954, 1963b, 1966c): "Wittgenstein's *Philosophical Investigations*", *The Philosophical Review 63, 4*: 530-559. In: Malcolm 1963a: 96-129. In: Pitcher 1966: 65-103

Malcolm, Norman (1956): "Dreaming and Skepticism", *The Philosophical Review 65, 1*: 14-37

Malcolm, Norman (1958a, 1966a, 1984): *Ludwig Wittgenstein. A Memoir (with a biographical sketch by Georg Henrik von Wright)*. London: OUP

Malcolm, Norman (1958b, 1963d, 1966b): "Knowledge of other minds", *The Journal of Philosophy 55, 23*: 969-978. In: Malcolm 1963a: 130-140. In: Pitcher 1966: 371-383

Malcolm, Norman (1963a): *Knowledge and Certainty: Essays and Lectures*. Englewood Cliffs, N. J.: Prentice-Hall

Malcolm, Norman (1963c): "A Definition of Factual Memory". In: Malcolm 1963a: 222-240

Malcolm, Norman (1964): "Behaviorism as a Philosophy of Psychology". In: Wann 1964: 141-162

Malcolm, Norman (1970): "Memory and Representation", *Noûs 4, 1*: 59-70

Malcolm, Norman (1977): *Memory and Mind*. Ithaca, New York: Cornell UP

Malcolm, Norman (1986): *Wittgenstein: Nothing Is Hidden*. Oxford: Blackwell

Marc, Edmond; Picard, Dominique (1984, 1991): *L'école de Palo Alto*. Paris: Éditions Retz. Translation into German by Hans Günter Holl as: *Bateson, Watzlawick und die Schule von Palo Alto*. Frankfurt am Main: Hain

Martin, Charles Burton; Deutscher, Max (1966): "Remembering", *The Philosophical Review 75, 2*: 161-196

McGuinness, Brian F. (1972): "Bertrand Russell and Ludwig Wittgenstein's »Notes on Logic«", *Revue International de Philosophie 102, 4*: 444-460

McGuinness, Brian F. (1988a, 1988b): *Wittgenstein: A Life. Young Wittgenstein (1889 - 1921)*. London: Duckworth. Translation into German by Joachim Schulte as: *Wittgenstein's frühe Jahre*. Frankfurt am Main: Suhrkamp

McGuinness, Brian F.; Schulte, Joachim (Eds.) (1989, 2001): *Ludwig Wittgenstein. Logisch-philosophische Abhandlung. Tractatus logico-philosophicus. Kritische Edition*. Frankfurt am Main: Suhrkamp

Meggle, Georg (1991): "Kommunikation und Reflexivität". In: Kienzle & Pape 1991: 375-404

Minsky, Marvin L. (1968a): *Semantic Information Processing*. Cambridge, Mass.: M. I. T.

Minsky, Marvin L. (1968b): "Matter, Mind, and Models". In: Minsky 1968a: 425-432

Monk, Ray (1990, 1991): *Ludwig Wittgenstein. The Duty of Genius*. London: Jonathan Cape et Vintage

Morris, Charles W. (1938): "Foundations of the Theory of Signs". *International Encyclopedia of Unified Science, Foundations of the Unity of Science I, 2*: iii et 1-59

Morris, Charles W. (1975): "Sprechen und menschliches Handeln". In: Gadamer & Vogler 1975: 235-251

Müller, Roland (1983): "Zur Geschichte des Modelldenkens und des Modellbegriffs". In: Stachowiak 1983a: 17-86

Mulligan, Kevin; Simons, Peter; Smith, Barry (1984): "Truth-Makers", *Philosophy and Phenomenological Research 44, 3*: 287-321

Nagel, Ernest; Newman, James R. (1958, 1984, 1992): *Gödel's Proof*. New York: NYUP. Translation into German by Hubert Schleichert as: *Der Gödelsche Beweis*. Scientia nova. Wien: Oldenbourg

Nardone, Giorgio; Watzlawick, Paul (1990, 1994): *L'Arte del Cambiamento. Manuale die terapia strategica e ipnoterapia senza trance*. Firenze: Ponte alle Grazie. Translation into German by Erika Frey Timillero as: *Irrwege, Umwege und Auswege. Zur Therapie versuchter Lösungen*. Bern: Hans Huber

Nedo, Michael (1993): *Ludwig Wittgenstein. Wiener Ausgabe. Einführung – Introduction*. Wien: Springer

Neurath, Otto; Carnap, Rudolf; Morris, Charles W. (Eds.) (1939 ff., 1970): *Foundations of the Unity of Science. Toward an Encyclopedia of Unified Science (former title: International Encyclopedia of Unified Science)*. Chicago: UCP

Nientied, Mariele (2001): "Autonome Grammatik – Linguistischer Idealismus? Ein Versuch mit Wittgenstein und Peirce". In: Haller & Puhl 2001b: 122-129

Nyíri, Kristóf J. C. (2001): "Wittgenstein's Philosophy of Pictures", *Wittgenstein Research Revisited. Reflecting upon 50 years of work on Wittgenstein and investigating future perspectives. Conference at the University of Bergen, Norway, Dec. 2001* (Unpublished electronic typescript read at the Wittgenstein Archives at the University of Bergen in summer 2002; publication of transactions forthcoming; see also *http://www.fil.hu/uniworld/nyiri/bergen/* (unaccessable in Feb. 2003, read in Jan. 2003))

Nyíri, Kristóf J. C. (2002): "Pictures as Instruments in the Philosophy of Wittgenstein". In: Haller & Puhl 2002: 328-336

Ogden, Charles Kay; Richards, Ivor Armstrong (1923, 1985): *The Meaning of Meaning. A study of the influence of language upon thought and the science of symbolism.* London: Routledge

Ortner, Hanspeter (2000): "Wittgenstein als Schreibstratege", *The Wittgenstein Archives' Discussion Forum, http://www.hit.uib.no/wab/el_texts/ortner/* (electronic documents, last access April 2003)

Peirce, Charles Sanders (1865-1903, 2000a): *Semiotische Schriften.* Band I (edited and translation into German by Christian J. W. Kloesel and Helmut Pape). Frankfurt am Main: Suhrkamp

Peirce, Charles Sanders (1903-1906, 2000b): *Semiotische Schriften.* Band II (edited and translation into German by Christian J. W. Kloesel and Helmut Pape). Frankfurt am Main: Suhrkamp

Peirce, Charles Sanders (1906-1913, 2000c): *Semiotische Schriften.* Band III (edited and translation into German by Christian J. W. Kloesel and Helmut Pape). Frankfurt am Main: Suhrkamp

Peirce, Charles Sanders (1885): "On the algebra of logic. A contribution to the philosophy of notation". *The American Journal of Mathematics 7*: 180-202

Peirce, Charles Sanders (1983, 1993): *Phänomen und Logik der Zeichen. (Syllabus of Certain Topics of Logic).* Frankfurt am Main: Suhrkamp

Perceval, John Thomas (1838-1840, 1961): *A Narrative of the Treatment Experienced by a Gentleman, During a State of Mental Derangement; Designed to Explain the Causes and the Nature of Insanity, and to Expose the Injudicious Conduct Pursued towards many Unfortunate Sufferers under that Calamity.* London: Effingham Wilson, Royal Exchange. Edited by Gregory Bateson as: *Perceval's Narrative. A Patient's Account of His Psychosis. 1830 - 1832.* Stanford, Calif.: SUP

Piaget, Jean (1954): *The Construction of Reality in the Child.* New York: Basic Books

Pichler, Alois (1992): "Wittgensteins spätere Manuskripte: einige Bemerkungen zu Stil und Schreiben", *Mitteilungen aus dem Brenner Archiv 12*: 8-26

Pichler, Alois (1993): "What is Transcription Really?", *The 1993 Joint International Conference, The Association for Computers and the Humanities, The Association for Literary and Linguistic Computing Georgetown University, Washington D.C. 16th-19th June 1993. Conference Abstracts* 88-91

Pichler, Alois (1994): "Untersuchungen zu Wittgensteins Nachlaß". *Skriftserie fra Wittgensteinarkivet ved Universitetet i Bergen 8*

Pichler, Alois (1995): "Transcriptions, Texts and Interpretation". In: Johannessen & Nordenstam 1996: 690-695

Pichler, Alois (1997a): "Wittgensteins PHILOSOPHISCHE UNTERSUCHUNGEN: Zur Textgenese von PU §§1-4", *Skriftserie fra Wittgensteinarkivet ved Universitetet i Bergen 14*

Pichler, Alois (1997b): *Wittgenstein und das Schreiben: Ansätze zu einem Schreiberporträt.* Diplomarbeit, Universität Innsbruck

Pichler, Alois (2000): "Tekster og fortolkninger eller homo hermeneuticus", *Lecture at the University of Bergen, Norway, May 2000. Sammelpunkt. Elektronisch archivierte Theorie: http://sammelpunkt.philo.at/* (electronic documents, last access May 2003)

Pichler, Alois (2001a): *Wittgensteins »Philosophische Untersuchungen«: Vom Buch zum Album.* Overworked, unpublished version of doktoravhandlingen, Universitetet i Bergen

Pichler, Alois (2001b): "5 Thesen zu der Entstehung und Eigenart der Philosophischen Untersuchungen". In: Haller & Puhl 2001b: 167-174

Pichler, Alois (2002): "Drei Thesen zu der Entstehung und Eigenart der *Philosophischen Untersuchungen*: Fragment, Album, Polyphonie". In: Haller & Puhl 2002: 355-365

Pitcher, George (Ed.) (1966): *Wittgenstein. The Philosophical Investigations. A Collection of Critical Essays*. Modern Studies in Philosophy. Garden City, N. Y.: Anchor

Pollok, Konstantin (2001): "Aggregatzustände des Wissens. Die Grundlagen der Wissenschaft im Lichte Wittgensteins Bemerkungen *Über Gewißheit*". In: Haller & Puhl 2001b: 193-201

Popper, Karl Raimund (1930-1933, 1979, 1994a): *Die beiden Grundprobleme der Erkenntnistheorie* (aufgrund von Manuskripten aus den Jahren 1930 - 1933 herausgegeben von Trøls Eggers Hansen). Tübingen: Mohr

Popper, Karl Raimund (1934, 1959, 1966, 1980, 1994b): *The Logic of Scientific Discovery*. London: Hutchinson; New York: Basic Books. Translation into German by Leonhard Walentik as: *Die Logik der Forschung*. Tübingen: Mohr

Popper, Karl Raimund (1945a, 1958a, 1992a): *The Open Society and Its Enemies*. Vol.1: *The Spell of Plato*. London: Routledge. Translation into German by Paul K. Feyerabend und Klaus Pähler as: *Die offene Gesellschaft und ihre Feinde*. Band I: *Der Zauber Platons*. Tübingen: Mohr

Popper, Karl Raimund (1945b, 1958b, 1992b): *The Open Society and Its Enemies*. Vol.2: *The High Tide of Prophecy: Hegel, Marx and the Aftermath*. London: Routledge. Translation into German by Paul K. Feyerabend und Klaus Pähler as: *Die offene Gesellschaft und ihre Feinde*. Band II: *Falsche Propheten. Hegel, Marx und die Folgen*. Tübingen: Mohr

Popper, Karl Raimund (1957, 1965, 1987): *The Poverty of Historicism*. London: Routledge. Translation into German by Leonhard Walentik as: *Das Elend des Historizismus*. Tübingen: Mohr

Popper, Karl Raimund (1963, 1989): *Conjectures and Refutations. The Growth of Scientific Knowledge*. London: Routledge & Kegan

Popper, Karl Raimund (1984, 1990): *Auf der Suche nach einer besseren Welt. Vorträge und Aufsätze aus dreißig Jahren*. München: Piper

Popper, Karl Raimund (1995): *A World of Propensities*. Bristol: Thoemmes

Puhl, Klaus (Ed.) (1993): *Wittgensteins Philosophie der Mathematik. Akten des 15. Internationalen Wittgenstein-Symposiums II, August 1992 in Kirchberg am Wechsel (Österreich)*. Wien: HPT

Putnam, Hilary (1975, 1979): *Mathematics, Matter and Method. Philosophical Papers* Vol.1. New York: CUP

Quillian, M. Ross (1968): "Semantic Memory". In: Minsky 1968a: 227-270

Quitterer, Josef (2001): "Wittgenstein und die Cambridge-Theorie der Repräsentation". In: Haller & Puhl 2001b: 208-214

Redpath, Theodore (1990): *Ludwig Wittgenstein. A Student's Memoir*. London: Duckworth

Resnikow, Lasar Ossipowitsch (1968): *Erkenntnistheoretische Fragen der Semiotik*. Berlin: VEB

Rey, Yveline; Prieur, Bernard (Eds.) (1991): *Systèmes, Ethique, Perspectives en thèrapie familiale*. Paris: ESF éditeur

Rhees, Rush (1977); edited and introduced by Phillips, Dewi Zephaniah (1996): "Discussion. On Editing Wittgenstein", *Philosophical Investigations 19*: 55-61

Rosenhan, David L. (1973, 1981, 1984): "On being sane in insane places", *Science 179*: 250-258. In: Watzlawick 1984a: 117-144. Translation into German as: "Gesund in kranker Umgebung". In: Watzlawick 1981a: 111-137

Rothhaupt, Josef G. F. (1996): *Farbthemen in Wittgensteins Gesamtnachlaß. Philologisch-philosophische Untersuchungen im Längsschnitt und in Querschnitten*. Weinheim: Beltz Athenäum

Rudich, Norman; Strassen, Manfred (1971): "Wittgenstein's Implied Anthropology: Remarks on Wittgenstein's Notes on Frazer", *History and Theory*, 10: 84-89

Ruesch, Jurgen; Bateson, Gregory (1951, 1987): *Communication. The Social Matrix of Psychiatry.* New York: Norton

Russell, Bertrand (1908): "Mathematical Logic as Based on the Theory of Types", *American Journal of Mathematics 30, 3*: 222 262

Russell, Bertrand (1921, 1989): *The Analysis of Mind.* Muirhead Library of Philosophy. London: Allen & Unwin

Säätelä, Simo (2001): "Art, Opinions, and Attitudes". In: Haller & Puhl 2001b: 258-263

Sartre, Jean-Paul (1943, 1962): *L' Être et le Néant.* Paris: Gallimard. Translation from French into German by Justus Streller, August Ott, and Alexa Wagner as: *Das Sein und das Nichts. Versuch einer phänomenologischen Ontologie.* Reinbek bei Hamburg: Rowohlt

Savigny, Eike von (1969, 1993): *Die Philosophie der normalen Sprache. Eine kritische Einführung in die "ordinary language philosophy".* Frankfurt am Main: Suhrkamp

Savigny, Eike von (1988): *Wittgensteins 'Philosophische Untersuchungen'. Ein Kommentar für Leser.* Bd. I und II. Frankfurt am Main: Klostermann

Savigny, Eike von (1991): "Self-Conscious Individual versus Social Soul: The Rationale of Wittgenstein's Discussion of Rule Following", *Philosophy and Phenomenological Research 51, 1*: 67-84

Savigny, Eike von; Scholz, Oliver R. (Eds.) (1995): *Wittgenstein über die Seele.* Frankfurt am Main: Suhrkamp

Savigny, Eike von (1996a): *Der Mensch als Mitmensch. Wittgensteins "Philosophische Untersuchungen".* München: dtv

Savigny, Eike von (1996b): "Psychological Facts: Social Facts about Individuals". In: Johannessen & Nordenstam 1996: 218-231

Savigny, Eike von (2002): "Private Language – Private Rules – Private Sensations: A Draw Position?". In: Haller & Puhl 2002: 389-398

Sayward, Charles (2001): "On Some Much Maligned Remarks of Wittgenstein on Gödel", *Philosophical Investigations 24, 3*: 262-270

Schäfer, Lothar (1987): "Der Konventionalismus des beginnenden 20. Jahrhunderts: Entstehungsbedingungen, Einsichten, Probleme". In: Stachowiak 1987a: 59-82

Schulte, Joachim (1987, 1993, 1995a): *Erlebnis und Ausdruck. Wittgensteins Philosophie der Psychologie.* München: Philosophia. Translation into English by Joachim Schulte as: *Experience and Expression. Wittgenstein's Philosophy of Psychology.* Oxford: Clarendon

Schulte, Joachim (1989): *Wittgenstein. Eine Einführung.* Stuttgart: Reclam

Schulte, Joachim (1995b): "Memory". In: Schulte 1995a: 95-119

Schulte, Joachim; Nyman, Heikki; Savigny, Eike von; Wright, Georg Henrik von (Eds.) (2001): *Wittgenstein, Ludwig: Philosophische Untersuchungen. Kritisch genetische Edition.* Frankfurt am Main: Suhrkamp

Schulte, Joachim (2002): "Wittgenstein's »Method«". In: Haller & Puhl 2002: 399-410

Searle, John R. (1995): *The Construction of Social Reality.* New York: Free Press

Seekircher, Monika (1995): "Arbeit, Technik, Sprache: Die Bedeutung von 'Tacit Know-ledge' in der experimentellen Physik". In: Johannessen & Nordenstam 1995: 418-425

Semon, Richard (1904): *Die Mneme als erhaltendes Prinzip im Wechsel des organischen Geschehens.* Leipzig: Engelmann

Shannon, Claude E.; Weaver, Warren (1949, 1963): *The Mathematical Theory of Communication.* Urbana, Ill.: Illini Book

Spencer-Brown, George (1969, 1994): *Laws of Form.* London: Allen & Unwin; Portland, Oregon: BookMasters

Stachowiak, Herbert (1965, 1969): *Denken und Erkennen im kybernetischen Modell.* Wien: Springer

Stachowiak, Herbert (1973): *Allgemeine Modelltheorie.* Wien: Springer

Stachowiak, Herbert (Ed.) (1983a): *Modelle – Konstruktion der Wirklichkeit.* München: Fink

Stachowiak, Herbert (1983b): "Erkenntnisstufen zum Systematischen Neopragmatismus und zur Allgemeinen Modelltheorie". In: Stachowiak 1983a: 87-146

Stachowiak, Herbert (Ed.) (1987a): *Pragmatik. Handbuch pragmatischen Denkens. Band II: Der Aufstieg pragmatischen Denkens im 19. und 20. Jahrhundert.* Hamburg: Meiner

Stachowiak, Herbert (1987b): "Neopragmatismus als zeitgenössische Ausformung eines philosophischen Paradigmas". In: Stachowiak 1987a: 391-435

Stachowiak, Herbert (Ed.) (1989a): *Pragmatik. Handbuch pragmatischen Denkens. Band III: Allgemeine philosophische Pragmatik.* Hamburg: Meiner

Stachowiak, Herbert (1989b): "Theorie und Metatheorie des Gesellschaftlichen und das pragmatische Desiderat". In: Stachowiak 1989a: 315-342

Stachowiak, Herbert (Ed.) (1993): *Pragmatik. Handbuch pragmatischen Denkens. Band IV: Sprachphilosophie, Sprachpragmatik und formative Pragmatik.* Hamburg: Meiner

Stachowiak, Herbert (Ed.) (1995): *Pragmatik. Handbuch pragmatischen Denkens. Band V: Pragmatische Tendenzen in der Wissenschaftstheorie.* Hamburg: Meiner

Stadler, Friedrich (1997): *Studien zum Wiener Kreis. Ursprung, Entwicklung und Wirkung des Logischen Empirismus im Kontext.* Frankfurt am Main: Suhrkamp

Stern, David (2002): "Nestroy, Augustine, and the Opening of the *Philosophical Investigations*". In: Haller & Puhl 2002: 425-445

Stroll, Avrum (2002): "Understanding *On Certainty*: Entry 194". In: Haller & Puhl 2002: 446-456

Tichý, Pavel (1988): *The Foundations of Frege's Logic.* Berlin: de Gruyter

Turing, Alan M. (1936/37): "On Computable Numbers, with an Application to the Entscheidungsproblem". *Proceedings of the London Mathematical Society, Series 2, 42*: 230-265

Varga von Kibéd, Matthias; Matzka, Rudolf (1993): "Motive und Grundgedanken der »Gesetze der Form«". In: Baecker 1993: 58-85

Vesey, Godfrey (1978): "Memory and Mind. Review", *Mind 28, 110*: 80-81

Vossenkuhl, Wilhelm (Ed.) (1992): *Von Wittgenstein Lernen.* Berlin: Akademie-Verlag

Vossenkuhl, Wilhelm (1995): *Ludwig Wittgenstein.* München: Beck

Wann, T. W. (Ed.) (1964): *Behaviorism and Phenomenology. Contrasting Basis for Modern Psychology.* Rice University Semicentennial Series. Chicago: UCP

Watzlawick, Paul; Beavin Bavelas, Janet Helmick; Jackson, Don D. (1967, 1969): *Pragmatics of Human Communication. A Study of Interactional Patterns, Pathologies, and Paradoxes.* New York: Norton. Translation into German as: *Menschliche Kommunikation. Formen, Störungen, Paradoxien.* Bern: Huber

Watzlawick, Paul; Weakland, John H.; Fisch, Richard (1974a, 1974b, 1992): *Change. Principles of Problem Foundation and Problem Resolution.* New York: Norton. Translation into German as: *Lösungen. Zur Theorie und Praxis menschlichen Wandels.* Bern: Hans Huber

Watzlawick, Paul (1975, 1988b, 1990b): "Wesen und Formen menschlicher Beziehungen". In: Gadamer & Vogler 1975: 103-131. In: Watzlawick 1988a: 9-33. Translated into English as: "The Nature and Structure of Human Relationships". In: Watzlawick 1990a: 11-44

Watzlawick, Paul (1976a, 1976b): *Wie wirklich ist die Wirklichkeit? Wahn Täuschung Verstehen.* München: Piper. In English as: *How Real is Real? Confusion, Disinformation, Communication.* New York: Random House

Watzlawick, Paul (1997): "Die psychotherapeutische Technik des »Umdeutens«". In: Watzlawick & Nardone 2001: 136-145

Watzlawick, Paul (1977): *Die Möglichkeit des Andersseins. Zur Technik der therapeutischen Kommunikation.* Bern: Huber

Watzlawick, Paul; Weakland, John H. (Eds.) (1977, 1980, 1990, 1997): *The Interactional View. Studies at the Mental Research Institute, Palo Alto, 1965 - 1974.* New York: Norton. Translation into German as: *Interaktion.* Bern: Hans Huber; München: Piper

Watzlawick, Paul (1978, 1993): *The Language of Change. Elements of Therapeutic Communication.* New York: Norton

Watzlawick, Paul (Ed.) (1981a, 1984a, 1994): *Die erfundene Wirklichkeit. Wie wissen wir, was wir zu wissen glauben? Beiträge zum Konstruktivismus.* München: Piper. Translation into English as: *The Invented Reality. How Do We Know What We Believe We Know? Contributions to Constructivism.* New York: Norton

Watzlawick, Paul (1981b, 1984b): "Selbsterfüllende Prophezeiungen". In: Watzlawick 1994: 91-110. Translation into English as: "Self-Fulfilling Prophecies". In: Watzlawick 1984a: 95-116

Watzlawick, Paul (1981c, 1984c, 1988f, 1990e): "Bausteine ideologischer »Wirklichkeiten«". In: Watzlawick 1981a: 192-228. In: Watzlawick 1988a: 156-186. Translation into English as: "Components of Ideological »Realities«". In: Watzlawick 1984a: 206-247. In: Watzlawick 1990a: 207-252

Watzlawick, Paul (1983): *Anleitungen zum Unglücklichsein.* München: Piper

Watzlawick, Paul (1985, 1988c, 1990c): "Wirklichkeitsanpassung oder angepaßte »Wirklichkeit«? Konstruktivismus und Psychotherapie". In: Gumin & Meier 1985: 89-108. In: Watzlawick 1988a: 103-116. Translated into English as: "Reality Adaption or Adapted »Reality«? Constructivism and Psychotherapy". In: Watzlawick 1990a: 131-151

Watzlawick, Paul (1988a, 1990a): *Münchhausens Zopf oder: Psychotherapie und »Wirklichkeit«. Aufsätze und Vorträge über menschliche Probleme in systemisch-konstruktivistischer Sicht.* Bern: Huber. Translated into English as: *Münchhausen's Pigtail or Psychotherapy & »Reality«. Essays and Lectures.* New York: Norton

Watzlawick, Paul (1988d): "Verschreiben statt Verstehen als Technik von Problemlösungen". In: Gumbrecht & Pfeiffer 1988: 878-883

Watzlawick, Paul (1988e, 1990d): "Münchhausens Zopf und Wittgensteins Leiter. Zum Problem der Rückbezüglichkeit". In: Watzlawick 1988a: 135-155. Translated into English as: "Münchhausen's Pigtail and Wittgenstein's Ladder: On the Problem of Self-reference". In: Watzlawick 1990a: 179-206

Watzlawick, Paul; Nardone, Giorgio (Eds.) (1997, 1999, 2001): *Terapia breve strategica.* Milano: Raffaello Cortina Editore. Translation into German by Michael von Killisch-Horn as: *Kurzeittherapie und Wirklichkeit. Eine Einführung.* München: Piper

Weingartner, Paul; Schurz, Gerhard; Dorn, Georg (Eds.) (1997a): *The Role of Pragmatics in Contemporary Philosophy. Papers of the 20th International Wittgenstein-Symposium, Kirchberg am Wechsel 1997. Vol.1 Contributions of the Austrian Ludwig Wittgenstein Society* Vol.V. Kirchberg am Wechsel

Weingartner, Paul; Schurz, Gerhard; Dorn, Georg (Eds.) (1997b): *The Role of Pragmatics in Contemporary Philosophy. Papers of the 20th International Wittgenstein-Symposium, Kirchberg am Wechsel 1997. Vol.2 Contributions of the Austrian Ludwig Wittgenstein Society* Vol.VI. Kirchberg am Wechsel

Wiener, Norbert (1948, 1949, 1961, 1965, 1996): *Cybernetics: or Control and Communication in the Animal and the Machine.* Cambridge, Mass.: M. I. T. *et* New York *et* Wiley *et* Paris: Hermann et Cie

Wiener, Norbert (1952, 1954): *The Human Use of Human Beings (Cybernetics and Society).* New York: Da Capo Press. Translation in German by Gertrud Walther as: *Mensch und Menschmaschine.* Frankfurt am Main: Metzner

Wiener, Norbert (1956, 1971): *I am a Mathematician. The Later Life of a Prodigy. An Autobiographical Account of the Mature Years and Career of Norbert Wiener and a Continuation of the Account of his Childhood in Ex-Prodigy*. New York: Doubleday. In German as: *Ich und die Kybernetik. Der Lebensweg eines Genies. München: Goldmann. Et qua: Mathematik — Mein Leben*. Düsseldorf: Econ

Wittgenstein, Ludwig (1913, 1957): "Notes on Logic", "Introduction" by Costello, Harry T., *The Journal of Philosophy 54, 9*: 230-245

Wittgenstein, Ludwig (1921, 1961a, 1974a, 1992a): *Tractatus Logico-Philosophicus* (translation into English by D. F. Pears and B. F. McGuinness, introduced by B. Russell). London: Routledge

Wittgenstein, Ludwig (1953, 1958a, 1963, 1991): *Philosophical Investigations* (translation into English by Gertrude Elizabeth Margaret Anscombe). Oxford: Blackwell

Wittgenstein, Ludwig (1956, 1967c, 1978, 1994b): *Remarks on the Foundations of Mathematics* (edited by Georg Henrik von Wright, Rush Rhees, and Gertrude Elizabeth Margaret Anscombe, translation into English by Gertrude Elizabeth Margaret Anscombe). Oxford: Blackwell

Wittgenstein, Ludwig (1958b, 1969a, 2000): *The Blue and Brown Books. Preliminary Studies for the »Philosophical Investigations«*. Oxford: Blackwell

Wittgenstein, Ludwig (1961b, 1979b): *Notebooks 1914 - 1916* (translation into English by Gertrude Elizabeth Margaret Anscombe). Oxford: Blackwell

Wittgenstein, Ludwig (1967a, 1993b): "Bemerkungen über Frazers *Golden Bough*. Remarks on Frazer's *Golden Bough*", *Synthese 17*: 233-253. In: Wittgenstein 1993a: 115-155

Wittgenstein, Ludwig (1967b, 1975b, 1981, 1990c): *Zettel* (edited by Gertrude Elizabeth Margaret Anscombe and Georg Henrik von Wright, translation into English by Anscombe). Oxford: Blackwell

Wittgenstein, Ludwig (1969b, 1974c, 1975c, 1997): *Über Gewißheit. On Certainty* (edited by Gertrude Elizabeth Margaret Anscombe and Georg Henrik von Wright, translation into English by Denis Paul and Gertrude Elizabeth Margaret Anscombe). Oxford: Blackwell

Wittgenstein, Ludwig (1973): *Letters to C. K. Ogden with comments on the English translation of the Tractatus Logico-Philosophicus*. Edited by G. H. von Wright, with an appendix of letters by Frank Plumpton Ramsey. Oxford: Blackwell

Wittgenstein, Ludwig (1974b, 1990d): *Philosophical Grammar* (edited by Rush Rhees, translation into English by Anthony Kenny). Oxford: Blackwell

Wittgenstein, Ludwig (1975a, 1990a): *Philosophical Remarks* (edited by Rush Rhees, translation into English by Raymond Hargreaves and Roger White). Oxford: Blackwell

Wittgenstein, Ludwig (1977, 1980c, 1994a, 1998c): *Vermischte Bemerkungen. Culture and Value* (edited by Georg Henrik von Wright in collaboration with Heikki Nyman, revised edition by Alois Pichler, translation into English by Peter Winch). Oxford: Blackwell

Wittgenstein, Ludwig (1979a, 1982a): *Wittgenstein's Lectures. Cambridge, 1932 - 1935* (edited by Alice Ambrose from the notes of Alice Ambrose and Margaret MacDonald). Oxford: Blackwell

Wittgenstein, Ludwig (1980a, 1998a): *Bemerkungen über die Philosophie der Psychologie. Band I. Remarks on the Philosophy of Psychology*. Volume I (edited by Gertrude Elizabeth Margaret Anscombe and Georg Henrik von Wright, translation into English by Gertrude Elizabeth Margaret Anscombe). Oxford: Blackwell

Wittgenstein, Ludwig (1980b, 1998b): *Bemerkungen über die Philosophie der Psychologie. Band II. Remarks on the Philosophy of Psychology*. Volume II (edited by Gertrude Elizabeth Margaret Anscombe and Georg Henrik von Wright, translation into English by Gertrude Elizabeth Margaret Anscombe). Oxford: Blackwell

Wittgenstein, Ludwig (1982b, 1990b): *Letzte Schriften über die Philosophie der Psychologie. Vorstudien zum zweiten Teil der Philosophischen Untersuchungen*. Band I. *Last Writings on the Philosophy of Psychology. Preliminary Studies for Part II of Philosophical Investigations*. Volume I (edited by Georg Henrik von Wright and Heikki Nyman, translation into English by C. Grant Luckhardt and Maximilian A. E. Aue). Oxford: Blackwell

Wittgenstein, Ludwig (1984 ff.): *Werkausgabe*. Bände 1 - 8. Frankfurt am Main: Suhrkamp

Wittgenstein, Ludwig (1991): *Geheime Tagebücher: 1914 – 1916* (edited by Wilhelm Baum). Wien: Turia und Kant

Wittgenstein, Ludwig (1992b): *Letzte Schriften über die Philosophie der Psychologie. Das Innere und das Äußere. 1949 - 1951*. Band II. *Last Writings on the Philosophy of Psychology. The Inner and the Outer. 1949 - 1951*. Volume II (edited by Georg Henrik von Wright and Heikki Nyman, translation into English by C. Grant Luckhardt and Maximilian A. E. Aue). Oxford: Blackwell

Wittgenstein, Ludwig (1993a): *Philosophical Occasions. 1912 - 1951* (edited by James C. Klagge and Alfred Nordmann). Indianapolis: Hackett

Wright, Georg Henrik von (1951a): *An Essay in Modal Logic*. Studies in Logic and the Foundations of Mathematics. Amsterdam: North-Holland

Wright, Georg Henrik von (1951b): "Deontische Modalitäten". In: Wright 1951a: 36-41. In: Berka & Kreiser 1984: 172-177 (abbreviated translation into German of Wright 1951a)

Wright, Georg Henrik von (1982, 1986): *Wittgenstein*. Oxford: Blackwell. Translation into German by Joachim Schulte: *Wittgenstein*. Frankfurt am Main: Suhrkamp

Wright, Georg Henrik von (1983): "On Causal Knowledge". In: Ginet & Shoemaker 1983: 50-62

Wrinch, Dorothy (1920): "On the Nature of Memory", *Mind 29, 113*: 46-61

Zemach, Eddy M. (1968): "A Definition of Memory", *Mind 77, 308*: 526-536

Index